THE COLOUR OF MURDER

THE COLOUR
OF MURDER

One family's horror exposes a
nation's anguish

HEIDI HOLLAND

PENGUIN BOOKS

PENGUIN BOOKS

Published by the Penguin Group
Penguin Books (South Africa) (Pty) Ltd, 24 Sturdee Avenue, Rosebank,
Johannesburg 2196, South Africa
Penguin Books Ltd, 80 Strand, London WC2R 0RL, England
Penguin Group (USA) Inc, 375 Hudson Street, New York, New York 10014, USA
Penguin Group (Canada), 90 Eglinton Avenue East, Suite 700, Toronto, Ontario,
M4P 2Y3, Canada (a division of Pearson Penguin Canada Inc.)
Penguin Ireland, 25 St Stephen's Green, Dublin 2, Ireland (a division of Penguin
Books Ltd)
Penguin Group (Australia), 250 Camberwell Road, Camberwell, Victoria 3124,
Australia (a division of Pearson Australia Group Pty Ltd)
Penguin Books India Pvt Ltd, 11 Community Centre, Panchsheel Park, New Delhi
– 110 017, India
Penguin Group (NZ), Cnr Rosedale and Airborne Roads, Albany, Auckland 1310,
New Zealand (a division of Pearson New Zealand Ltd)

Penguin Books (South Africa) (Pty) Ltd, Registered Offices:
24 Sturdee Avenue, Rosebank, Johannesburg 2196, South Africa

www.penguinbooks.co.za

First published by Penguin Books (South Africa) (Pty) Ltd 2006
Reprinted 2008

Copyright © Heidi Holland 2006

All rights reserved
The moral right of the author has been asserted

ISBN-13: 978-0-143-02512-2
ISBN-10: 0-143-02512-0

Typeset by CJH Design in 10.5/13 pt Melior
Cover photographs: Copyright © SABC
Picture section: Top and centre photographs on page 2 and all photographs
on pages 5 to 8 © SABC. Photographs on pages 5 to 8: Michael Brennan
(photographer) and Isa-Lee Jacobson (director of documentary 'Sabrina: Daddy's
Girl')
Printed and bound by Interpak Books, Pietermaritzburg

For
A

Preface

The first time I heard the name Van Schoor was when an Australian magazine asked me to write a profile of a young woman, Sabrina van Schoor, who had murdered her mother. It sounded familiar but, having been immersed in another project at the time of the matricide a year earlier, I must have paid it scant attention. When I looked her name up on the Internet, I discovered to my surprise that Sabrina was the daughter of Louis, the most notorious mass murderer of the apartheid era.

At the time of his trial, the story had huge capital in South Africa as an apt compression of what the whole country was going through, and everyone in it; no one involved was simply themselves; they also represented over three hundred years of history and through their actions, rightly or wrongly, spoke the actions of their predecessors, glorious or otherwise. The same would be true in Sabrina's case, although as the South African story had moved on by then it was accordingly a much more complicated case, and more bizarre, so much so that the act of murdering her mother would win Sabrina comparison in some quarters to Nelson Mandela and the freedom fighters of the liberation era.

But the story was also personal to me. I am not outside of it; as the child of a British father and a Swiss mother who migrated to South Africa, where I was born, and then went farming in what used to be Rhodesia – rapidly becoming as racist in their attitudes as the whites who had been exploiting and tormenting their African labourers for generations – I grew up feeling superior to black people. By the age of 15, however, thanks to my father's efforts to discourage my rampant materialism by continually pointing out how poor the farm workers were in comparison with us, I became aware of just how unequally my adopted country treated its citizens. This led me not only to campaign for opposition parties during elections that excluded blacks, but to socialise across the colour line. It led my father on occasion to heckle at the political meetings I attended as a minor functionary, much to my embarrassment. I remember him taking me aside once when I dated a black man (who subsequently became Minister of Finance in liberated Zimbabwe) and warning me not to throw away my future prospects by being spotted dining with him.

The Van Schoor cases made me ask questions of myself, and tough ones at that. Where does racism reside now that the language used to signpost it has changed? Is it racist not to have black friends? Is it racist to know the entire family history of the white shopkeeper in your street but nothing about the African beggar who sits outside the same shop you enter day after day? The story I have written is of a family, but it is also the story of a divided country and of the people of that country trying to find new ways to live with each other. In a world in which these questions are avoided as too difficult or too embarrassing, or too dated in a supposedly post-race era, we as South Africans cannot afford to avoid them; our future ultimately depends on the answers we come up with.

Acknowledgements

Material in this book not derived from my own observation is taken either from court records, newspaper and magazine articles or is the result of interviews with the people directly concerned, in some cases numerous interviews conducted over two and a half years. These collaborators are identified within the text so it is redundant to name them here; nevertheless, I want to thank them for their cooperation, without which my task would have been impossible. Equally, I will not attempt a roll-call of all the East London and Queenstown residents who, though not named in these pages, provided me with insight and hospitality.

I would like to thank specifically Alex McGregor, my informal editor in Sydney, whose judgement and encouragement helped me enormously from the outset; Adam Roberts of *The Economist* in London, who challenged my assumptions so beguilingly from beginning to end; Emma Brockes of *The Guardian* in London for her dazzling observations; Rory Carroll, also of *The Guardian*, for the title and assorted inspirations; Justina Mashiya of Queenstown for introducing her community to me in many revealing ways; David Pitman, a South African human rights lawyer who was involved in Louis van Schoor's case and is now living in America, whose assistance in legal matters was invaluable; psychologist Ruth Rice for raising crisp questions about the human condition during our numerous discussions on the Van Schoor cases. And my late father, Les Holland, for teaching me to examine my values.

Those who helped in less specific ways include my sons Jonah Hull and Niko Patrikios, the late Anthony Sampson, Richard Johnson, Peter Struiff, Sue Armstrong, Emma Guest, Sophie MacGregor, Duncan Campbell, Ellen Windemuth, Adele Lucas, Issy Dowden, Simon Pike, Anne Hammerstad, Fran Saunders, Christian Jennings, Nicky Wimble, Marion McNeilage, Janina Masojada, Tim Butcher, Gail Leschinsky, Oystein Meland, Claudia Rizzi, Skye Lucas, Franki Black, Isa-Lee Jacobson, my agent Camilla Hornby of Curtis Brown and my editors and publishers Pam Thornley, Alison Lowry and Jeremy Boraine of Penguin Books.

Chapter One

I had never met a murderer before and wasn't sure how to conduct myself. Although I smile readily as a rule, I did not smile on encountering Sabrina van Schoor. She was a startling sight in prison uniform, with her dyed red hair, carefully made-up face, fingernails painted black. Her gaze and voice were steady although the eyes she had described in a note she sent me as 'blue or green, depending on my mood' looked close to tears. I realised from the way she watched me so closely, as if looking for vital clues on my person, as well as the way she leant forward to speak to me confidentially, that she was searching for approval. The last thing on my mind, which was crammed with grotesque images of her dead mother, was the possibility of empathising with her.

A year to the day since she committed matricide on March 22, 2002, 23-year-old Sabrina began to tell me about the morning of the murder. She woke at 5.30 to run an errand for her mother. She washed hurriedly, pulled on a pair of leggings and a T-shirt and went into her mother's bedroom. Announcing that her baby was still asleep in the cot beside her own bed, Sabrina watched her mother turn over and open her eyes. Crossly, she told Sabrina not to be long and then went back to sleep. As Sabrina walked outside to her car, she paused on the kitchen steps to phone the man who had agreed to kill Beverley.

After driving across town to her mother's florist and bridal boutique, Lady B, Sabrina unlocked the shop to admit an employee who had arrived early to arrange flowers for an unusually long list of weekend funerals. She turned off the night light, closed the front door and waited in her car for a call from the hitmen to say it was all over. When her mobile rang, however, she froze. It rang again. Stunned to hear her mother's angry voice demanding to know what was taking her so long, Sabrina told Beverley she was on her way home. Another call immediately afterwards was from the man who had helped her plan the murder, saying that the killer had been unable to enter Beverley's home because the dogs were barking frantically. He directed Sabrina to the local graveyard, saying that the assassin, Feza Mdutshane, was waiting there to get into her car.

'We were two houses away from Mom's house,' Sabrina recalls. 'Feza was lying on the back seat, saying nothing. It was about 6.30. I drove down the driveway – our house was set back from the road – and stopped at the gate. My dogs were standing by the gate, waiting for me. Feza was walking behind me. I unlocked the back door and we walked into the kitchen. My mom's TV was playing. She was busy putting on her make-up as she did every morning before work. She'd always sit on the bed watching *Morning Live*.

'I left Feza in the kitchen. He did not seem to have a weapon. He had on black tracksuit pants and a plain yellow T-shirt. I went down the passage, past my bedroom and into my mom's room. She started shouting at me because I had taken so long and I hadn't answered the phone. I was nearly crying, thinking, "Mom, please stop shouting at me", because

I wanted to say goodbye to her properly. Driving in the car with Feza, I'd been thinking about my last words to her. I wanted to say to her that I was sorry for everything I'd done to her, for all the hell I'd put her through, and tell her that I loved her lots.

'Feza was standing in the kitchen doorway, down the passage from Mom's room, having taken one of my baby's pink pants from the laundry basket and pulled it over his head. One of her tops – a new lilac one Mom and I had bought together – he had pulled over his right hand and another of her little tops was covering his left hand. I saw him putting something in his pocket. He came towards me down the passage. My daughter was asleep in my arms. I passed him without looking at him or saying anything. As I was putting my baby down on my bed, quickly turning on the radio, I heard my mother shouting, "Sabrina, run!" That's when I put the TV on very loudly, as well as the radio.'

When Sabrina opened the door of her room ten minutes later, she asked the murderer: 'Are you sure she's dead?' He answered yes. When she asked again if he was sure, he returned to Beverley's bedroom to check the half-naked, bleeding corpse. Later Sabrina would say in court that she felt regret when she saw her mother's body and immediately phoned for an ambulance.

It went against the natural order of things, said Judge Eric Leach when he sentenced Sabrina to 25 years' imprisonment for taking 'the life of the person who gave her life'. Sabrina – a 'normal girl who baked cakes and listened to Roxette', according to her best friend – sobbed while her brothers were giving their tearful evidence against her. In mitigation of sentence, Sabrina told the court that she believed her mother had to die because she was a racist.

After my first interview with Sabrina at Fort Glamorgan prison outside East London, and having decided to investigate the circumstances surrounding Beverley van Schoor's murder, I begin the drive inland to Queenstown, where the crime took place. The road from East London, a run-down South African port that calls itself The Friendly City, winds steeply through the Amatola mountains. Lining the route on either end of the two-hour journey are clusters of makeshift houses; little hovels situated close enough to town for poor black people to catch the crumbs flung out by their rich white neighbours. These rickety villages used to be cited by anti-apartheid activists as evidence of the country's uncaring government. Now that South Africans know they are unlikely to get better rulers than the ones chosen in the first democratic election in 1994, these homes made from plastic bags and slivers of corrugated iron are sometimes called creative solutions. Despite the poverty they represent, the precariously perched shacks blend into the green slopes, their tones of rust, mud and dung being easy on the eye if not on the mind.

Drizzle turns to rain. The sky has darkened so much that headlights are on at midday. Fog blocks the horizon, enveloping the car. It feels suddenly lonely on a road devoid of its landscape, the uncertainty of what to expect in Queenstown beginning to make me uneasy.

Matricide is a rare crime, accounting for less than one per cent of the world's murders. Even in crime-ravaged South Africa, the investigating officer in Sabrina van Schoor's case was unable to find a single precedent in the police reference library. As a mother, I had wondered since first hearing the news of Beverley van Schoor's murder what would provoke a daughter to so brutally end the life of 'the person who gave her life'. Why does a child kill? Is it a reflection of the values of a lost generation, as the Menendez brothers in California, who killed both their parents, were viewed by some as symbols of the empty amorality of 1980s spoilt American youth? Matricide brands the killer an outcast beyond not just the family but their humanity. It is a monstrous crime, but are the killers monsters?

Sabrina told Judge Leach that her motive was to free herself from Beverley's oppressive opposition to Sabrina's black and 'coloured' (mixed race) friendships. Beverley's first grandchild was the result of Sabrina's brief affair with a coloured lover – a bitter blow to her mother's pride as a businesswoman who had won the respect of Queenstown's white establishment. In much of South Africa, even ten years after the abolition of apartheid, a mixed-race baby is at the very least an embarrassment to a white family. In Queenstown, a conservative agricultural backwater, it is seen as an assault on the integrity of the former ruling race.

What makes the murder of Beverley van Schoor so quintessentially South African is the violent legacy of the Van Schoor family. In 1991, eleven years before Sabrina went to prison for matricide, her father, security guard Louis van Schoor, was sentenced as the worst mass murderer in the country's history. The killing of Beverley van Schoor ought to have led to a great deal of heart-searching. Did the daughter simply copy her father's cold-blooded methods of achieving his ends? Or was Sabrina's attempt to escape racism through violence a symptom of South Africa's deepest problems?

Among Louis van Schoor's victims in 1988, when apartheid seemed unstoppable, were two teenagers. Louis said it was too dark to see that the boys were children. The response of the police and judiciary was much the same as it had always been. For years, violent people like Louis got away with murder under a South African law that permitted anyone to shoot dead a person fleeing the scene of a serious crime. Included in the definition of 'serious' was petty theft if it involved trespass.

Magistrates conducting inquests routinely cleared Louis van Schoor of criminal acts, even though survivors gave sad accounts of trying to surrender when they were shot. Or of Louis grabbing innocent people as they were walking in the street, dragging them onto the premises he was guarding and shooting them. The victims were all black. Their word did not count against that of a former white policeman. As apartheid imploded, the establishment was finally forced to deal with Louis van Schoor. It did so by arguing that the police and magistrates had erred all along. Louis was eventually tried for 19 murders, convicted of seven and sentenced to 20 years. It was the biggest murder trial in South African history but it hardly mentioned most of the 39 killings the security guard had boasted about.

Many white East Londoners protested that Louis was apartheid's fall guy, though he said in court that his only regret was being parted from his 12-year-old daughter Sabrina. Eleven years later, it was Sabrina's turn to be locked away for murder, again amid protests from some of her community. This time, though, the South Africans who once lived in fear of Sabrina's father gave her their support. Black and coloured residents of Queenstown packed the public gallery during Sabrina's trial to applaud Louis van Schoor's daughter for the matricide they described as a blow against racism. Sabrina's attorney, Siphiwo Burwana, hailed her as a 'heroine' for hiring an assassin to slaughter her mother.

Every witness testifying in Sabrina's case swore to tell the whole truth and nothing but, yet the truth remained fuzzy at the end of the trial, especially in regard to the mother-daughter relationship and Sabrina's motive for killing Beverley. After reading the court transcript and not knowing who to believe or whose side to take, I could not offer my usual ambivalent excuse of being on the side of common sense since that was a notion in particularly short supply. Was there such a condition as absolute truth in this case or was my search limited to fragments of each witness's own truths?

And what of the truth about their truths? Is it based on a temporal interpretation of events: the more shared their interpretation, the more factual it seems at the time? In South Africa, arguably the most complex society on earth, the truth you hear is often dependent on the colour of your skin. How often can blacks and whites actually agree about the truth of the same events? Perhaps the truth in this case, no matter how assiduously sought, just did not exist in the muddle of conflicting opinions. What I was hoping to find instead was the motive: why did a daughter kill her mother? Was there provocation, or enough provocation, for Sabrina to kill Beverley? Is there ever enough provocation for a daughter to kill her mother? Leave town, change your identity to escape your mother ... but hire a killer?

I have no doubt that Sabrina belongs behind bars. Yet her story fascinates me and, despite the lengthy court case and media coverage, remains largely untold. As soon as I learnt how whites in East London applauded Louis for killing blacks on the grounds that he was a crime-fighter protecting white-owned property, while blacks in Queenstown cheered Sabrina for murdering her mother on the grounds that it struck a blow against racism, I wanted to write about these dark events – a whydunnit rather than a whodunnit. Why do two murderers in a family that would have been ostracised in any normally functioning society become elevated by one group or other as heroic in South Africa?

Racism is a subject close to anybody growing up in Africa. Some struggle self-consciously through adult life to discard ingrained discriminatory tendencies; most accept the affliction as inevitable. As a child, I remember my father, a kind and generous man in all other respects, keeping a long baboon tail with a big safety pin on the end, which he would sometimes attach to the pants of a recalcitrant farm labourer when he felt he needed to endorse his authority. The workers fell about laughing at this stinging humiliation, as did we white kids because my father thought it a joke.

One of the reasons I have long had the itch to explore racism through personal stories is to see how the actions of someone like Sabrina – and perhaps Louis, too – are the result of the prejudices of the world that surrounds them. Are we just pieces of clay moulded by our environment? One of the questions raised by the Van Schoor murders is where does external intervention come from, if it comes at all.

Many questions spill out of the two cases titled State vs Van Schoor – public disasters that mesmerise as much by their improbability as by their horror. Is the proclivity to murder genetic? Is racism still endemic in its headquarters, South Africa? How have developed democracies like the United Kingdom and the United States of America managed their prejudices? Was Sabrina provoked beyond endurance? What role did their communities play in Louis' and Sabrina's crimes?

I squirm at some of the raw reactions and forthright statements of white South Africans, like the policeman in East London who told me he is now able to call a wealthy black man sir, which would have been unthinkable for him ten years ago. Yet it is such moments of emotional nakedness that reveal how race is lived in South Africa today and how far the country has come from the presumptions of superiority that span racism – the enduring fault line in South African life. Onlookers may wince at the way South Africans, from the president down, still categorise each other by race but they should know that it is impossible to tell this story – or any other contemporary South African story – without constant reference to skin colour because race remains a strong feature of the national mindset.

This is the story not only of a family corrupted by apartheid but of a country so perverted by racism and violence that it will take a long, long time to overcome its terrible history. While similar to Truman Capote's classic American murder story *In Cold Blood* in its forensic detail, this one is the opposite in terms of its central theme: *In Cold Blood* is about society being unable to insulate us from random acts of violence, whereas this is the story of how society can create them.

The Van Schoor murders happened in South Africa but could have occurred in America. There, the Ku Klux Klan and American Neo-Nazis, with thousands of supporters, shared the moral responsibility for 20 equally outrageous racist murders committed between 1977 and 1980. The killer was Joseph Paul Franklin, the man who shot and paralysed Larry Flynt because his magazine ran an issue celebrating interracial sex. A chilling dedication to Franklin in a novel called *The Hunter*, written in 1989 by the same author who wrote the *Turner Diaries* – the racist screed that inspired Timothy McVeigh to plant his bomb in Oklahoma City ten years ago – referred to him as 'a devoted son of his race, who did what any white man should do, without regard for the personal consequences'. Like Louis van Schoor's belief that he was a crime-fighter rather than a racist mass murderer, Joseph Franklin insisted he did not fit the profile of a racist serial killer since he was motivated by political conviction.

Violent acts between black and white characterised South African life for years, to the extent that whites became international outcasts and civil war was widely predicted. Over a decade after the repeal of apartheid's hateful laws, blood-letting in the name of race still occurs even though, to much of the world, the country has come to represent the possibility of human progress through reconciliation. The man who gave South Africans their unexpected moral authority, the country's first black president, Nelson Mandela, addressed a joint session of the United States Congress in 1990 soon after his release from 27 years' political imprisonment, when South Africa was still in the grip of what he called 'the apartheid crime against humanity'. Speaking of a society '... which has known nothing but racism for three centuries', Mandela envisaged a future in which 'the black shall to the white be sister and brother, a fellow South African, an equal human being, both citizens of the world'.

Apartheid, meaning 'separateness' in Afrikaans and today used to describe bigotry throughout the world, began as a policy of geographically separating whites from blacks and grew into an atrocity of tragic proportions. It was first implemented in the Cape on a minor scale, following the arrival in 1652 of the Dutch East India Company. Its representative, Jan van Riebeeck, was ordered to provide fresh produce for the company's ships and to maintain good relations with the natives. However, skirmishes between the Dutch and the local people broke out after the foreigners took more and more land for their project and the indigenous Bushmen responded by stealing the white men's cattle. Van Riebeeck planted a bitter-almond hedge around his trading station to keep the locals at bay but they refused to be contained beyond the prickly barrier, insisting that all the land belonged to them.

Apartheid developed over the next 150 years when whites of Dutch descent – the Afrikaners who were proud to call themselves Boers (farmers) – began venturing further into the interior. Moving southwards at the same time was the vanguard of a great sweep towards the Cape by the black tribes of Africa, who had inhabited the continent for centuries. Both needed land and water, the disputed resources of age-old frontier struggles everywhere and the cause of ongoing confrontations between the Boers and the Bantu people.

When the British took the Cape Colony in 1795, they abolished Dutch as a language in their administration and enforced a vigorous policy of anglicisation. From 1820, when the British government funded large-scale emigration to the Cape, English settler towns sprang up alongside Cape Dutch homesteads in places like East London and Grahamstown and the two language groups began an uneasy coexistence.

Although the British oversaw the implementation of several race laws which furthered apartheid, a growing humanitarianism was soon to abolish slavery throughout the Empire. At the same time, the Bantu people kept pressing south, a threat to which the British seemed irresolute in the minds of Afrikaners. Affronted by demands that people with darker skins be given what one prominent Boer described as 'an ungodly equality', the heirs to Jan van Riebeeck looked further into the interior.

Around 1838, clinging to a dream of racial exclusivity but leaving behind their homes and the fields they had cultivated, the Afrikaners set out to escape the British by migrating northwards across the Drakensberg mountains into Natal and over the Orange River into the Transvaal. The Great Trek, some bloody nineteenth-century battles with Zulu warriors, and their defeat in the war with the British 70 years later helped create a fierce nationalism among the Afrikaners. The concentration camps of the Anglo-Boer War, in which women and children perished at the hands of the British, left Afrikaners a profoundly defeated tribe with a defensive psyche that was to have disastrous repercussions in later years.

Not long after the Anglo-Boer War the country became a self-governing dominion within the British Empire. Tensions between Afrikaans and English-speaking whites continued unabated until 1948 when the dissident National Party, advocating a programme of separate racial development, came to power. A speech given in parliament in 1951 by Hendrik Verwoerd, then education minister but later the leader of the country, made it clear that blacks were to remain 'hewers of wood and drawers of water'. Thereafter, whether classified black, white or coloured by the new government, one's race became the crucial factor in South African life. It had to be declared on all transactions from post office applications for telephone lines to marriage certificates and hospital admission forms. It determined where one could live and swim, on which bus one could travel, where one could urinate. And it led to a culture of violence.

*

Queenstown, which has begun to take shape through thinning mist, was the adopted home of Beverley van Schoor. It is a business centre serving the rich white farming region of the Eastern Cape, the province where many legendary political figures, including Nelson Mandela, rose to challenge apartheid. There is one main street in Queenstown, which was named in honour of Queen Victoria and founded in 1847 by Sir Harry Smith, a British governor well remembered in the folklore of these parts because he insisted that African chiefs kiss his feet as a mark of respect.

Sandwiched between a barren rural region called the Transkei and its clone, the Ciskei, Queenstown is one of 500 small South African towns where a large proportion of the country's population lives. The quaint Victorian outpost recently made local headlines as the cleanest city in the Eastern Cape, a far cry from its earlier flamboyant reputation as a frontier town in the successive wars between the British, the Afrikaners and black South Africans. It was from Queenstown that apartheid's bureaucrats, determined to confine blacks to underdeveloped, remote parts of the country, conducted their fraudulent 'homeland' experiment in the Seventies; an attempt to create the illusion of self-government in border areas comprising several million people, some spectacular mountains and an unsustainable economy.

I have reserved a room at a guest house called Longview Lodge, chosen after a search through the Automobile Association's guidebook. Queenstown's original hexagonal layout, the AA book explains, was planned so that the town's inhabitants could defend themselves against the natives. They could fire from the centre at attackers who might be approaching on any of the six roads leading into town. 'Fortunately it was never necessary to fire a shot in anger,' says the travelogue. 'Subsequently the hexagon became the marketplace and later, with its beautiful fountain and gardens, was declared a national monument.'

There are no beautiful fountains and gardens at Longview Lodge. Outwardly plain, its interior veers from nondescript to garish. My room is decorated in yellow and neon pink, all florals and crochet and fuss, which I assume to be rural Afrikaner style. Somebody has fixed little seashells around the frame of a large hanging mirror in the bathroom but the glue into which the shells are embedded has turned grey with dust and age. I am tempted to hand back my keys and flee, yet I continue to pace around the alien though somehow familiar room. The view from the window, which looks out on to stolid suburbia, is framed with curtains flounced and frilled. They are the type of curtains I suddenly recall seeing in the homes of the upwardly mobile in Soweto, the vast black township in Johannesburg.

I reconsider my response to the decor, thinking that if Longview Lodge is a black-owned rather than an Afrikaner guest house it might prove an asset in my quest to make some sense of the myriad stories I have heard about Sabrina and her family. It bemuses me to find black and Afrikaner style suddenly indistinguishable. Is this universal kitsch a sign of a blurring of the races? Its importance to me is a sign of my own prejudice, I realise, even if the superiority of my taste is so common a form of self-deception as to be unremarkable. My interest in the decor is purely pragmatic on this occasion, however. A white writer without African languages will be needing a friendly black translator-cum-referee to coax insights from the domestic workers, gardeners and office cleaners who worked over the years in the Van Schoor homes and businesses, and who may not readily trust me with their stories.

I go downstairs hoping to discover the race of the guest house owner. She is called Justina, the receptionist tells me, which could be either an Afrikaner or a black African name. I ask if I can meet her, but she is out. There are plaques bearing trite messages on the walls – 'Life is a journey not a destination' and 'Love is a strange thing … but we cannot live without it'. Unable to decide if I am staying or going, I get into my car and drive around Queenstown's hexagon, taking in the town's only claim to fame, the world's largest array of car badges at the Collector's Museum.

There are a number of once-gracious Victorian hotel buildings in Queenstown, including one called The Hexagon that served 118 breakfast courses every morning in its heyday. Built in gentry mode for use by British army officers, visiting businessmen and bureaucrats from London, the hotel's classic English family silver that characterised an elegant colonial lifestyle was subsequently sold off in the early days of apartheid by men with windfall aspirations who had no use for such frivolities. The hotels now house offices and shops and are mostly run down. I drive slowly past two businesses where Beverley and Sabrina worked together – the Queenstown franchise of Pam Golding Properties, one of South Africa's top real estate agencies, and Lady B, a florist and bridal boutique. A block away is Red Guard, the security company founded by Beverley and run for some time before her death by Allister and Lester, two of her three sons from a previous marriage.

Back at Longview Lodge, there is no one at the reception desk. I poke my head around the open doorway of a room from which a lot of noise is emanating. Justina is not there but her identity becomes clear: the dining room is full of her daughters and tiny grandchildren and a lot of informal feeding is under way. Adorning the fireplace is a large print of Robben Island, the prison where Nelson Mandela and other champions of the anti-apartheid struggle were incarcerated for 27 years.

It still amazes me that so many whites living in Cape Town claim to have been unaware for so long of the political prisoners languishing on Robben Island, despite seeing the island every day of their lives. Did they not wonder what went on there or why they could not go there? Part of the explanation is that whites were programmed through indoctrination not to notice, while blacks were programmed through oppression not to show that they objected. There is, of course, much hardship that we continue to ignore: the manifest poverty of the townships and rural areas, for example; the beggars on our streets.

Longview Lodge's owner, Justina Mashiya, turns up later. We chat about her guest house, which she says is frequented by 'government people', an indication along with the Robben Island picture that she has political credentials. A smiley woman with whom I relax very quickly, she tells me she knows a lot about the Beverley van Schoor case.

Justina remembers the East London murder trial of Sabrina's father, Louis van Schoor, a famous case during which the former policeman-turned-security guard's support-ers drove around with 'I love Louis' stickers, decorated with three bullet holes through a heart, on their cars. While many whites in East London at the time of Louis' trial believed he was a scapegoat for apartheid, few realised that his daughter was also being punished at Queenstown Girls' High for his sins. Sabrina's father's imprisonment signalled the start of a tormented life for the schoolgirl. 'Black kids began to tease me, calling my dad "*kaffir* killer". I used to cry and didn't want to go to school until eventually the headmistress called them in and threatened to expel them,' she told the court.

At home, according to Sabrina, her life was equally fraught. 'Mom didn't want me to have anything to do with my dad,' she said. In a diary written when she was 14, Sabrina referred to her family having been forced to flee East London for Queenstown after her parents' divorce because her father assaulted her mother and threatened to kill Beverley. Subsequently, Sabrina claimed in court that she had no recollection of her father's abuse, saying she believed the diary entry was the result of Beverley's campaign to poison her against her father. She said she longed to see Louis. 'My half-brothers didn't like my dad, except Shane, the youngest. He went to visit my dad in prison once when I was 18 and I was adamant I must go with him. I threw a tantrum and cried and cried until my mom couldn't stop me.'

According to Sabrina's court testimony, the people who befriended her were hardly ever whites. She told the judge that she was molested during her childhood on three occasions by white men, one of them a boyfriend of Beverley's. When she told her mother and brothers about the sexual abuse, they laughed and called her a liar, Sabrina claimed. The court realised there was too much controversy over memory of sexual abuse in children to evaluate the truth of Sabrina's claim that her mother betrayed her by not taking the sexual abuse charges seriously. A coloured man listened, however, which marked the start of a double life that few whites understood.

While still at school, Sabrina became pregnant by a

coloured man – the average white South African's nightmare. She told the judge her mother forced her to have an abortion by threatening to charge the father, a married policeman, with rape. A year later, she was pregnant again by another coloured man. Sabrina said in court that her mother urged her to abort this child even when she was five months into the pregnancy. She ran away from home. 'My mother found my coloured boyfriend by threatening his family. She told his mother I was a whore and, because his mother was a Christian, she made her son bring me back,' Sabrina said at her bail hearing.

Shunned by her half-brothers after refusing to terminate her pregnancy, Sabrina recalled: 'They called me to a meeting and told me it was my last chance to have an abortion. They said if I went ahead and had the baby, my child would never play with theirs.' From prison, Sabrina's father telephoned Beverley to announce his opposition to the abortion on the grounds that it was against the law. Sabrina gave birth to a girl, Tatum, three days after her 21st birthday. 'That baby was black – really black – when she came out,' Beverley's best friend, Maggie Riggien, told the court. 'And Bev just wept. I said something crazy, stupid, that we could make its skin lighter by putting it under a light; anything to console her. Things got worse after that.'

Sabrina told the judge: 'Every time we used to fight, it was always about coloureds ... She beat me with a shoe, a wooden spoon, anything she could find. She called me a whore. My mother has tried to shoot me, but she stopped before it got that far. She even stopped me from going to church because it was on a farm and I could meet people there she didn't approve of.'

Maggie Riggien agreed that Sabrina's mother used to lock her in her bedroom to stop her mixing with people of other races. 'Sabrina was hurt and scared, and a prisoner in her own home,' she explained in court. 'Bev used to call her a whore for "running around with *kaffirs* and *hotnots*". Bev hit her in the face, a lot. I saw how she treated her and I did nothing. This town will say I betrayed Bev, but she would have expected me to tell the truth.'

The facts of Sabrina's case became clear to the investigating officer, Inspector Stephen Rheeders, the day after Beverley van Schoor's funeral, when Sabrina corroborated his pieced-together theory in a confession following her arrest. But when Judge Leach turned his attention to the question of sentencing, he admitted he did not know how much of Sabrina's evidence to believe. Nor did I after reading the court transcript. Was Sabrina lying? A pathological liar perhaps, which is how the prosecution assessed her. What was her motive – Beverley's abuse, her mother's racism, monetary gain, or all the above? Was Sabrina sorry for what she had done?

The judge summoned Mark Welman, a professor at Rhodes University in nearby Grahamstown and a registered clinical psychologist, to help him understand the accused's personality. A respected South African expert in the prediction of criminal behaviour, Professor Welman explained the context of his psychological profile on Sabrina van Schoor. 'The defendant pleaded guilty to a charge of murder but contends that there are mitigating factors in so far as she was a victim of verbal, emotional and physical abuse directed at her by her mother and that her actions were motivated by fear of a "demonic" mother.'

The charges Sabrina made against her mother in a number of interviews with Professor Welman were checked by his office: some proved true, some false, others debatable. In the daughter's mind, it seems, the mother was a threatening, manipulative figure – the superpower in her life. For some reason, Sabrina could not look at Beverley realistically as an ordinary middle-aged woman who was not even powerful in her own street.

Many of us have turned on our mothers at some point: it has been a respected rite of passage in the West since Freud first incriminated the female breast. Yet love usually triumphs in the end. Most mothers are essentially the same, recognising themselves in each other from generation to generation. Most love their children despite the intense daily labour of mothering and the terrifying emotions of anger, fear and frustration that lurk among the romantic ideals of child-rearing. Most know the agony of ambivalence in the face of the motherhood myths of unremitting gentleness and goodness. All of us are wounded by our childhoods, as Freud told us, and made an industry out of telling us. Still, most of us survive intact, more or less fond of our parents. It takes years to kill the love children automatically feel for parents, especially their mothers. There are cases of mothers snapping and killing their children and creating crimes so terrible they are supposed to be beyond understanding. Occasionally, sons and daughters snap and kill their mothers, supposedly forfeiting the right to be understood because they have breached a powerful taboo.

Professor Welman looked closely at the question of whether Sabrina regretted murdering her mother and concluded: 'While the defendant exhibited a degree of remorse, this appears to be related more to the consequences that the offence holds for her, particularly her loss of freedom, than to the actual committing of the offence. For instance, she displayed intense dysphoric emotion when talking about "paying for what she had done" but her emotions were far more subdued when relating details of the murder and of the planning of the murder. My clinical impression is that there is an important sense in which the defendant feels that her actions were justified by the circumstances that she found herself in.'

On the 'vexed question of motive', Professor Welman told the court: '... it must be stated that despite intensive discussion with the defendant and with several key witnesses, this report is unfortunately unable to offer conclusive insight into the reason why the defendant had her mother murdered. It is conceivable that the defendant herself does not clearly understand the combination of thoughts, desires, conflicts and tensions that led to her actions, and her inability to offer a clear explanation of events may bear this out. The defendant insists that material gain was not her motive, and this may be true. But what is then equally apparent is that the deceased was not murdered because she posed a real or perceived threat to the defendant.'

One man who believes that money was Sabrina's motive is Inspector Stephen Rheeders of Queenstown's Murder and Robbery Unit. We meet outside Buffalo Springs Spur – one of Queenstown's smartest eateries and a place chosen as a bomb target by anti-apartheid activists during the turbulent Eighties. It is closed at nine in the morning so I follow him in my car to the police station. Light rain is falling and I am wearing Justina's raincoat with fake fur around the collar, having left my own plainer mac at home in dry Johannesburg. Walking behind Inspector Rheeders along a veranda at police headquarters, I am surprised by my flashy reflection in his office window and I think how odd it is to be investigating a disturbing crime in a strange town in somebody else's clothes.

Stephen Rheeders often investigates politically sensitive or otherwise difficult criminal cases. Described as the Eastern Cape's top cop by one journalist covering State vs Van Schoor, he is a manly Afrikaner with a brush-cut, a scar on his cheek and a confident stride: the sort of policeman you would trust to help you through thick and thin provided he thought you were innocent. He speaks English with flattened vowels, saying of his job, 'I like hunting the suspects. That's the best part.'

A shiny brass statue of a uniformed policeman, inscribed Best Non-Commissioned Officer Serious Crimes Eastern Cape 2002, is displayed on a bookcase beside Inspector Rheeders' desk. Answering the phone which rings incessantly the day after his return from leave, he is doing his best to remain patient with an obtuse colleague to whom he repeats the same advice over and over. He rolls his eyes heavenward for my benefit, his tone becoming increasingly patronising as he tells the caller, 'I don't know why I must come there, really. I'm going to tell you the same thing I'm telling you now. Seven counts of attempted murder: it's 3 to 9, not 3 and 9. I don't think it's so difficult but it seems difficult for you.'

Inspector Rheeders says it was easy to catch Sabrina; 'an open and shut case'. He tells me: 'We knew as soon as we arrived at the scene that it was an inside job because there was R2 500 still in the wallet on the deceased's bed.' Beverley's missing cellphone was the initial focus of the police investigation against Feza Mdutshane – the hitman hired by Sabrina via a gangster called Gino Redcliffe. She was caught five days later when Mdutshane agreed to Inspector Rheeders' request to call her and demand payment. Police arrested her at a local motor dealership moments after she handed Feza R3 000 to 'get out of town'.

Inspector Rheeders reaches for a file. Leafing through it, he looks up and asks, 'Do you want to see the photo album of the murder scene?' I recoil, saying no emphatically. He grins and pages on, the pictures informing his commentary of the ghastly events at 73 Berry Street on a cold morning in March a year ago.

Shortly after he arrested her, Sabrina admitted to Rheeders that she was aware of R170 000 missing from Pam Golding Properties' bank account. In the investigating officer's view, the missing money was stolen by Sabrina. Rheeders, as well as the public prosecutor and Sabrina's brothers, believe that, knowing she was about to be accused of stealing the money, Sabrina decided to kill her mother and put the blame for the shortfall on Beverley. That was Sabrina's motive for murder, they believe. 'Her mother gave her everything money could buy,' says Rheeders. 'That was the problem. That's what happens. She was spoilt. On the Monday before the murder, they discovered the money was missing and arranged an internal investigation. She knew she was about to be caught.'

During the trial, Allister van Schoor, Sabrina's half-brother, told the judge of a meeting that had been arranged between auditors, himself, his mother and Sabrina. It was to take place on the Friday when Beverley was murdered. Missing bank statements were subsequently found in a drawer of Sabrina's desk, he said.

'I am convinced Sabrina took that money,' says Inspector Rheeders. 'She used it to buy friends. Those people she used to drink with – she paid for everything. That's why they liked her.' What of Sabrina's plea in mitigation of sentence that she plotted the murder because her mother humiliated and beat her for sleeping with boyfriends of another race? Rheeders wrinkles his nose and laughs. 'Her lawyer just wanted to make a name for himself,' he says.

The telephone rings and rings. We arrange to meet again when Inspector Rheeders has caught up with the backlog on his desk. As I turn to go, I realise I have to brace up and look at the photographs. He smiles when I ask him to show them to me. I walk back and stand behind his chair as he pages slowly through the file. There is a young black man standing in the veld, pointing into the grass. He is wearing black trousers, trainers, a grey sweater and a black baseball cap. 'That's the co-accused pointing out where he threw away the knife,' explains Rheeders. Several more of Feza Mdutshane and then the subject changes to a large, young, white woman carelessly dressed in jeans and a shapeless pullover, also pointing. 'That's Sabrina, showing us where she parked her car ... there she's showing us where she passed Feza in the passage just before her mother was murdered.'

Then comes a monstrous sight, a picture of Beverley van Schoor's half-naked body, the nightdress pulled up to her chest, her neck slashed, a crimson tangle of muscles, veins and tendons. I gasp and turn away. 'It was a shocking sight even for me,' Rheeders says grimly. 'I knew Beverley well. She was a very nice person.' He continues to study the photographs. 'This is exactly as it was that morning when we arrived,' he explains. 'Baby clothes on the carpet beside the body, and a bloody T-shirt where the killer wiped his hands.' He glances up, sees me hovering at a safe distance, sighs and slams the file shut.

My next meeting the same day is with Sabrina's defence attorney, Siphiwo Burwana. I have already learnt a bit about his background from Justina: she says he was a political activist during the apartheid years. I wait for him at Buffalo Springs Spur, having discussed the case briefly with him on the phone and offered to buy him lunch. When he arrives with his sister and girlfriend, I register my irritation by saying, 'Oh, you brought your whole family?' He replies, 'You never know who to trust. I go everywhere with witnesses.' I look for humour but cannot tell if he is joking.

We order steaks and chat, sizing each other up. I see a man in his thirties, his eyes hidden behind stylish shades, wary and self-conscious. Both of his trendily dressed companions seem to think he is fabulous, seldom taking their eyes off his face, smiling indulgently whether he is being aggressive, serious or flippant. I listen to him in all three modes for a long time and then ask about the money missing from Pam Golding Properties: did Sabrina take it, as Inspector Rheeders believes?

'The brothers made accusations they were unable to prove. One thing I realised about the Van Schoor family is they love money. We know that Sabrina's mother sometimes took money from that same trust fund that Sabrina is alleged to have defrauded. Sabrina testified that the mother was going to charge the brother with theft of money from the same account.'

Which brother?

'I don't know. I can't differentiate between these whites,' he replies.

They all look the same to you? He nods and we both laugh at the reversal of an old racist joke. He seems to have relaxed but when the sunglasses come off, his eyes have an unexpectedly angry look. 'You should know that Stephen Rheeders, the investigating officer in this case, is the bosom friend of one of those brothers,' he continues. 'I don't have anything against Stephen as a person. I wrote a recommendation for him. He's a very good policeman. Most of the cases I represent are from his unit. We work together a lot. But people in Queenstown and in this whole country must change. I tell Stephen all the time: you are a very good policeman but you must just get rid of your racial prejudice. He just laughs.

'Even the judge in this case was not free of racism. Every individual in this country is a product of a certain environment. Despite the fact that Judge Leach – who, by the way, is one of the best judges in South Africa: he knows the law and he knows how to apply it – despite the fact he knew Sabrina had done wrong, he felt sympathetic to her because she was white. If she had been black, he would have been harsher.' He pauses, searching my face for a response. 'I don't blame Inspector Rheeders or Judge Leach. I don't even blame Sabrina's father for what he has done. There were certain ideas implanted in people's minds by apartheid. The white community has never been rehabilitated from such ideas. If they have been thinking the black man is subhuman since their childhood, how can they now be sentenced for that belief? All of us are victims of apartheid, blacks and whites.'

Does this mean that blacks can be racists as well, I wonder. 'Those to whom evil is done do evil in return', according to W H Auden. There was a time when the accusation of racism could only be levelled at whites in South Africa because it reflected the prevailing power relationship between the races. Now that the country has a black government and a growing black middle class, are black racists emerging?

Siphiwo Burwana came to live in Queenstown three years ago, partly to ply his profession but also to get involved in 'local civic structures as an activist for the governing party', the African National Congress. 'This town is still run by whites,' he says. 'The black people who have been elected to office are still very much afraid of white people and so they are only rubber-stamping.'

He met Sabrina van Schoor at Queenstown police station, having gone there at the behest of her co-accused, Feza Mdutshane, shortly after her arrest. 'Stephen Rheeders was also there because Sabrina wanted to go before a magistrate to make a confession. She was crying. She asked me to help her. She told me she was very much ill-treated by her mother. She stated categorically that her mother was a racist. I believed her then and especially after I investigated her claims around Queenstown. The black and coloured people I interviewed said they loved Sabrina very much. They confirmed she was not a racist. Stephen Rheeders will tell you they loved her only because she bought them drinks. You cannot ask the white people of this town about racism, because they are all suffering from the same sickness. They are all racists.'

Burwana reminds me of the evidence of racism he presented in court in Sabrina's defence. One of Sabrina's former boyfriends, Navin Neermul, described how Beverley attempted to intimidate him while they were dating. 'Her mother came over with two security guards to tell me that if I didn't stop seeing her daughter, something would happen to me. She was a very arrogant and racist person,' he said. Beverley had not approved of their relationship 'because I was not white', he claimed. Questioned by the prosecutor on whether Beverley's disapproval did not stem from the fact that he, as a working man, was in an intimate relationship with a schoolgirl at the time, he replied: 'I would have understood that if that had been the reason.'

Beverley's friend, Maggie Riggien, told the judge that Beverley believed her daughter's attraction to black men was a reaction to her father's crimes. 'Bev said that maybe it's because her father shot those blacks that she's trying to rectify it by sleeping with blacks and coloureds.' The prosecutor tried hard to get witnesses to admit that it was the 'low morality' of Sabrina's boyfriends that her mother objected to, not their race. But none in the courtroom apart from Beverley's sons and friends could be shaken from the belief that it was all about colour.

A crowd of black and coloured supporters cheered as Sabrina confessed to matricide in court. Among them was Maria Phillips, who had never met Sabrina but wanted to encourage her. 'She was just doing exactly what Mr (Nelson) Mandela said – making friends with people of different colours. But her mother tried to stop it. She was a very rude lady,' Phillips told a local newspaper.

'She liberated herself from racial oppression, just as Africans in this country had to do,' Siphiwo Burwana told the court. 'I was very happy to represent Sabrina,' he tells me. 'It was a very unusual situation for me, a black man defending a white woman – especially in Queenstown. The court was packed out with black and coloured people because the feeling of the whole black community was to support her.'

Siphiwo's sister and girlfriend have barely spoken during the meal, not least because he has shot them stony looks on the few occasions they have ventured an opinion. If Siphiwo Burwana is a democrat by political persuasion, as he claims, it is not reflected in his stranglehold on the lunchtime conversation.

I tell Siphiwo that I am going to visit Louis van Schoor in prison the following day. He says he was not impressed by Louis as a witness in Sabrina's trial, having called the father to give evidence in the hope that he would paint a damning picture of the deceased's character. 'He was only interested in wiping his own slate clean,' Siphiwo says of Louis' contribution to Sabrina's defence. The lawyer describes how the mass murderer, brought to court for Sabrina's trial in shackles, told the judge that he wanted parole after serving only half his sentence so that he could adopt his baby granddaughter Tatum while Sabrina was in prison. Sabrina spoke in support of his plea for parole, saying that, even if evidence were produced to prove that her father had assaulted her mother during their marriage, she would still be happy if he looked after her baby. 'I don't believe he would assault my child. She is his first grandchild,' Sabrina told the judge.

When we get up to leave the restaurant, a young waitress – whose Buffalo Springs Spur badge gives her name as Elinah – sidles up to me and asks in a barely audible voice, 'Are you American?' It might as well have been a whisper, a secret confided: you are white, talking and laughing with blacks in Queenstown ... Where on earth do you come from? When I tell her I am from Johannesburg, we stand staring at each other for a moment as if one wishful thought unites us. Then she smiles and hurries away.

The weather has cleared for the 100-mile drive back to the coast early next day. The rain-soaked browns and greens of the veld glitter in the morning sun; the Amatolas on the horizon are sharp and blue. I am on my way to meet Louis van Schoor for the first time.

*

On the outskirts of East London is Fort Glamorgan, where father and daughter are imprisoned within a stone's throw of each other. A low-slung sprawl of sand-coloured buildings, it opens its multiple gates for one hour per visitor on Saturdays, Sundays and public holidays. Visitors gather in a reception area near the outer entrance where, having surrendered their cellular phones and personal details, they board a bus that shuttles to and from the heavily guarded, double-fenced and electrified main gates of the prison itself. I am the only white among forty visitors apart from a man of seventy-something, who looks of indeterminate origins and is trying as hard to attract my attention as I am trying to avoid eye contact with him.

We are herded into two prefabricated huts immediately inside the top security zone – women in one, men in the other – to be body searched. My camera and tape recorder are confiscated, along with some backache pills. It is a short walk to the women's prison on the left, the men's on the right. I turn right to visit Louis. In the entrance stands the man I avoided talking to earlier, wanting to know: 'Have you come to see Louis?' I nod. 'How do you do,' he beams, hand outstretched, clearly assuming we have a lot in common. 'I'm his father.' I smile back, wondering how he would react if I revealed that I mistook him for a coloured. How long would our smiles last if I struck up a conversation about the hypocrisy of the former ruling class as evidenced by

28

the proliferation of coloured children among rural Africans wherever a lonely white man lived.

There has been a power cut at Fort Glamorgan. Beside the reception window is a heavy metal door with an opening through which I can see a dark passage into the cells. I say I have come to visit Louis van Schoor and the warder calls him by his first name on the intercom. I wait, glancing into the black hole, expecting to see him in suitably contrite mode through the impenetrable door. Instead, he suddenly appears among the milling visitors, tall, dark-haired and authoritative despite the slightly ridiculous bright orange pyjama-like prison garb, striding towards me as if he owns the joint.

The sense of sheer physical power I get on meeting Louis van Schoor is scary. He shakes my hand with such force that I feel my teeth will chatter and I clamp my jaw to stop my mouth trembling. Staring straight into my face, he looks a portrait of confidence. Alfred Hitchcock's description of '... the moral imbecile, who takes pride in his own utter recklessness and depraved ingenuity' comes to mind.

I follow him into a communal visiting room where he immediately takes charge of the interview, telling me he is no longer locked up during the day but running the tuck shop for visitors because his parole is imminent. I am holding my notebook but as soon as I open it, he tells me not to record our conversation. 'I can't say very much,' he confides, lowering his voice a bit, 'because I am at a very sensitive stage of my parole hearing and people might take it the wrong way.' I commit this sentence to memory as he is explaining, self-evidently, that his pre-parole privileges include seeing his visitors face-to-face rather than through glass.

At the time of Sabrina's trial, Louis sent a message to the court via his spiritual adviser: 'I let her down; I wasn't there for her. Please tell her that I love her.' Now he tells me he blames the community and the family for the murder. 'They knew what was going on between Bev and Sabrina. But they did nothing. In a small place like Queenstown, everybody knew.'

When I ask him to describe his feelings about Sabrina's crime, he says carefully: 'I don't approve of what happened but she's my daughter, I love her and I'll always support her. I understand why it happened but I can't say much.' Then he remembers his former wife and goes on more passionately, nodding when I waggle my notebook: 'Bev was a domineering, possessive and manipulative woman. She would do anything to get her own way; otherwise all hell broke loose. For example, there was a period during our marriage when I worked nights on police duty. Bev didn't like this: she wanted attention. So she started to break windows in our home, then called the police station and said someone was attacking the house. It worked for a while and she would be the centre of attention night after night. But then I got suspicious and caught her red-handed, throwing the stones herself.'

He goes on: 'If she wanted your friendship, she'd get it. She would convince you. She knew the only way to hurt me was through my kids. She turned them all against me, except Sabrina and Shane (one of Beverley's three sons, who were all formally adopted by Louis during the marriage). She was an out and out racist. She didn't like them (black people). There was no place in her life for them.'

She was a racist! What about him? I close my notebook and ask about his crimes, to which he responds smoothly: 'I can't say much. I have learnt, in here. I am a changed man.' He is so guarded that I decide to leave the substantive part of the interview for a subsequent visit. I stand up, telling him I am going to see Sabrina.

As I walk towards the open doorway, he tells me he is writing a book himself, a parting shot that may signal another reason, apart from his parole hopes, for his reluctance to discuss his crimes. I ask Louis if he will live in the East London area after his release, which seems a foregone conclusion if he genuinely intends to adopt his granddaughter. 'No,' he replies. 'I'm moving to Cape Town.'

With little Tatum?

He looks indignant. 'No, I'll have to get established first.'

Chapter Two

Each time I saw Sabrina I was struck by her size. Although she was standing back from the bulletproof glass window in the visitors' cubicle at Fort Glamorgan prison in East London, she was so tall that I had to bend forward to see her face. On one occasion, amused by my bowing, she mimicked it, leaning towards me, her bejewelled hands holding on to the back of the chair, pinkies sticking up. She was smiling coyly and tilting her head to one side as if to say, here I am in all my glory. Her hair was yanked back and I remember thinking that she was the kind of girl who would have trouble finding a partner at a dance. At well over six feet tall and weighing 328 pounds – having inherited her father's height and her mother's width – she was an awkward shape for a girl from Queenstown, where conformity is everything.

I had already told Sabrina about the book I was writing but I decided to outline my intentions again to be sure that she understood our relationship. She did not respond when I asked if there were perhaps as many questions on her mind about me as on mine about her. Looking bemused at the idea that she might want to examine my motives, she seemed far from canny. She spoke unexpectedly pukka English through a microphone behind the thick glass exactly a year to the day since she murdered her mother. 'When I woke this morning, I didn't want to get up. The first thing I saw when I opened my eyes was a hallucination of my mother's body lying on the floor. I don't know what I feel. I still feel I wasn't part of her murder. I can't really believe that I was part of it. I loved my mom but I despised what she did to me and my daughter. If I could go back, I'd rather kill myself than organise the death of my own mother. Life without Mom is too difficult. I'm too used to her. Sometimes I even miss her shouting at me.

'I regret it very much,' Sabrina continues. The words are tumbling out as if rehearsed. I keep wondering if I have ever seen a bigger woman. To be the size she is in a conservative community of an unfair country that categorises people purely on their physique, whether it be the colour of the skin or the dimensions of the body, conjures immediate images of a lonely child and an outcast adult. Sabrina's eyes, surprisingly beautiful, never leave my face. Is this perhaps the 'frozen watchfulness' psychoanalysts notice in severely traumatised patients who no longer trust anybody? The intensity of her stare makes it a relief for me to avert my own eyes while jotting down her comments. 'I had got to the stage in my life where I couldn't handle it any more,' she goes on. 'The way Mom tormented me, the way she threatened my child in front of me, the way she was always trying to turn me against my father.'

Sabrina admits that she provoked her mother by being promiscuous and drunk almost every night. When I point out during our second interview that any mother would worry and rail about such behaviour, she shakes her head, tilting it sideways a bit, trying to look appealing. 'I wanted to prove to my mother and to myself that men did want me because she used to say to me that I was ugly. Her problem was just with the colour of the men I fooled around with, nothing else. I went with blacks and coloureds because I liked the way they treated me but also because I didn't like white men because of what happened in the past to me. I spent my whole life with black people. When I walked to town holding our maid's hand as a young child, I used to call her Mom. My mother knew this and it didn't bother her – until I got older. I am more a part of them (blacks and coloureds) than the white community. They accept me with open arms.

'My whole family is racist except me, maybe because only I had a black mother, Gladys, our maid. My mom worked just about 24 hours a day. I was never looked after by my mother. Everybody will tell you I'm lying because my mom gave me a car and she put diamond rings away for me. She bought my loyalty by giving me things but I wanted someone to show me love rather than buy it. That's probably why I went for the coloureds and blacks. They are poor; they haven't got money but they do give you love.'

Sabrina stresses her resentment at being prevented by Beverley from seeing her father. She is clearly haunted by her first visit to Louis at Fort Glamorgan, years after last seeing him on his smallholding in East London, the site of her idyllic childhood fantasies. She remembers standing in tears on the prison steps, not knowing what to expect. 'I didn't know how he felt because Mom had always told me he didn't love me or care about me. All the letters I sent him and the letters he sent me were destroyed by Mom. She insisted he didn't care about me but I discovered when I finally met him in prison that it wasn't true.

'I wanted to leave home after Tatum was born. But Mom said she'd go to the (social) welfare (authorities) and dispute my fitness as a mother. She said she would keep my baby. My brothers did what they liked but Mom wanted me to stay with her until Lord knows when. Then I realised that, although she loved the baby in front of people, she used to hit Tatum. She used to take her stress out on my daughter while I was at work.

'I remember the night I realised I had had enough. Mom phoned me at the club; she was always phoning me there and shouting at me to come home, even though it was her club and I was working there for her. She told me my baby was crying and wouldn't stop. She said if my child didn't learn some manners, she was going to kill her one night.'

When I ask Sabrina why her mother referred to the baby's 'manners', a curious notion to apply to an eighteen-month-old, she gives a bitter little laugh. 'That's because Tatum was coloured. Mom always said blacks and coloureds have no manners. So if Tatum was getting on Mom's nerves, it was the baby who had to learn some manners, not Mom who had to learn some patience.'

Our time is up and I am about to leave when I notice that Sabrina's eyes have become glassy with tears. I hover in front of the door while she blows me kisses, thanks me lavishly for coming and stares at me, perhaps imploring me to say something. Her neediness and the speed of her affection are disconcerting. I am wondering if I should remind her that I am a professional doing a job, not her friend, when the head of the prison puts his face around the door and I hurry away.

By the time I next visit Sabrina at Fort Glamorgan, I have learnt a lot more about her history during a second visit to Queenstown. My plan on that occasion is to confirm the broad details of the family with her. After spending many hours talking to Beverley's closest friend, Maggie Riggien, and to Sabrina's school chum, Cherie van Heerden, as well as to one of her brothers, Allister van Schoor, among others, I realise that Sabrina never got on well with her mother and that her abiding characteristic is catastrophically low self-esteem. Perhaps it is that debilitating though common psychological affliction that will help explain her shocking crime. Most people's feelings about themselves fluctuate but those who feel inadequate all the time are unable to direct their lives because they are perpetually reacting to others. If never affirmed by their parents, the adults who do not feel good about themselves are always looking for acceptance, according to a psychologist I talked to about the syndrome.

It is a cool, cloudless morning at the end of April 2003. Two giant steel doors just inside the prison entrance are being dragged open. A beefy female guard herds a group of uniformed prisoners out into the reception area, where I have been told to wait on a bench. I scan the faces of the seven silent women, searching for signs of evil, but they all seem blank and ordinary. As they look back at me impassively, I wish my instinct had been to say good morning rather than to stare at them.

While waiting in another bench-lined room for Sabrina to be brought from her cell, I greet a black woman beside me, who introduces me to her two friends and asks who I have come to see. Clapping her hands at Sabrina's name, she says, 'Give her our greetings.'

Sabrina is wearing her hair in jaunty bunches caught above her ears by twinkling pink clips and my initial impression of her shifts. She is no looker but I can see the appeal of this big-boned, buxom woman. The regulation denim looks fashionable enough on a person her age. Having heard from everyone I talked to in Queenstown how promiscuous Sabrina was, including an account from an indignant journalist who had been amazed to see her flirting at the height of her disgrace with a prison warder outside the courtroom at her bail hearing, I wonder if Sabrina's story is more of a commentary on sexual stereotyping than deep layers of racism. Perhaps she was simply interested in being popular with the blokes, whatever the wagging tongues might say about the colour of her boyfriends.

It does not take much to ignite gossip among Queenstown's 4000 white residents. The Van Schoor family was particularly vulnerable to small town envy and malice because Beverley had gone to great lengths to set herself up as a pillar of society. When she first came to Queenstown in 1984 – a penniless, battered divorcee and mother of four young children – she was determined to establish herself financially and ensure her children lacked nothing. In order to free herself from time-consuming child-rearing duties, Beverley went so far as to leave Sabrina in East London with her mother and place her three sons in a boarding school.

She worked hard and achieved rapid success, buying a number of businesses in Queenstown including a private security company called Red Guard, which she reckoned was ripe for expansion, a florist shop she called Lady B in tribute to her grandiose self-image, and a franchise from the prestigious international realtor Pam Golding Properties, which immediately bolstered her status among the town's elite. She was soon well enough established to send Sabrina's brothers to swanky Queen's College alongside the sons of wealthy white farmers. Maggie Riggien remembers all three of them receiving cars from their mother as soon as they acquired driving licences at 18. Sabrina, having moved back to her mother's home following her grandmother's death in East London, was also given everything she wanted – materially.

Beverley's sons were good-looking, gifted athletes. Like any parent, Beverley was proud of their sporting achievements, which made them popular at school and drew favourable attention to her. The three boys, who had each other for support while Beverley was building her career, got along well with their mother but bullied and taunted Sabrina. 'They saw how Bev treated Sabrina and probably thought it was okay,' says Maggie. 'Sabrina was just like the maid's child to all of them.'

Virtually everyone I spoke to in Queenstown described Beverley as 'respected' or 'ladylike'. For 20 years, she maintained her position in the town's upper echelon with several hairdresser's appointments each week and a full-time seamstress to stock her wardrobe. While much was known about Beverley's business acumen and genteel appearance, it was also general knowledge in Queenstown's close-knit white community that Beverley had been at odds with Sabrina virtually all her life. Maggie, who first met the family when Sabrina was four, remembers friction between the two even then. Sabrina was a large, clumsy child, according to Riggien when she testified at Sabrina's bail hearing. 'She didn't fit (Beverley's) image of beauty and success and she was often sworn at.'

Maggie remembers that she and Beverley, both divorcees, used to go on dates together in Queenstown when Sabrina was six or seven. 'Bev would be there, full of fun, sitting on the bed doing her make-up, and Sabrina would be hanging around, looking for attention. It hurt me that Bev always waved her away, saying, "Just go, just go." She would call the maid to take Sabrina for a walk or something. Bev had no time for Sabrina. She was never accepted. She was a problem for Bev. If she had been cuter, more like the porcelain dolls Bev used to make, it would have been different.'

By the time Sabrina left school in 1997, aged 17, Maggie says Beverley's dismissive attitude towards the child had hardened. However, Sabrina had grown into an imposing six-footer who gave Beverley as good as she got verbally. Although Sabrina was capable of protecting herself, she told the judge at her trial that she never dreamt of hitting her mother in retaliation for the back-handers sometimes dealt her by Beverley and witnessed on occasion by Maggie.

At an early age, Sabrina already had a small town infamy for the time she spent with her black and coloured friends at school. She seemed to regard the disdain of the upwardly mobile circles in which her mother moved in Queenstown as a small price to pay for the acceptance and affection of her unconventional friends, according to Cherie van Heerden, Sabrina's only remaining white friend from her days at Queenstown Girls' High. Cherie remembers Sabrina becoming socially isolated around the age of 12 because she was prevented by her mother from participating in school activities outside the classroom. One afternoon, at the start of the school year when both girls were hoping to be picked for the hockey team, Cherie recalls asking her own mother to collect Sabrina for practice. 'Aunty Bev came to the door and told us Sabrina wasn't coming. She didn't explain why: that was just the way it was. Sabrina was not allowed to have a social life, and so she became an outcast. The blacks and coloureds were then her only option. They were flattered by the attention of a white girl. And later on, her boyfriends followed the same racial pattern.'

It does not seem to occur to Cherie that Sabrina's black and coloured friends might have been her first choice of companions. Like most of her community, Cherie's aversion to black people and the assumption of their inferiority make it improbable for Sabrina to have chosen a coloured boyfriend. Despite telling me several times that Sabrina was raised by Gladys, a black woman on whom Cherie knows Sabrina relied for mothering, there is never any hint from Cherie that Sabrina might have preferred the company of the maid to her mother.

Cherie is, nevertheless, acutely conscious of Sabrina's painful world. Even as a child, she was struck by the contrast in Beverley's public demeanour and the private humiliation to which she subjected Sabrina. 'She would order Sabrina around like a slave. When she came home from work, she would plonk herself on the sofa in front of the TV and tell Sabrina, do this, fetch that. Sabrina was expected to wait on her like a servant. And she never trusted Sabrina, even on trivial things. Once, I remember her sending Sabrina to Pick 'n Pay with a shopping list. Sabrina came back with everything except avocados, which were sold out. Aunty Bev went mad, accusing her of lying. I couldn't believe it when she picked up the phone and called Pick 'n Pay to check if Sabrina was telling the truth. Though the supermarket confirmed that the avos were sold out, there was no apology to Sabrina.'

When Sabrina became pregnant by one of her boyfriends while still at school, Beverley was incensed. According to Maggie, she subsequently insisted on knowing Sabrina's whereabouts virtually hour by hour. 'After the first pregnancy, Sabrina was a prisoner in the house,' says Maggie. 'I remember on one occasion, a year before the murder, Sabrina phoning while I was with Bev to tell her mom that she had had a car crash. The first question Bev asked was, "Why are you there, in that street, when you are supposed to be at Pick 'n Pay? Are you with the coloureds again?" Only after those questions, and in a loud, angry voice, did Bev ask, "Are you injured?" To be around those two was very, very hurtful.'

For the most part Sabrina was tormented by her mother and, Maggie speculates, she began to suffer from depression. 'She was always in her bedroom. She even ate her meals in her bedroom. Now and then, Bev would mention, "Sabrina ate with me last night", but I know it didn't happen often because I was there at the house a lot of the time and I saw and heard how it was between them. One day I went into my office, crying, and I told my colleagues: "The way Bev talked to Sabrina last night was terrible. I can't take it any more."

'Bev was an important lady in Queenstown and Sabrina's looks and her friendship with blacks and coloureds were an embarrassment to her. I remember one day I was at my father's butchery. Chris, the guy serving behind the counter, is quite a small guy. Sabrina was on the other side, ordering meat for Bev in the same polite way as her mother had in public, even though each of them could swear and talk ugly in private like people who grew up in a township like Soweto, or somewhere like that. When Sabrina left, Chris was shaking his head and he said to me, "What a giant of a woman!" Those were the comments she got from white men, whereas the black and coloured guys thought, "What a trophy, a white lady, and with money under the table for everything we ask her for!" So Sabrina had become an increasing embarrassment to Bev, now that she was not only friends with blacks and coloureds but sleeping with them. But that was not all.'

Maggie's gravelly voice sounds outraged most of the time she is talking during our second interview in June 2003. We are sitting in a coffee shop in Johannesburg shortly after her move to the city. A businesswoman of fifty-something, Maggie left Queenstown in disgust after being the only person to give evidence about the true nature of the relationship between mother and daughter at Sabrina's bail hearing. She tells me that Beverley's life was in crisis the year before her murder. 'She was middle-aged, overweight and frightened of the future. She still had a pretty face but men were no longer lining up to court her. She was still respected in the business community but what the people of Queenstown did not know was that she had lost everything that mattered most to her.

'Bev had given her security company, Red Guard, to two of her sons on condition that they continued to pay her life insurance and pension premiums and that they gave her an agreed monthly allowance, sufficient to cover her overheads,' explains Maggie. 'This arrangement worked for a couple of years while her sons built up the business. But then they both got married the year before the murder and decided they needed all the income from Red Guard. So they stopped paying her insurance premiums and her allowance.'

Although Beverley continued to run her auction business, estate agency and florist, these had become only marginally profitable and she had been relying for some time on the monthly payments from Red Guard to finance her extravagant lifestyle. In an attempt to boost her income, she began to sell insurance policies at night, secretly, to black and coloured staff and patients at Komani Hospital on the outskirts of Queenstown. 'She would not have done that at night in mid-winter if she had not been desperate,' says Maggie. 'I arranged for my daughter's fiancé to go with her because it was not safe for her to be out late at night on her own. She was exhausted, mentally and physically.

'The same thoughts were burnt into her head, day after day: "I've got nothing. How am I going to get profitable businesses going in the next ten years before I'm too old? I'm so tired," ' recalls Maggie. 'She felt betrayed by two of her sons and sought legal advice with a view to suing them for ownership of Red Guard. She was lonely because those sons, Lester and Allister, seldom invited her for Sunday lunch or to share their beach holidays, as they had done in the past. The problem there was that Bev came with Sabrina and the baby – a package – and Tatum wasn't white. Lester and Allister were big businessmen in Queenstown and the coloured baby was a problem for them and their in-laws.'

Meanwhile, Sabrina was pleading with her mother to be allowed to leave home. Beverley refused, saying she could go but Tatum must stay. Remembering the appalling arguments between the two, Maggie's voice reaches a crescendo of indignation: 'I told Bev in December, a few months before her death, when she and I spent a whole month together talking about her problems, "Let Sabrina go." But she wouldn't. Partly, it was because she needed Sabrina to run around her doing the things she was too tired to do: "Sabrina, get the flowers; Sabrina, lock this, open that; Sabrina, do the shopping at Pick 'n Pay, Sabrina, cook my supper ..." And partly it was because Bev was frightened of being alone.'

Although ashamed of Sabrina's baby initially, Beverley grew to love Tatum, according to Maggie. 'But there were none of the usual bonds between her and Sabrina because Bev never knew Sabrina. She left her with the maid all her life and when the problems started, Bev and Sabrina didn't know how to talk to each other. So there was no companionship with Sabrina – that wasn't what Bev was hanging on to. She was hanging on to the baby for company, for a purpose in life, even though Tatum was the reason Bev was no longer invited as often to her sons' homes.'

Around the same time, Beverley made an ill-fated business decision to buy a mini-cricket business and bar situated in a corrugated iron warehouse in Factory Road, at the heart of Queenstown's industrial area. Called Action Quicket, the business was drawn to Beverley's attention by Sabrina when she heard it was for sale from a friend who was a regular at the bar adjoining the mini-cricket pitch. Beverley's sons, who had formed a team called the Red Devils when mini-cricket was first launched in Queenstown, regularly drank there too, though on different nights from the black and coloured patrons because the business had been informally segregated on racial lines under the original management.

Sabrina encouraged her mother to investigate the viability of the business with a view to easing the financial woes that had become Beverley's obsession. Privately, though, Sabrina saw Action Quicket as a social opportunity for herself. 'When Mom saw the figures and saw that she could make loads more money, she decided that she would go ahead with my project and buy Action Quicket so that it would provide more publicity for her as well as more money,' Sabrina told me.

Maggie believes the mini-cricket was Beverley's final undoing. 'Even her murder was planned there, and Sabrina's ultimate betrayal of her mother came because of that business. Since she was a young child, Sabrina had been stealing money from Bev's purse. She didn't want it to buy things for herself, because she had everything she needed and she didn't want any more things. What she wanted was acceptance and she used the stolen money to buy friends. If she had money in her pocket, she could buy each one in the group at school a hamburger and then they would play with her. The same happened at Action Quicket. She would buy pizzas all round, costing R300 or more each time. The coloureds and the blacks used the phone whenever they felt like it – Bev told me the bill was over R12 000 one month. Sabrina let them do that, and she gave them free drinks. So Action Quicket, which was supposed to save Bev, was a flop.'

Although Action Quicket was a club designed principally as a venue for mini-cricket, its main source of income was the bar under Sabrina's management. Maggie says Sabrina was determined to have the social life Beverley had denied her – at any price. The money Sabrina used to buy pizzas and drinks for friends who could not always afford to pay, as well as the copious amounts consumed by Sabrina herself, came out of the till, Maggie believes, while the cash Sabrina presented to Beverley each night as takings from the club's cover charge and sale of drinks – so that Beverley would be fooled into thinking Action Quicket made a profit – was stolen by Sabrina from Beverley's property business. In Maggie's opinion and that of the investigating officer, some of the property rentals and sales deposits received by Sabrina at the counter from customers on occasions when Beverley was out of the office, which Sabrina was supposed to bank into the account of Pam Golding Properties, went into Sabrina's pocket instead.

Action Quicket had seemed to offer Sabrina the opportunity to mix with people her own age until she realised that Beverley was determined to keep an eye on her even while she was tending the bar. 'I thought I would have some sort of night life and she tried to mislead me to think I would have freedom. But no such luck. The Quicket was the only way I could get out of the house but I was always guarded by someone reporting to my mother that I was doing this with the coloureds or doing that with the blacks.'

It was obvious to Beverley that Action Quicket had been a disastrous investment but she could not dispose of it, her son Allister tells me. He says his mother still owed R60 000 of the purchase price and the previous owner was threatening legal action to repossess it. Beverley had consulted a lawyer, who told her the creditor could force her to sell even her own home to recoup the debt if she had no other assets. For a time, Beverley tried to run Action Quicket herself but long hours spent on her feet behind the bar after a busy day at Pam Golding Properties exhausted her. The coloureds who frequented the place when Sabrina was in attendance stayed away when Beverley was on duty, which meant Action Quicket was sometimes empty without Sabrina.

Adding to the tension and distrust that had dogged the mother-daughter relationship for years, Beverley's concern about Sabrina's mismanagement of the bar meant they were constantly quarrelling. Then, to exacerbate her accumulating financial problems, Beverley discovered the large sum of R170 000 missing from one of her estate agency bank accounts.

*

Fort Glamorgan's rules permit visits with prisoners on weekends and public holidays. I have chosen two public holidays, one of them Freedom Day on April 27, commemorating the achievement of democracy in South Africa, and the other May 1, which celebrates workers' rights worldwide. During this four-day visit, I am hoping Sabrina will talk me through the three weeks prior to the murder, from the moment she first considered killing her mother to the morning of Beverley's death.

She sits opposite me behind the glass, her arms folded on the narrow counter in front of her most of the time, leaning earnestly towards me and speaking mainly in a relaxed voice. I record what she tells me in my notebook, glancing up at her often, no longer bothered by her devouring stare but occasionally feeling that I am putting her under pressure by making her go over certain details surrounding the murder.

She begins: 'I was sitting one evening with a group of friends at Action Quicket. Mom phones. She phoned me all the time, all night, every night. Her quarrelling was getting worse and worse. She was hysterical that night. I really took her seriously when she said she would murder my daughter one night if Tatum carried on crying. I thought I would find my baby beaten black and blue by the time I got home. My daughter's father, Shaun Ortell, was there that night. I was very upset and I called him aside and told him I couldn't stand it any more. He was upset, too, and he said he knew someone who could help "once and for all". He said he would get that person to come and see me.'

Shaun Ortell, a young coloured man among several with whom Sabrina had a brief relationship which, she guesses, led to her second pregnancy, introduced her the following night to a man known to her and throughout her trial simply as Gino. She describes him as 'a good-looking guy with long black hair which he sometimes wears loose and sometimes ties up – a womaniser. He doesn't work as such: he sells drugs.'

Gino and Sabrina sat next to each other that night at Action Quicket. She remembers playing music as usual, mainly rhythm and blues, and sponsoring one of the drunken games her patrons enjoyed. Called down-down, it involved drinking as many neat tots of alcohol from different varieties of liquor as each player could tolerate before collapsing. Sabrina says she was smoking non-stop, her nerves frazzled. 'We were drinking rum and sambuca, sitting in a circle of friends. After a while, Gino signalled to me to meet him outside. He went downstairs first. I waited a bit and then followed. We sat together on a bench under a tree. It was about 9.45. He said to me, "Sabrina, what is wrong?" I explained the situation between me and my mother, how she was always shouting at me, how she tried to control me all the time, and especially how she loved my baby one minute and threatened to harm her the next.'

After listening to her complaints, Sabrina recalls, Gino remained silent for a while before telling her that Shaun Ortell was also worried about Tatum's safety. 'Then he said he could take care of her (Beverley). I knew he meant murder, even though we didn't use the word, because Gino is quite a dangerous guy.'

They returned upstairs, one at a time, and continued drinking. Sabrina remembers feeling so tense after the conversation with Gino that she couldn't sit still among her friends. She suggested they all dance. The tables and chairs were pushed aside and a party got under way. 'I kept playing the Shaggy song *It Wasn't Me*, over and over. I remember that because I caught the eye of the father of my daughter while I was singing the words and we both laughed.'

Sabrina says she could not sleep at all that night despite being very drunk when she went to bed. While part of her wanted to go ahead with the murder, she says she feared the consequences. The following evening, she sat with the same group to drink and listen to R&B. Gino arrived early but took no notice of Sabrina, who was chain-smoking and gulping her drinks. Waiting for his signal, her heart thumping, she wondered if her friends might begin to think she and Gino were having an affair. She grins as she tells me that this was a pleasant prospect because she was attracted to Gino.

Eventually, Gino leaned over and whispered that they needed to talk. He strolled downstairs and, after a few minutes, Sabrina followed. He told her the price was R250 000 and said that the man who would 'take care of it' would be coming from Johannesburg with a group of people the following evening. Sabrina says she baulked at the price and Gino suggested she think it over.

'I got home at about 1.45. I went straight to Mom's room as usual to fetch Tatum. My mother was awake and started arguing with me, saying I was so late because I had been whoring. She never went to sleep before I got home because she wanted to check what I looked like; if I still had make-up on. She was convinced that I slept with some coloured guy every single night.

'The next morning, we left the house for work at about 7.00 as usual. In the car, Mom was criticising me again. She said I stank of smoke. I had started smoking when I was still at school, but I never admitted it to her or my brothers. She would have had a fit and so would they. I gave up while I was pregnant, but started again after my daughter was born. I told Mom that everyone smoked at the club so obviously I was going to smell of smoke. She went on and on. It was the same every morning on the way to work. If I waved to a black or coloured friend, she would say, "You only greet coloureds, not whites, Sabrina. What is wrong with you?" '

There was indeed something wrong with Sabrina; something that Beverley recognised as her fault. According to Maggie Riggien, Beverley often admitted her inability to relate to her daughter. It bothered her constantly that she could not accept Sabrina, Beverley told her friend, but she was unable to manipulate her own feelings. Part of the reason for Beverley's ambivalence was Sabrina's marked physical resemblance to Louis, whom Beverley loathed. Sabrina was not only extremely tall for a girl but she bore many of Louis' mannerisms. It was the ungainly way she sat, with her legs wide apart, hands spread over her knees, that particularly reminded Beverley of her former husband. She could not stop criticising Sabrina, who was also teased and ridiculed at school to the point where she lost both the power to believe in herself and the courage to try new things, says Maggie. As her development became stunted, her immaturity made her less and less able to meet life's challenges.

In a way, as Maggie noted frequently, Beverley bullied Sabrina much as she treated the black people who worked for her, dominating and controlling those she saw as unequal in value as human beings rather than relying on the subtle influence and cooperation she applied to relationships with people she respected. If Beverley's harsh style of parenting Sabrina was a reflection of her own demoralising childhood, as is usually true of persecuting mothers, it also mirrored apartheid's muscular ethos and its devastating effects on the self-esteem of entire generations of South Africans.

Self-esteem is, arguably, the principal dynamic in all human behaviour. To love oneself is the beginning of a lifelong romance, according to Oscar Wilde. And the converse is equally true: to doubt oneself is to feel unworthy of happiness. Sabrina grew up feeling insignificant to both her parents. She identified instead with a surrogate mother who belonged to a group characterised by negative attributes in South Africa. Sabrina's understanding of the relative value of people in her world came from watching Beverley's conduct towards Gladys, who was ordered around rudely, given exhausting and demeaning tasks, and scarcely ever thanked. It was Gladys who, despite being distraught when her long-time employer died a violent death, was told by Allister to mop Beverley's blood from the carpet of her bedroom hours after the murder; then dismissed a few weeks later with only one month's pay despite her devoted service. If anything was likely to disturb a child following rejection by her biological mother, it was her community's rejection of the loving surrogate. Yet it was Gladys who told me laughingly that, years earlier, she had enjoyed taking Sabrina by the hand to a shop where, among the toys, one little black doll sat on a shelf with several white ones. 'Ask ma'am to buy you this one,' she would whisper, pointing to the dark doll as Sabrina sobbed. Although I questioned Gladys repeatedly about the meaning of this anecdote, I could not understand from her account whether Sabrina was crying because she could not have a doll or because she could not have the black doll that she knew Beverley would never consider buying in preference to a white one. What was clear, though, was that Gladys found the discomfiting story amusing.

*

A few days before Beverley's murder, while at work at Lady B, Sabrina received a telephone call from Gino. 'I remember I accidentally spilt my coffee over the computer keyboard because I was so nervous when I saw his number on my cellphone. I told him R250 000 is a lot for "that". I was talking quietly, nobody was near my desk, but it was not unusual in the office to talk about large amounts of money because we were dealing with property sales. Mom had gone to Queenstown Auctioneers, one of her businesses.'

Gino chastised Sabrina for her indecision, telling her the gangsters from Johannesburg were staying with him and costing him money to entertain while she stalled. As she tells me this, Sabrina leans closer to the microphone at the centre of the glass panel to confide that she was scared of Gino because he was known to the Queenstown police as a ruthless gangster. I listen impassively, careful not to encourage dramatic embellishments or to appear either sympathetic or judgemental.

At this point in the interview, Sabrina has become distracted, glancing at someone standing to her left, out of my sight, in the narrow passage connecting the prisoners to the row of visitors' cubicles. Whoever is waiting there has said something to her, to which she replies in Xhosa. I guess out loud that it is the woman who wheeled a trolley piled high with items for sale behind Sabrina a few minutes earlier: the middle-aged black prisoner with tightly coiled hair dyed the colour of corn, who is in charge of the mobile shop from which visitors can buy gifts of chocolate, cigarettes, tea and biscuits for the prisoners in an anteroom at the start of the dual passages on either side of the visitors' cubicles. Sabrina nods enthusiastically, saying: 'She is my prison mother. She was just telling me to tell you the truth, even though she is listening. She told me she will not repeat anything she hears to the other prisoners.'

I ask what her 'prison mother' is in jail for and she replies matter of factly, 'Murder, like me,' as if this is a hobby they have in common. Trying not to react since the older woman is now peeping at me with a shy grin on her round face, I take up my pen and remind Sabrina where we have got to in the story of her plot to kill her mother.

She continues: 'That night, lying in bed, I tried to decide. When I came home from the club earlier, Mom and I were fighting again. She said somebody saw me at Clicks that morning, flirting with a coloured guy ... It made me mad because I was not at Clicks flirting with anybody. I tried to figure out how I could pay Gino the money. I thought I could sell the Action Quicket to pay for it because Mom had told me that business was mine. There was also a life insurance policy that would pay up if Mom died. I could sell Lady B and my car, and I could take out a loan ... But it was still too much money.

'The next day, I was ducking and diving. I didn't want to talk to Gino because I couldn't make up my mind about doing it, never mind the price. I was scared, very nervous, smoking whenever I got the chance. Gino was trying to talk to me. I didn't answer my phone when I saw it was him. He came by the office a few times and I ran into Mom's office. Once, when she wasn't there, I hid under her desk so that nobody would see me and call me to speak to Gino. I would be driving in town and suddenly see him speeding towards me. Then I'd drive quickly home or to the office. In the evenings, I invited my brothers to the Action Quicket so Gino wouldn't try to talk to me there.'

Part of the reason Sabrina did not want to face Gino was because she and her mother were suddenly getting along quite well. There were occasions, she admits, when they enjoyed each other's company, usually when Beverley's boyfriend, Danie Nel, was out of town. 'Mom used to quarrel a lot with him and then take it out on me. That was part of the problem. This time, Uncle Danie was away visiting his children and Aunty Maggie, Mom's friend, had gone to live in Jo'burg, so she really wanted to be with me'.

They shopped together for clothes for Tatum, and then went home to swim and barbecue in the garden. 'I didn't want to think about the business with Gino. It was hard to think I had even discussed the plan with him. Then Danie came back and told Mom I had been seen with coloureds by a policeman, and the arguments started again.'

After avoiding Gino for five days, Sabrina says she was

finally confronted by him at the club. He was very angry when he told her to stop playing games with him, she recalls. But instead of telling Gino that she remained unresolved about the murder, as she now claims, Sabrina blamed the high price of the crime for her failure to agree to it. Gino told her he could either do it for less himself or find a cheaper assassin. Later, he suggested payment of R150 000 for the killing. Sabrina says she agreed to think about it. However, she goes on immediately to describe their discussion about how the murder might be committed. 'I told Gino that Mom often drove along the road to Komani Hospital just outside Queenstown, where she sold insurance to the staff and patients. I was thinking we could arrange a hijacking. But Gino said it was too risky. He preferred to do it in town at my house. He told me to go home and study the house so I could describe it to him.'

Two days later at Action Quicket, when the death of her mother had already been the subject of conversation with Gino for nearly a fortnight, Sabrina again discussed the murder plot with him. She says he asked her to leave the sliding doors in the sitting room of her home open so that the killer could jump over the wall and enter the house late at night. 'I went home, drunk again, but it was now in my mind all the time. I just couldn't drink enough to chase it away. I thought the plan would work. I never thought it wouldn't work because Gino had said he would do it himself, and I knew if he hired someone else it would also work because he would plan it properly. I convinced myself that we wouldn't be caught.'

Gino was at Action Quicket almost every night, chatting to Sabrina about other matters so as to allay any suspicion about their relationship that might arise in the wake of the killing. A week before Beverley's death, Gino confirmed that he would commit the murder himself. The following night, a

Thursday, Sabrina waited for her chance to unlock the sliding doors. 'I came home from work at Lady B as usual, bathed and fed Tatum. Mom said I must cook her dinner before I went to the club so I made her seafood pasta and took it to her in the lounge. She got cross with me, I remember, because she said there was too much salt in the pasta. "Are you trying to poison me?" she asked, but not in a joking way. I remember her saying that.

'When I was washing the dishes, Mom went to fetch Tatum from my bedroom. While she was gone, I unlocked the sliding doors. I didn't eat anything myself at home that night because I was too nervous. I went to the Quicket, and the first thing I did was eat several chocolates so that I wouldn't get too drunk, and then I poured myself a long glass of rum and drank it, neat, because I was so scared. The chocolate was a regular thing I ate before I started drinking in the evenings but, no matter how many chocolates I ate, I usually still got drunk. Every night at around 1.00 in the morning, just before I went home, I ate three packets of salty biltong to be sober when I got home and saw my mother.'

Throughout the evening, Sabrina sat on a bench in the downstairs toilet at Action Quicket, leaving the barman to cope on his own because her nerves were uncontrollable. She recalls smoking two packs of cigarettes, sometimes two at a time in her anxiety. Half an hour after calling her mother to confirm that Tatum was asleep, her phone rang. 'I got such a fright. It was Gino, saying: "Sabrina, it didn't work. I'm coming over there now." I went outside and waited for him. He arrived in a red Golf, driven by a friend called Kello. He came and sat next to me on the bench and told me he had jumped the wall but my three dogs went for him, making a lot of noise. Then the neighbours' dogs started barking, going crazy. So he went back over the wall. He told me he would try again the next week.'

The following Tuesday, Gino approached Sabrina quietly at Action Quicket to tell her he had hired a local man to murder Beverley. Two days later, after supper at Allister's home with her mother and baby, Sabrina drove to the club where Gino's friend, Kello, was waiting to tell her that a hired hitman named Feza, who was not afraid of dogs, was going to try to get into the house that evening.

'But again, my dogs and the neighbours' dogs went mad and the three of them came back to the club,' says Sabrina. I interrupt her to ask what type of dogs had guarded Beverley's home in Berry Street. I have in my mind's eye Rottweilers or German shepherds – large, aggressive beasts to scare away dangerous criminals. When she replies, 'French poodles', I drop my pen and laugh helplessly. She laughs too, welcoming the unexpected levity before continuing her ghastly tale.

Describing how she sat in the red Golf with Feza and Gino, planning yet another attempt to murder her mother, Sabrina says she gave Gino the kitchen door key. Although she claimed in court to have tried repeatedly to pull out of the death deal at this stage, saying that Gino had threatened to harm her baby if she backed out, there is no such suggestion in our interview so far. 'I explained where the bedrooms were, and told them not to go into the first one but the second on the right, which was Mom's. I told them she would be lying on her bed watching TV. They said they'd go at 11.00. I never spoke to Feza directly.

'I waited, smoking non-stop. Half an hour later, Mom phoned and said the sliding doors were open. She was angry and upset with me because she insisted Uncle Danie had checked them earlier in the day and found them locked. I told her not to worry because my maid sometimes forgot to lock them. Mom knew this wasn't right. She phoned me back a little later, sounding scared because she said, "There's a noise outside my window. People are walking around the garden." I said, "Mom, it's your imagination. It's just because you noticed the sliding door was open that you're scared."

'I was sweating, hot and cold. I saw Shaun sitting by himself at the club and I went over to him and said, "I don't want to go through with this." He told me to phone Gino and call it off. But Gino's phone was switched off. I messaged him, and five minutes later he called me back. While I was answering his call, Mom phoned. I told Gino I'd call him back. It was about midnight. I answered Mom's call. She asked, "Sabrina, when are you coming home?" I could hear she was scared. I told her, "Mom, we're busy. I'll be home now now." But I knew I didn't have my back door key so I couldn't go home, even if I wanted to. And I did want to by then. I was so confused, and very, very scared. I thought I was going to panic and do something stupid.

'I called Gino and asked him to bring me the keys, saying, "I have to get home". He came to the club, gave me the keys and told me to phone him. I don't know if he was cross or what. I didn't notice because I just wanted to get home to my mom and my baby.'

Throughout Sabrina's detailed account of half-starts, constant drinking and panicky phone calls, she has remained dry-eyed, her voice steady, only occasionally animated when she talks of quarrels with her mother. I wonder if it is her tragic inability to win Beverley's acceptance that has soaked up all her tears, or if a more sinister, pathological explanation lies behind her disquieting composure.

'I walked into the house, down the passage,' she continues. 'Tatum was asleep on Mom's bed. I picked her up, trying not to wake her as I carried her to my bed. Mom was screaming at me. Gino phoned three times while we were quarrelling. I didn't answer because I knew it was him. Mom thought it was a lover or something and she was shouting, "You're late home again because you have been whoring. I'm going to put a stop to this, Sabrina. I'll close the Quicket, send you overseas, keep your baby and tell your brothers."

'Then she calmed down and told me to double-check the sliding doors. I walked into the lounge to the doors, and made sure one of them was open. I walked down the passage, went into my room and closed the door. Quietly, I dialled Gino's number and whispered to him: "Listen, Gino, let's not do it now because my nerves are shot. I don't want to be in the house when the killer comes. Let's do it tomorrow. I'm going to work at 6.00 to unlock Lady B so that Joyce, one of our maids, can go in to prepare the coffin sprays." '

Sabrina describes her drive to Lady B early the following morning; her anxiety while waiting for Gino's phone call outside the flower shop; the return journey with Feza lying on the back seat of her car. Her eyes are staring fixedly at me. She is lost in the dramatic memory, hiding in her bedroom while Feza attacks her mother and Beverley shouts for Sabrina to save herself.

'It was exactly 7.00 when I heard Feza walk back down the passage and stop outside my bedroom, where the floorboards creaked. I opened the door,' she recalls. 'He said she was dead. Then he said he wanted to tie me up to make it look like a break-in. I said, "No, it's not part of the plan. You must leave immediately." I was actually scared of him. I didn't know if he might harm me or my daughter. He looked so calm. I walked with him to the kitchen. I gave him my car keys, which were lying on the kitchen table, so that it would look like a robbery, and told him to go. He said I must give him ten minutes before I called the police.

'He left. I was alone in the house with my baby. And my Mommy. I thought maybe she wasn't dead but just on the way to dying. I don't know what I thought, actually. I was numb, almost dead myself. I walked slowly towards her room, like a ghost. As I came towards her door, which was half open,

I pushed it slowly and then I saw her feet on the floor, on the carpet.'

Sabrina begins to cry. I feel inexplicably relieved to see tears glisten in her eyes and spill down her cheeks, silently, while she continues to describe the death of her mother. 'I walked in a bit more and saw blood all over, and then I saw he'd slit her throat. I ran out, grabbed my daughter from my bed and ran out of the house, down the driveway, screaming. My garden boy, Tony, was coming towards me down the driveway, arriving for work. I said to him, "Go and help Mommy. Somebody broke in and hurt Mom." He replied that she had just driven away in my car. By that time I was hysterical. "No, that wasn't her. That was the person who hurt her," I yelled.'

The gardener ran into the house while Sabrina called Red Guard, her brothers' security company, on her cellphone. She remembers telling the switchboard operator, 'Please phone the police, call an ambulance … somebody's broken into my house and hurt my mother.' Then she switched her phone off.

Gladys, the family's domestic worker, was not living on the premises at the time. For a while Sabrina was alone with Tatum sitting on her hip, watching her crying. 'I couldn't believe I had had something to do with what I saw in my mom's bedroom, really. I couldn't believe it. It felt like this stranger had broken in and hurt my mother. That's what it felt like, and that's what I believed had happened.'

Neighbours heard Sabrina screaming and came running. 'The garden boy came out of my house, very shaken up,' she recalls. Sabrina's use of 'boy' for a grown man – once common but as insensitively racist a term as you can utter in South Africa today – gives a bizarre spin to her attorney's portrayal of her as a pin-up for anti-racists. Though guilty of the reviled crime of matricide, she is patently innocent of South Africa's definitive sin – racism – since she chooses black friends in preference to white ones. Ironically, Sabrina's genuine colour-blindness has earned even a mother-killer widespread sympathy among non-white South Africans despite her typically racist language.

Although I have stopped taking notes and have been glancing at my watch repeatedly since the visiting hour expired, Sabrina carries on telling me exactly who arrived at her home on the morning of Beverley's murder, what they said and how much they cried. I shuffle and fidget and finally stand up to leave as I do not wish to incur the wrath of the prison boss, who makes no secret of regarding me with suspicion even though I have every intention of obeying his rules. Sabrina carries on as if in a trance, repeating again and again the disbelief she claims to have felt on achieving the death of her mother.

Throughout my interviews with her, Sabrina has given the impression of not being really convinced that she did what she did; otherwise, how on earth could she have done it? Aware that denial is a classic symptom of post-traumatic stress disorder I write a reminder to myself to ask the psychologist, Professor Mark Welman, about the syndrome as well as Sabrina's childlike reversion to 'mommy' instead of her usual 'mom' after seeing Beverley's corpse.

Something else is bothering me, though: a disquieting question that has been lurking just below my conscious thoughts, which suddenly pops up. I am not as repelled by Sabrina as I should be. Am I beginning to sympathise with somebody who murdered her own mother? Or am I just a sympathetic observer of Sabrina's hapless stand against racism? Though certainly no radical, she has, in her own muddled way, challenged the taboo long surrounding intimate contact between the races not only in apartheid South Africa but in the southern states of America – albeit less so in the US today than half a century ago. Its existence, for the same reasons in both countries, was not only to ensure that authorities intent on segregation could tell at a glance who was who by dint of unambiguous skin colour but also to suppress the shared humanity that intimate contact implied.

As I turn to leave, the three black women I had met earlier in the visitors' waiting room dash to my side. They have been talking to a prisoner in another cubicle some distance away. 'Good luck, sweetie,' one of them calls as she waves to Sabrina.

Sabrina laughs and says to me, 'You see?' Then she beckons me to the microphone, the stricken expression back on her face. Recalling the advice of the psychologist who counselled her about lesbianism and prison gangs when she first arrived at Fort Glamorgan, Sabrina says: 'She told me I had had a terrible life but now I must try to put it behind me. It is still a shock to think I murdered my own mother. I still can't believe it some days. But when I see where I am, then I realise I did do it.'

Chapter Three

Rather than work late into the night, Inspector Stephen Rheeders prefers to start his job before daybreak to stay ahead of the criminals he hunts. He wakes at 4.30, showers, kisses his sleeping wife goodbye, lights the first of a chain of cigarettes and drives a few kilometres across Queenstown to the former military base that houses specialised sections of the South African Police Service. His office is a small room in one of several barrack-like rows of low-cost structures under corrugated iron roofing. His door bears a small sign – Murder and Robbery – that is barely visible from the parking area a few paces away.

Inside, his office is strictly functional. One desk, one chair, a wooden bench where colleagues, suspects and informers impart their opinions, confessions and lies. A green metal filing cabinet stands alongside shelves stacked with files. An empty revolver holster lies in the in-tray. Propped against the wall is the blue bulletproof vest Rheeders is supposed to wear at all times, even driving to and from the office. In the event of a fatal shot, his life is not insured by the police unless he is wearing the flak jacket. Apart from a shiny award for excellent detective work and a radio permanently tuned to a local station, there is nothing to indicate that this room, reeking of stale smoke and bitingly cold even on a late winter morning in August, is where a man with a comfortable home spends most of his time.

Although Inspector Rheeders works mainly in and around Queenstown, his reputation as one of the country's best detectives means he can be deployed to solve difficult cases anywhere in the Eastern Cape – the portion of South Africa that stretches 800 kilometres along the Indian Ocean coast north-east of Cape Town.

He tells me that Queenstown was once an elegant provincial centre in the English tradition of teashops and roses. It became a beacon apartheid constituency during the early Sixties when the Afrikaner government's resentment of liberal-leaning white voters, who had previously prevailed in the area, turned to revenge. During one particularly decisive election, the nationalists defeated the moderates by packing the town with railway workers and other artisans loyal to apartheid's policies. Then they turned their attention to another liberal stronghold nearby, King William's Town, with the slogan: Now that we've got the queen, let's get the king.

The region became the site of apartheid's most malevolent purges, where people were regularly dragged from their beds in the dead of night or arrested in the streets in broad daylight. Detained for long periods without trial, activists were sometimes assassinated. Queenstown became the outpost from where apartheid's masterminds tried in vain to confine the rebellious black majority to the Transkei and the Ciskei, rural 'homelands' that served as apartheid's dumping ground. Unwanted black people were regularly 'resettled' in the open veld, many of them turning to crime as their only hope of survival. Some white farmers living in the area today were apartheid-era opportunists who, by keeping their ears close to the ground, were able to identify the white landowners who had become fearful of the region 'going black' during the consolidation of the 'homelands'. By deliberately fuelling anxiety over the encroaching, albeit fake, black empowerment, they were able to grab farms at a discount from the simple families who had worked the land for generations.

Such a history of trickery and betrayal in the country's poorest province has made the Eastern Cape one of South Africa's crime centres, yet its police force is perennially understaffed. Stephen Rheeders shrugs when I ask if his punishing workload gets him down. 'Somebody has to do it,' he says.

Every weekday morning, Inspector Rheeders joins the policemen of Queenstown's specialist units in what is curiously called the 'parade room', a bleak lecture theatre where they discuss the cases under investigation with their commanding officers. The meeting had barely begun on March 22, 2002, when a colleague appeared at the open door and announced that members of the Murder and Robbery Unit should go to Beverley van Schoor's house because she had been murdered. The victim's name was familiar to all the detectives in the parade room: she was the girlfriend of one of Queenstown's senior policemen, Superintendent Danie Nel.

'When we arrived at the scene we found members of the family and Sabrina standing outside the house. Sabrina was crying hysterically,' recalls Rheeders in heavily accented English. 'I spoke to some of the policemen already there and they took me inside. We found the body lying on the floor between the bed and the dressing table in Bev's ...' He rummages through his English vocabulary, trying to find the word.

Bedroom?

'Ja, her bedroom.' Rheeders points to the pictures of the corpse in the photo album on his desk. 'There she is lying. You can see lots of blood coming out of her neck. There was a pink baby top lying next to Bev with blood on it. We suspected the killer wiped his hands on it before leaving the room after the murder. Her handbag was lying on the bed and there were some cosmetics on the floor. Three wallets belonging to Bev lay next to the handbag. When we checked them, we found they contained R2 500, cash that wasn't taken, which is very strange if you're committing a murder in order to rob. The TV was on and the remote control for it was lying on the bed. The cupboard doors were all closed except for the one containing the TV. Bev's jewellery was still on the dressing table. The bed was moved away a bit from the thing for the head … the headboard … as if there had been a struggle. There was nothing abnormal about the bedroom apart from the immediate murder scene and the scene of the struggle. There was no sign in it that someone had been looking for something to steal. Nothing else in the house was disturbed. The hi-fi was not taken; the TV was not taken.

'We didn't believe the killer even went into any of the other rooms. Only Sabrina's car, a red Citi Golf, was missing, and Beverley's cellphone. We couldn't speak to Sabrina, who had been there during the murder, because she was in a state of shock – or putting on a good show. But we talked to her brothers.'

When the police searched the deceased's house, they found the glass sliding door leading to the pool area closed but unlocked. One knife in a set of four on the kitchen dresser was missing. Beverley's bedroom door appeared to have been forced open. There were bloody fingerprints on some pharmacy receipts lying next to Beverley's handbag on the bed.

The police spoke to Allister, who told the investigating

team that the lock on his mother's door had been broken years earlier when the children locked themselves in by mistake. Danie Nel said he had personally checked that the sliding door to the pool was locked the previous night after Beverley expressed concern at having found it open a few evenings earlier. 'The family members also told us that it was very strange to find that door unlocked, even though we could see that the murderer had not entered through that door but through the kitchen door,' Inspector Rheeders tells me.

How did you know he came through the kitchen door?

Rheeders sighs and looks straight ahead for a moment, summoning patience. I assume he must already have given me this information, which I somehow missed, though later when I play back the tape there is no talk of the kitchen door prior to this point in our interview. He replies tonelessly: 'It was the only door that was open. If you break into somebody's house and you leave in a rush, you don't wait to close the door.' He points to close-ups in his photo album of the swimming pool door closed but unlocked and the kitchen door wide open.

'Sabrina's room was in a mess, confirming what she told us: that she left early in the morning to go to the shop to let in the girl who was going to make flower arrangements for some funerals that weekend. We at first thought Bev was raped because her nightgown was pulled up above her breasts, close to her neck – close to where the cut was, actually. We took some smears to establish whether or not she had been sexually assaulted.'

Rheeders reads through the pocketbook in which detectives are required to note their observations on first inspecting the scene of a crime. 'On top of the bedside table in Bev's bedroom was a clock knocked out of its normal position. A small calendar was lying on its side between the bed and the wall where the headboard was. The deceased was lying on her back with her legs wide open and her head facing towards the bed. We lifted fingerprints, did a video, took photos. The family doctor came in to declare Bev dead at the scene. Estimated time of death was 7.00 or 7.30. Then the body was removed.'

Inspector Rheeders and two other investigating officers went from Beverley's home in Berry Street back to their headquarters to complete the paperwork entailed in opening a murder docket: a detailed crime report, covering letters to the Forensics Unit, statements from the witnesses, several exhibits reports. At about 11.30, Rheeders was phoned by the Dog Unit who told him they had found the missing vehicle next to a broken-down liquor store in Ezibeleni township. 'The vehicle was locked. There was nothing wrong with it. Even the radio was still in it, which was very strange for a robbery,' Rheeders tells me.

'I came back to my office and applied to the Director of Public Prosecutions for a reward of R50 000 because it was a high profile case and the public expected an arrest soon. When a prominent person like Bev gets murdered, they want the case solved now,' Rheeders explains. 'This was later approved for R20 000. I immediately phoned the media for assistance in the matter.'

*

The next morning when I meet Allister van Schoor he greets me with an amiable smile. His mother's deep-set blue eyes, the same as Sabrina's, look at me from across the table in a noisy roadside diner. It is the only place in Queenstown open for breakfast at 7.30am. I have felt from the moment I first met Allister a few months earlier, sitting in his office behind his immaculately ordered desk, that, despite his smooth and friendly manner, he distrusts me and my questions just as much as his older brother, Lester, who was openly hostile on the couple of occasions I had tried to talk to him.

Not knowing what to make of Allister, I remember a conversation I had by chance in Johannesburg with a man in his early thirties who was a contemporary at Queen's College of two of the Van Schoor brothers: Lester and Allister were both star rugby players, he told me, and they became millionaires within a few years of taking over the security firm, Red Guard, from their mother. According to their former school mate, Allister was always pleasant and responsible while Lester was an aggressive character. Much was made of the Van Schoor name at Queen's College in those days, he recalled, because Louis was a symbol of strength in a community that had become increasingly scared of black power. The Van Schoor brothers enjoyed the macho image this gave them at school and were quick to associate themselves with Louis, the legendary killer of blacks.

Sabrina had told me during one of our interviews that her brothers played the Louis card whichever way it suited them: when Louis was being condemned for his crimes, Lester and Allister said they had no time for him; that he was not their real father anyway. But when, more often, Louis was being hailed as a brave defender of the white right to kill indiscriminately, Lester and Allister claimed him as their own. Shane chose not to be involved in the security business set up by Beverley but Lester and Allister relished it. In the country with the highest murder rate in the world – apart from societies involved in armed conflict – they made a fortune from fear of violent crime.

All three of Beverley's sons resented Louis for regularly assaulting their mother during her marriage to him, I was told by a Cape Town documentary film-maker who introduced herself to me in Johannesburg when she heard we were working on the same subject. During our discussions about

Beverley's murder, she revealed that she had managed to interview Lester and Shane by promising to show them her footage before it was screened. She also told me that Shane remembered Louis teaching him where to shoot an enemy, just below the neck, in order to kill with one bullet.

Over breakfast, Allister explains that he was the first family member to arrive at 73 Berry Street on the morning of Beverley's murder in response to a frantic call from Sabrina. Although she was incoherent on the line, gasping and sobbing, he tells me he was not unduly alarmed at first because he had received similar calls from Sabrina in the past after she and her mother had quarrelled and Beverley had ended up fainting from stress. It wasn't until a neighbour took the phone from Sabrina and told Allister to come quickly that he realised something more serious had happened.

When he got to Beverley's house within twenty minutes of the murder, Allister found Sabrina sitting outside, sobbing. A neighbour was shouting for his domestic worker to fetch Sabrina and bring her into his home. Another neighbour tried to stop Allister from entering Beverley's house. 'I ran straight in and saw my mom lying there,' recalls Allister. 'I'm not going to try to explain the whole picture ... I didn't know how long she had been dead. I felt for her pulse but her skin was very cold.'

He ran outside in a daze. Not knowing if anyone had contacted the emergency services, Allister phoned his office to ask his staff to call an ambulance. A lawyer living across the road heard the commotion and ran to the house. He and Allister went back into Beverley's room together. 'That's when we threw a sheet over my mom because we knew there were going to be a whole lot of people coming in and out, and we knew at that stage that it was too late ... that it must have happened quite some time before. Immediately after that, I phoned my brothers – who were in East London. I told Lester what had happened. He picked up Shane and they arrived in Queenstown two hours later.'

Allister remembers his frustration at having to wait for the ambulance to arrive. 'Although I had felt for her pulse and I thought it was too late, you never know ... I kept thinking the ambulance people must come quickly and look. So when they didn't come and didn't come, I was getting really pissed off, to say the least. The police had also taken a long time before they came, finally. When I had first phoned the police station, they asked where I was calling from. When I said 73 Berry Street, the cop asked, "Where is that?" And then, "How do you spell that?" '

Lester and Shane were prevented from going into Beverley's home when they arrived from East London. The police told them that 73 Berry Street had become a protected crime scene while photography and fingerprinting were under way. 'I'm sure if they wanted to go in they could have because we know everybody in Queenstown,' Allister explains. 'I'm actually glad it was me and not one of them who saw my mom because I am a child of the Lord and I have been helped through this. I don't know how badly they would have taken it – probably a lot worse than me.'

Soon after their arrival, Lester and Shane began to work with the police. Having listened to Sabrina's version of events as she related it to the investigating officers – that a black man came out of the house brandishing a knife, forced her out of her car and drove off in it – they volunteered to join the hunt for the killer. 'We wanted to get him,' says Allister. 'Fortunately, we have a lot of friends in town and we organised two guys with their own planes to go up in the air and look for the red Golf. The entire police force in Queenstown was deployed on the case.'

Allister's wife Lucinda took Sabrina and baby Tatum to her home, where friends began to arrive on Friday afternoon to comfort the family and hear the grisly details of Beverley's death. 'Sabrina at that stage seemed like she was in shock – not crying, though,' recalls Allister. 'The terrible thing for me was that the people arriving actually wanted to know exactly what happened. That was the worst part of it, having to describe ...'

I notice that Allister's breakfast is getting cold because he has been doing most of the talking. Urging him to eat his eggs, I comment that, from what he has told me, he and his brothers initially believed everything Sabrina said about the killing. It just shows how people can get away with murder, I remark idly; how primed we are to feel sympathetic rather than suspicious especially when we are white South Africans and can blame a black person. Sabrina didn't get away with it, but, I speculate, there must be many murderers who escape detection on this basis. He gives a wry snort as he eats.

I ask who else among his relatives I should interview, Lester and Shane having declined. Allister warns that his family is inclined to trust only the young film-maker from Cape Town since she has promised to show them her footage for their approval. I know he is trying to entice me to match this offer and I feel like telling him the film-maker is either inexperienced or naive. Instead, I explain why it is impossible for an author to relegate her judgement to a committee of interviewees, telling him that if the writer notes that someone has bad table manners, for example, that interviewee will almost certainly strike the observation from the manuscript if invited to do so. Wouldn't we then be left with boringly bland books, I suggest, to which he nods hesitantly.

After breakfast, Allister recalls that his wife felt increasingly uneasy when Sabrina moved into their home immediately after the murder. Unable to explain her discomfort, Lucinda asked him to increase the security in the house. At some point, Lucinda spoke to Beverley's boyfriend, Danie Nel, who revealed that Sabrina had stolen money and jewellery from Beverley on the occasion a couple of years earlier when she discovered she was pregnant and ran away to East London. 'My mom had not told us about this because she worshipped the ground Sabrina walked on and was always protecting her,' says Allister.

This is the first time I have heard, contrary to all other evidence, that Beverley adored Sabrina, though I do not comment. Allister continues: 'Lucinda got very upset when she heard this from Danie and she had a full-on argument with Sabrina, saying how could you have done this, look what has happened to your poor mother now, how could you put her through all that … stuff like that. Lucinda was really upset with Sabrina and couldn't stop herself. I also got very upset, but with my wife, because Sabrina was still grieving and here was my wife attacking her for something that was past. So I had words with Lucinda. So she went and apologised to Sabrina.'

Allister relates this incident to show how concerned he was for Sabrina's well-being in the wake of Beverley's murder. However, I am left wondering why Allister's wife and Danie Nel – who was said by a number of people I interviewed to have openly disliked Sabrina – were discussing Sabrina's integrity at a time when Allister was not remotely suspicious of her.

Allister says much of the detail of that weekend is a blur in his memory. 'I was half-hysterical myself, crying and shocked, but at that stage I was trying to stay calm for Sabrina and everyone else. If I'd known what I know now, obviously it would have been totally different. I was more worried about Sabrina than anyone else at the time because she saw it and she was quite young still.

'The first time we were struck by anything strange about Sabrina was when she started to smoke that Friday morning at my house. She never used to smoke in front of any of us, or my mom, but she did it outside and I was fine with that. If she needed to smoke to calm her nerves, fine. But when my wife went with her to my mom's house to collect some clothes for herself and Tatum, Sabrina lit up a cigarette the second she walked in – no emotion, no crying, nothing. Like nothing had happened. My wife came back to me and said, "I can't believe what's just happened." It immediately struck her as odd behaviour. She said to me, "It's not right", but she was not suspicious. She just thought Sabrina was in such a state that she couldn't function properly.'

During the Friday evening of the murder, the Van Schoor family – including Beverley's sister Val and her husband from East London – was gathered at Allister's house discussing funeral arrangements with the undertaker when Sabrina again behaved strangely. 'She cracked a joke,' says Allister, barely able to hide his disgust even a year after the event. 'Once again, it wasn't the right time; it wasn't the right behaviour. Afterwards, Aunty Val, who was very upset, and somebody else came to me and said, "How can Sabrina crack a joke at a time like this?" '

What was the joke?

Allister looks appalled at the question and shakes his head. He doesn't recall Sabrina crying much during the day. He does remember his mother's accountant saying how impressed he was with the calm way Sabrina was coping with the tragedy, although he said he was surprised when Sabrina told him, within hours of Beverley's murder, how she planned to reorganise her mother's businesses.

'Sabrina and I spoke a lot, first on the way to the office to tell the staff what had happened, and also at my mom's house,' says Allister. 'She told me that, when she arrived back at the house after opening the shop, she drove badly and hit the kerb by mistake, making a loud noise. As she was reversing, she looked up and this guy was at her door. He pulled her out and threw her on the ground – she even showed me some grazes she said she had sustained in the fall but which she had, we now know, inflicted on herself.'

Allister remembers Shane trying to ascertain from Sabrina if Tatum had witnessed anything traumatic apart from her mother's hysteria. 'Sabrina very calmly said, no. That was just a little bit suspicious, too: how would she know with such certainty that Tatum saw nothing. I'm obviously saying now what I wasn't thinking at the time. I was not suspicious then – not at all.'

At the end of our meeting, I comment on Inspector Rheeders' exemplary detective work while trying to confirm Siphiwo Burwana's claim of a friendship between Allister and the investigating officer by slipping in a reference to Rheeders being close to the Van Schoor family. Allister looks annoyed and corrects me quite sharply. 'I didn't say we were close. I said we knew him.'

On the Saturday morning after the murder, Inspector Rheeders took a statement from Sabrina. 'She was crying profusely,' he recalls. 'She described the killer to me in great detail – the marks on his face, his height, everything. That was strange because she saw him for a very short time when he pulled her out of the vehicle and threw her on the ground.'

Rheeders then tells me he began to hear rumours on Saturday morning that it was Sabrina who killed Beverley. When I try to substantiate these, he backs off. 'No, it was just rumours. I can't say I heard it from a certain person.' I recall Justina telling me on several occasions how incestuous Queenstown is, how remorselessly its residents discuss each others' affairs, and I try to press Inspector Rheeders.

It was a common assumption in Queenstown?

'Ja,' he agrees reluctantly.

Was it based on the town's people knowing that Sabrina

did not get along with her mother?

'I don't know. I think they were expecting the worst from Sabrina.' Suddenly, his eyes blaze and he continues at a feverish pitch. 'It was not the people she was hanging out with; it was the type of person. It wasn't about the colour of her friends. Bev gave her hairdressing shop to a coloured lady who was her close friend. If she was as big a racist as was claimed at the trial, why did she do that? She could have sold the shop.'

While jotting a quick reminder in my notebook to find out if Beverley 'gave' her hairdressing salon to a coloured woman, as Rheeders claims, I consider pointing out to him that Queenstown's cruelly skewed society would have been hard pressed to produce the sort of middle-class non-white friends Beverley might have considered suitable for her daughter. But Inspector Rheeders is looking flushed and stony. Perhaps he regrets having let his professional guard slip, revealing some of the anger provoked throughout Queenstown's white community at Sabrina's use of racism as her defence for matricide. Beverley's friend, Maggie Riggien, and Sabrina's friend, Cherie van Heerden, have both told me in earlier interviews how outraged local people were in their discussions about Sabrina's racism charge in the days following the murder. According to Cherie, the response of both her boss and her father was to scorn the racism allegation and finger Sabrina.

Rheeders pondered the case all weekend but it wasn't until Monday morning, while attending a lecture at police headquarters, he recounts, that he was given the information with which to solve the crime. 'One of our officers told me a man had called him on Saturday morning to say he had heard he was suspected of involvement in an armed robbery at Buffalo Springs Spur that occurred in the town centre at about the same time Beverley was murdered: 7.30 the previous

Friday morning. The man told the police officer his name was Feza Mdutshane, who was well known to us because we had previously arrested him for a cash-in-transit robbery. We knew his cellphone number and all his details.'

I look puzzled and Stephen Rheeders gives another of his big sighs. 'You see, this is an attempt by Feza to get some information out of us. It is like a child who does something wrong and goes to his father, saying: "Hey listen, what's the story? I'm hearing that you think this ..." Trying to get information because nothing seems to be happening about the crime or misdeed he has committed. But we didn't give Feza any information – nothing.'

Although Rheeders felt there was something fishy about Feza's eagerness to be implicated in the armed robbery, he was more preoccupied with solving Beverley van Schoor's murder. Then an informer, attracted by the offer of a reward for Beverley's killer amid details of the crime published in the local newspaper, approached him to report that he had seen Feza Mdutshane on the day of the murder carrying two cellphones, one of which was the same as Beverley's – a Nokia with a silver face. Rheeders noted this information in the docket.

He left Queenstown for East London the following day to give evidence in court in another case. Driving back on Wednesday, he began to connect the dots linking Feza to Beverley's murder and to consider pursuing Feza as a possible suspect. 'I talked to my colleagues about Sabrina's description of the man who had stolen her car. We had a photo of Feza from the previous arrest and I studied it when I got back to my office, noting that the scars Sabrina described exactly matched those on his face. He has lots of old fight scars; not like your ordinary thief.'

Rheeders then called Feza Mdutshane, asking him to come in and tell the police what he knew about the Buffalo

Springs Spur robbery. The interview took place in Rheeders' office. After questioning him as an informer in the steak house robbery, Rheeders was convinced that Mdutshane knew nothing about that case, which suggested he might be attempting instead to distract the police or to gain information from them.

'I then arrested him in connection with the murder of Beverley van Schoor. We interrogated him and he said he knew about the missing cellphone and he could show us where it was. So we drove around with him, from one friend's house to the next. Everyone we went to had a phone from him because Feza's job was fixing cellphones. Eventually I said to him, "No, we can't drive around like this looking at phones which are not even close to the one we want. We are going back to the office to interrogate you further." ' Rheeders' voice has a hard edge when he is recounting his words to Feza. 'His rights were explained to him and we 'cuffed him'.

That was brave, I say. You did not have much evidence against him.

Rheeders sighs. 'Feza was arrested for questioning. We can keep him for 48 hours and release him after that. I must warn him that he is a suspect in the Beverley van Schoor murder case. I must have some concrete suspicions to arrest somebody but I have to 'cuff him. To have a dangerous criminal in your office without handcuffs … and he grabs a gun … you are going to have troubles. That's why I arrested him at that stage.

'When I told him he was a suspect, he said, "What me? No, never, not me …" That type of response. I think he thought we knew more than we had told him. We had been questioning him about the cellphone, Beverley's phone, so he must have feared we were on his trail. We went with him to the room he rented at the back of somebody's house and found another cellphone but with a green face and a serial number that did not correspond with Bev's. Then we went to some other addresses he gave us; the same runaround as before. When we got back in the vehicle, I said to him: you must start telling the truth ... And then he agreed to speak to myself and one other officer.'

Rheeders pauses, drawing deeply on a cigarette, and then resumes in a more relaxed tone. 'Sabrina's brother Lester phoned me while I was talking to Feza in the vehicle, saying he had heard that we arrested somebody. I don't know how he knew this but I said, yes, we did arrest somebody and we were busy questioning the suspect. I told him I would get back to him with more information.'

Perhaps suspecting that the Van Schoor brothers were receiving classified information from Danie Nel, Rheeders decided to call Lester back and tell him that the police had arrested the wrong man. He sidesteps the question when I ask how he thought Lester knew about Feza's arrest, telling me that he felt obliged to lie to Lester as a precaution against Sabrina – whom he already suspected of involvement – leaving town if she thought Feza was under arrest.

'We went back to my office where Feza admitted being involved in the killing of Bev. He immediately mentioned Sabrina by name, which was very suspicious because how would somebody who goes and robs a place where the daughter is not even present know her name? Then he told us Sabrina took him to the house to kill her mother, promising to give him R200 000 from a life insurance payout.'

Feza also told the police that Sabrina saw him take a knife in the kitchen. He said she walked into her mother's room where Beverley – having seen Feza from her bedroom doorway, which looks straight into the kitchen – asked Sabrina what a black stranger was doing in the house. Questioned about the murder weapon, Feza told Rheeders he had thrown the knife away while driving the red Golf through Ezibeleni.

Later the same day, in Inspector Rheeders' office, Feza named the two coloured men he claimed had hired him on Sabrina's behalf to murder Beverley. 'I then arranged to set a trap for Sabrina,' says Rheeders. 'We have to obtain authority from a judge through the Director of Public Prosecutions in Grahamstown. The permission was immediately given to record everything that was said between Sabrina and Feza while they were in monitored conversation. It was granted for 24 hours only so we had to spark, to move, on this matter while Feza was cooperating. Often when you put the suspects back into prison, the cell attorneys tell them not to talk, not to sign confessions, not to do this or that. They try to influence prisoners not to cooperate with the police.'

While officers from the Technical Support Unit in East London were driving to Queenstown to help set the trap, Rheeders and Feza agreed on a detailed plan to lead police to Sabrina's accomplices, Gino Redcliffe and Kello Nieuwenhys. 'We drove to a dance club in the coloured township, Victoria Park, late that night,' says Rheeders. 'The two were standing outside, talking in a group. Feza pointed them out to us by describing their clothing and we arrested them.'

How did they respond?

'They were very shocked, denying everything, of course,' says Rheeders with a deep sigh. 'You see, when people commit a crime they don't think they're going to be caught. They don't expect to see a policeman walking towards them to question them about murder. That's why people commit crimes: they aren't expecting to be arrested.'

Keeping the two suspects apart, Rheeders questioned first Gino and then Kello. Both agreed to discuss the murder with him on condition they were given indemnity from prosecution. Rheeders explained that he could take statements from them under the Criminal Procedures Act only if they agreed to be state witnesses testifying against the other accused by implicating and incriminating themselves.

'At about two in the morning we finished taking their statements in my office. Both of them confirmed independently that Sabrina had orchestrated the whole thing. Gino told us that, two days before the murder, Sabrina was really pressuring them to get a killer for her and that was when he decided on Feza, a known robber.'

*

Having felt an overload of tension since arriving in Queenstown, which has left me wondering if I am imagining it because of the strange circumstances surrounding Beverley's murder, or if there is really something odd about the place, I am pleased to have met a man the previous day, a senior civil servant, who immediately vindicated my instincts. Asking me not to name him, he explained Queenstown in terms that made sense of the unease I was picking up wherever I went.

Over lunch, he told me that Queenstown has an unusually high rate of white-on-white violence, including the recent assassination in broad daylight of a crooked lawyer by one of his disgruntled clients; a murder that turned out to be based on an ancient grudge. Not long after Beverley van Schoor's death, a 19-year-old son murdered his father and shot his mother in the head and face in a farming area near Queenstown. 'People just snap here; the stresses are very great,' according to my companion. Part of his explanation is the get-rich-quick culture of the white community, as well as the lack of entertainment outlets for youth apart from the church and sports clubs in the 'little England on the veld tradition' of Queenstown.

He said that life outside the charmed circles inhabited by families like the Van Schoors 'was rather like being blackballed from a club you never wanted to join in the first place' because it was impossible to belong in Queenstown unless you conformed absolutely to the white community's norms. He and I were in a restaurant he described as one of Queenstown's few public places: the rest of the town's social life was hidden, he said. 'Apart from invitations to each others' homes, social acceptability is dominated by a couple of institutions – the private schools, the churches and the Rotary Club. If you don't join one or the other and preferably all three, you are an outcast. If you are invited to join the Rotary Club, you'll find there are three rate structures, depending on who you know. Long after you and your children have left school, your life continues to revolve around Queenstown Girls' High or the boys' equivalent, Queen's College, where only the rich can go.'

I told him I had clipped a *Daily Dispatch* advertisement for Queen's College, which highlighted not only the school's motto, *esse quam videri*, meaning 'be rather than seem to be', but also the boast that the school 'has an extremely powerful and influential Old Boys' Association'. He nodded vigorously, saying that the two schools epitomised the town's double standards. 'The old guard at Queenstown Girls' High upholds strong Victorian ideas of ladyhood – very strict codes, for public if not private display, which probably had a lot to do with the moulding of Sabrina's morality as well as her rebellion.'

The wealthiest people in Queenstown are Lebanese liquor and property dealers, he said. The death industry also flourishes in a time of Aids, monument masons and coffin manufacturers being among the town's most respected tycoons. It is ultimately money that talks to Queenstonians, never mind their religious vows. Amongst the elegant Victorian buildings and restrained public manners is the illusion of gentility and morality but in truth the whole place has been corrupted by pretence and state-sponsored immorality. In this environment, according to my lunch date, '... someone as over-the-top as Beverley, so carefully groomed and controlled but not really up to speed, couldn't quite grasp the ingrained dynamics of social viability in Queenstown. She was never really able to enter the power elite where she so desperately wanted to be.'

During the day of Beverley's funeral, her relatives gathered at Allister's home. Standing next to the hearse, the family huddled together as Allister said a prayer. Allister noticed that Sabrina was relaxed and unemotional, which he assumed to be the calm before the storm. 'She travelled to the church with Shane so I had a chance to speak to my wife and let her know that I was going to be distracted trying to comfort Sabrina as much as possible during the funeral.

'Sabrina did sob her eyes out during the service. We had each written a little message to be read out for us because none of us could face standing up ourselves. When Sabrina's message to my mom was read, she was crying uncontrollably on my shoulder, genuinely. Afterwards, we went to the church hall for tea. Everyone was crying as they came to us, especially to Sabrina, to express their sorrow. I didn't notice how she was behaving at the time but after her arrest, several people told me they were surprised how composed she was during that tea.'

Several people noticed, too, that Sabrina left the tea briefly to greet a carload of her coloured friends, who were parked some distance away, watching the proceedings. Allister had given permission for Tatum's father, Shaun Ortell, to attend the funeral but the others clearly felt unwelcome.

At Allister's house after the funeral, Lucinda again told her husband she was feeling edgy. 'She even asked me to get my firearm out of the safe,' according to Allister. 'She felt instinctively that something wasn't right in her home.

When she woke me in the night, I asked her to try and describe what exactly was wrong and she said she felt there was some evil in the house. Then she heard some footsteps in the early hours of the morning and woke me again. It was quite nerve-racking. I got up and checked all the doors and made sure the alarms were on. Neither of us was suspicious of Sabrina, not at all, although we later worked out that the footsteps Lucinda heard were Sabrina's as she paced around while talking to Feza.'

Inspector Rheeders did not go to bed at all that night. In the early hours of Thursday, the Technical Support Unit officers arrived at his office to discuss tactics for trapping Sabrina. 'We decided to ask Feza to call her from my office phone, which was tapped, and he agreed. It was about four in the morning. Feza told her the police are looking for him; they've been to his house twice and he's hiding in the bushes and he can see them from where he is lying, and he wants Sabrina to give him money to get out of town. She asked him how much he wanted and he said R1 000. She said okay but he must wait until the morning. They arranged the meeting. She told him: "Don't phone me again at this time of night because I am staying with my family and just now they'll suspect something." '

Rheeders took Feza back to prison. He then went home to wash and rest for a couple of hours before returning to the cells to book Feza out again and take him to a meeting with the police technicians in his office at 7.30. Having decided to set the trap at the Caltex garage in Cathcart Street, Rheeders placed a listening device in Feza's top left shirt pocket and sent him, accompanied by a plain-clothed policeman to ensure he did not escape, to meet Sabrina in an unmarked police car resembling a taxi.

'We were waiting with the tape recorder and the trapping technicians just around the corner,' Stephen Rheeders explains. 'Sabrina arrived at 9.00am as arranged. She spoke to Feza and handed him R3 000. You must remember Feza was only asking for R1 000, so this was strange. Sabrina was probably scared that he would come back asking for more so she gave him more than he had asked for.'

But he was owed R200 000.

'Ja, only once the insurance paid out. We pretended that Feza could not wait this long. He needed some money now. I think Sabrina thought Feza was now out of her hair. If she paid him to get out of town he would be too scared to come back because he now knew the police were looking for him.'

After pocketing the money, Feza and the undercover police officer drove away hurriedly. Inspector Rheeders received a phone call from his colleagues informing him that the transaction had taken place. Sabrina was about to leave the garage when Rheeders drove in. 'She was alone in the red Golf. When we stopped her she was friendly but you could see she was nervous. She asked, "What's wrong, Stephen? Are you looking for me? What did I do wrong?"

'I got out of the vehicle and went towards her and you could see she was very, very nervous. I told her we were arresting her for the murder of her mother. She was totally mind-blown. She was white, whiter than a page in the book you're writing. I 'cuffed her and one of the policemen drove her car while she came with me. She was crying, asking who told us, trying to get information. Then she saw Feza and the undercover policeman he had driven away with, standing outside my office. That's when she cracked. She was crying profusely, saying she was sorry, so sorry.

'I explained her rights to her, told her she could have a legal representative and that she doesn't have to say anything. But she said she wanted to talk to the three police officers present. Maybe it was a relief to her to be arrested; I don't know. She told us she never meant to kill her mother but only to hire

Feza to scare Bev. She agreed to make a confession and to do the pointing out to the police.

'We still had the authority to trap her by recording everything she and Feza said to each other. Feza still had the listening device in his pocket. We took them to the police station and locked them in adjoining cells. They spoke, blaming each other, discussing who was the most sorry of the two of them.'

Rheeders arranged for officers to conduct the pointing out by both Feza and Sabrina, a magistrate to take Sabrina's confession, and policemen to accompany her to the magistrate's court to endorse her confession because, he explains, the investigating officer is not allowed to do this. He then listened carefully several times to the recorded conversations between Sabrina and Feza to make sure he had got the facts straight.

'Then I spoke to Allister. He was trying to contact Sabrina on her cellphone, which was now in my possession, while she was being guarded outside my office. I informed him that she was under arrest. The three brothers arrived soon afterwards. Sabrina was crying and apologising.'

Recalling the dramatic events on that Thursday morning, Allister says he had arranged to meet Sabrina at his office at 8.30. He had some of Beverley's files on his desk because he wanted to show Sabrina how to manage the accounting records. 'When she didn't arrive, I called her office but they did not know where she was. When there was still no sign of her after 9, I rang her cellphone. A man answered but did not say who he was. I asked, "Who's that?" He still didn't identify himself but I realised who he was when he said, "I'm sorry, you can't speak to Sabrina because I have arrested her for the murder of your mother". That's how I found out.

'I was totally traumatised, so shocked because of all of us I was the closest to Sabrina. I immediately told Lester, who works with me, and I phoned my wife to tell her Sabrina had been arrested. Then I called the rest of the family to an urgent meeting in my office. I was disappointed, to say the least, and extremely hurt because of my close relationship with Sabrina, and deeply shocked. My immediate concern was: how involved was she? Did she hold my mom down, did she do this, did she do that? For the next three or four months, those questions tormented me. Lucinda was so worried about me that she had a dream in which I ended up in a loony bin. When I saw how small this Feza guy was, it worried me even more that Sabrina had been physically involved. My mom wasn't exactly a weakling but she would have been physically no match for Sabrina.

'The news that Sabrina arranged the murder quickly clicked into place for Lucinda but Shane and his wife, who often had Sabrina and Tatum to stay, just wept and wept.' The family sat around for hours trying to absorb the shock. Raking through the week since the murder for unseen clues pointing to Sabrina's guilt, Shane and Lester remembered her claiming that she had driven into the kerb, yet the police found no marks of this collision on either the car or the pavement. They discussed the uneasiness Lucinda had felt on several occasions: first, when Sabrina had walked into the room where her mother had died only a few hours earlier, forbidden cigarette in hand, rummaging through Beverley's cupboards as if nothing had happened; later, the joke while funeral arrangements were being discussed; Sabrina's composure during the funeral tea; her callous rearrangement of Beverley's business within days of the murder.

'What a shock! There's no way anything can ever, ever prepare you for something like that,' says Allister. 'In some ways, the shock of discovering that Sabrina had killed my mom was greater than the shock of finding her dead in the first place. I felt so betrayed. I was the one who opened up my home and my life to Sabrina. I sat her down and told her not to worry, we're going to buy a nice townhouse for you and Tatum. And we'll help you bring up Tatum. All that, and you get a huge slap in the face. I was incredibly upset and I decided there and then that I wanted nothing more to do with her.'

After the Van Schoor brothers had left his office, Stephen Rheeders told Sabrina and Feza they could each make one phone call before being taken to prison. He remembers Feza phoning his girlfriend, while Sabrina called a boyfriend named Mark.

What did she tell Mark?

'I can't say exactly. Basically, she told him she had been arrested for the murder of her mother.'

That's the quickest way to lose a boyfriend.

'Ja,' says Rheeders, laughing loudly.

The next morning, he drives me to various sites that mark important turning points in his investigation. We stare at the disused tavern in Ezibeleni township, where Sabrina's car was abandoned by Feza in front of a sagging Lion Lager sign. He points out the footpath in front of a humble grey house where Feza threw the serrated bread knife he used to cut Beverley's throat. As we stop to allow goats to cross the road, he tells me that most of his investigations take him into Ezibeleni: 'There's a lot of rubbish living here, but also a lot of ordinary people trying to live decently.' We talk about murder in general and he says, 'Anyone can turn into a murderer. There's a fine line before snapping here.'

Stephen Rheeders' modest little lemon-coloured house, where we pause on our tour of the murder sites while he dashes in to fetch something, is a long way below the Van Schoor family's aspirations. 'They had everything money can buy,' he tells me wistfully. We continue past Hangklip School for Afrikaans-speaking children on the right and down the hill, driving slowly past the graveyard at the bottom of Livingstone Road, where some of Queenstown's white youths were recently arrested for damaging tombstones and where Sabrina met Gino on the morning of the murder in order to let Feza into her car and drive him, lying on the back seat, to 73 Berry Street.

'Sabrina phoned Gino, urging him to fetch Feza in the early hours of that Friday morning,' Rheeders says. 'She was the one pushing for the job to be done, not the other way around, as she claims. This was because she knew her mother was going to find out that she had been stealing money from the business. They thought they had planned the perfect crime. Their big mistake was not to take the money from Bev's handbag,' says Rheeders, adding that Sabrina's biggest mistake was describing Feza too accurately to the police.

I don't think Beverley knew Sabrina was involved in her murder, do you?

Rheeders shrugs. 'I don't know. I hope not.' He parks his car outside his office. I ask if Sabrina told him that the last thing she heard when Feza went into her mother's bedroom, as Sabrina was turning up the volume of her television and radio to drown her mother's cries, was Beverley shouting, 'Sabrina, run.' He gives another shrug that speaks volubly about the mysteries of the human condition, then shakes his head and replies: 'It's ironic.'

Chapter Four

Sabrina was 12 years old when she heard on a lunchtime news broadcast in August 1991 during the dying days of apartheid that her father, the man she liked to describe as her 'knight in shining armour', was in fact a trigger-happy killer. 'I was sitting with my mom eating my lunch after school at our shop, Lady B, which was then in the Pick 'n Pay mall,' she told me during one of our interviews at Fort Glamorgan prison. 'It came over Radio Algoa through the public address system into our shop as well as into the supermarket next door and the concourse outside. It was the first item on the news: "East London security guard Louis van Schoor appears in court today charged with 19 counts of murder and 21 counts of attempted murder …." '

Sabrina remembers feeling stunned, 'almost dead', unable to speak as she stared at her mother. 'I had not seen my dad for a long time because my mom did not want me to see him. I worshipped my father. I was very, very upset,' she told me, explaining that she had felt close to Louis despite her divorced parents' ongoing feud. Louis used to drive to Queenstown to visit her until Beverley, in retaliation for his failure to pay child support, refused to speak to him. Thereafter, Sabrina occasionally managed to visit him by arranging to stay with her old friend Sonja Botha in East London over weekends. Sonja's family knew Louis and facilitated visits between father and daughter. 'When I reconnected with my dad, (Beverley) resented it. I dressed sloppily like him, wore no shoes, and she didn't like that. When I stayed with my dad, we'd go to town in shorts without shoes. I got on well with him. I liked his honesty, his hard-headedness and the fact that he was full of life.'

According to Sabrina, Beverley's response to her daughter's shock on hearing of Louis' arrest had been to shake her head helplessly, and then to grab Sabrina's arm, steer the dazed child briskly to the car park and drive her home. On the way, Beverley confirmed the radio report. Sabrina recalls her mother saying that Louis had shot a lot of people, '... but what was done could not be undone, and we would have to live with it'. Later that day, a policeman friend of the family told Sabrina that Louis had killed so many people because, as East London's top security guard, it was his job to curb crime. He told her that Louis was considered a hero in East London for protecting the town's citizens against criminals. She remembers him saying that her father had the superhuman reputation of a man who never slept because people used to see Louis on the beat in the middle of the night as well as during the day.

From newspaper reports, Sabrina learnt that her father was accused of shooting and killing on a scale far beyond the 19 counts of murder and 21 counts of attempted murder for which he had been charged in State vs Van Schoor. He was alleged by numerous witnesses, who had told their stories to reporters and human rights lawyers, to have shot 101 people, killing 39 of them, over just three years – a shocking tally that suggested a civil war in the Eastern Cape or at least a crime wave of unprecedented proportions. In fact, East London was the same sleepy place it had always been. And Louis was so self-righteous that he did not even bother to pretend that he had used his firearm to protect human life: he had killed 39 people, by his own admission, merely in the interests of protecting the town's business premises. After his arrest, journalists and jurists all over the world demanded to know how Louis van Schoor got away with so many murders for so long.

The Van Schoor case showed the impact of politics on the individual. Apartheid's systematically enforced codes of denial enabled white South Africans to differentiate effortlessly between human and what they considered subhuman, a dehumanising process that became a way of life for most of them. The Van Schoor case in the wider context of apartheid provided the world with an opportunity, a virtual laboratory experiment, to see what happens when people have to deny their humanity in order to function. The question echoing in the wake of Louis' arrest as a symbol of apartheid, and indeed after the Nazi holocaust, was: to what extent can people bring themselves not to know what they know? Part of the answer came a few years later from Archbishop Desmond Tutu when he tried to restore the conscience of South Africa: 'It's impossible to wake someone who is pretending to sleep,' he told the Truth and Reconciliation Commission during its attempts to honour the victims of apartheid violence while publicly shaming the perpetrators.

Wherever violence against a particular out-group is portrayed as a moral ideal shared by the larger society and sanctioned by its leaders – as in the aftermath of the US-led war against Iraq in 2003, some of South Africa's liberation movements' activities during the Eighties, as well as apartheid itself – violence becomes part of the psychological repertoire of what is acceptable. US soldiers torturing captured Iraqis at Abu Ghraib prison and black South Africans dancing and singing around burning human beings believed to have been consorting with the enemy, and therefore deserving of 'neck-lacing', are among the consequences of sanctioning racism, torture, repression or genocide.

*

In the Van Schoor family home in Queenstown, Sabrina and her brothers were forbidden from visiting Louis in prison because, not surprisingly, Beverley pronounced him a bad influence on her children. Sabrina became preoccupied not only with Louis' demise but her own fate as his daughter. Brooding alone in her room for hours at what she saw as the injustice of not being able to see her father, she recalls that she was simultaneously plagued by the taunts of some of the black girls at school who tried to hold her accountable for Louis' crimes. Already suffering from a poor sense of self, Sabrina's confidence plunged when Louis was sent to prison.

After reading a long magazine article about Louis' killing spree in East London, Sabrina realised how little she knew about her father. When her history class at school was asked to research a person who had had an evil influence on the world, Sabrina initially decided to study Louis. She telephoned the librarian at the *Daily Dispatch*, who sent her a pile of newspaper clippings about the trial. After reading them carefully countless times, however, she changed her mind about studying Louis. 'Most of my friends were blacks and coloureds by then and I thought it would look like I was praising him,' Sabrina says, adding disapprovingly that Louis had been 'reckless' while defending himself in court. 'I didn't do my project on my dad in the end. I did it on Hitler instead.'

The newspaper cuttings about Louis' trial nevertheless

became a focal point in her life because they contained the only photographs she had of her father. Over the next few years, Sabrina says she developed a ritual to cope with the quarrels she had with her mother throughout her teens. Locking herself in her bedroom whenever she missed her dad, she used to take the shoebox containing the stories about Louis from its hiding place and read each of them as she lay on her bed, usually crying. 'By the time I left school, I knew every one of those stories off by heart,' she recalls.

Ironically, in a letter she wrote to her father from prison, Sabrina asked Louis' forgiveness 'for all the disappointments and setbacks I have caused you ...' Louis claims he wrote often to Sabrina from his prison cell, perhaps begging her forgiveness, but there is no record of this exchange because Louis also claims that Beverley destroyed all his letters.

Recalling how she once made contact with her father by sending him a message over a Christian radio station, Sabrina says in another letter written to Louis from her cell at Fort Glamorgan: '... I listen to the song, *Butterfly Kisses*, that I dedicated to you a little while ago on Link-FM. I feel it both ways, Daddy; first as your baby girl and then also as my baby Tatum's parent. That song says a lot and it reaches out to me because it feels like both my father and my daughter have been taken away from me.' On another occasion when Sabrina, aged 15, and Louis communicated via public radio, Link-FM featured a festive greetings programme in which Louis sent a message to the families of the people he had murdered, saying he was sorry and wishing them a happy Christmas. Sabrina found comfort in her father's apparently sincere gesture towards those left behind to mourn for his victims. '(It) helped me to understand that, as most of our friends had explained to me, my dad was only doing his job when he hurt all those people.'

While it is understandable that a daughter might cling to

any explanation that softened her father's moral culpability, there are many whites in East London who defend Louis van Schoor on the same grounds to this day. Others, including John Stoltz, Louis' spiritual adviser during his prison years, make excuse after excuse but eventually run out of steam. When I met Stoltz while he was on a visit to Pretoria, he tried for nearly an hour to evoke sympathy for Louis van Schoor, a man who grew up longing for the approval of his bullying, hard-hearted father; who was spoon-fed racism with his cornflakes. When I became tired of listening to the excuses and wondered if Stoltz was speaking to me as a professional prison evangelist or possibly as a racist, I suddenly switched off my tape recorder and asked him abruptly what he actually thought of Louis. Stoltz replied without hesitation: 'He is a cold-blooded killer.'

The reason it took a tight-knit white South African community three years to apprehend a cold-blooded killer is simple: the white East Londoners who knew did not care and the black people who knew were powerless to intervene. It was left to a couple of young journalists and a few human rights lawyers to hunt Louis down and force the criminal justice system, that had covered his tracks for so long, to deal with him.

*

For my next trip in June 2003 to interview the Van Schoors in prison in East London, I caught an early flight from Johannesburg. Looking out of the window over the wing of the plane at 6.00am, I watched the sun light up the east side of each mountain range while the other half remained densely black so that the vast vista below seemed half-revealed, as if only so much was knowable. Slowly, the sun crept higher and the stark line across the top of the mountains began to soften, illuminating the dark side.

During the flight, I reread a pile of newspaper clippings about Louis. The beginning of the end of his killing career had come in 1989 when an East London estate agent, Des Nish, listened in astonishment to a burglar alarm salesman extolling the talents of one of his company's security guards. Explaining that the alarm system he was selling went off without the knowledge of intruders inside the guarded premises, the salesman boasted about the resultant armed response: 'Louis van Schoor has killed or wounded up to a hundred burglars.'

Nish knew Louis as the macho, short-tempered former husband of Beverley van Schoor, a local businesswoman who had been assaulted by her spouse throughout the marriage and who told her friends that she so feared for her life after beginning divorce proceedings in East London that she fled with her four children to Queenstown to start a new life. The idea that such a man was not only investigating burglar alerts but legally carrying a gun with which he shot suspects struck Des Nish as disastrous. He decided to report his concerns to the *Daily Dispatch*, where the journalist he spoke to immediately set about verifying the story.

Louis had been carrying a gun since the age of 16, when he left school without a basic leaver's certificate and joined the police. After completing his training during the heyday of apartheid, when white cops were used to keeping black civilians brutally in their place, Van Schoor became a handler in the Dog Unit. It was a simple job offering a lot of action, very little paperwork, and some satisfaction for the policemen who were suited to it. Louis enjoyed the work but, despite more than 12 years' service, a rampant desire for recognition and his friends achieving promotion all around him, he never rose above the lowly rank of constable. 'He was not a clever bloke,' recalls one colleague, 'but he would go to hell and back to get his man. It was his way of proving that he was as good as the others.'

On the sports field, the hulking Louis was able to show his physical talent more convincingly. Playing flanker for the police rugby team and earning provincial colours in the Eastern Cape's tug-of-war squad, he also starred in four-wheel-drive challenges. Racing over hillsides and beaches in his super-powered Land Rover with its monster mag wheels and heavy black roll bar, dressed in shorts with the ever-ready holster on his hip, Louis felt happy, according to his first wife. To keep fit, he ran cross-country barefoot. A beer-swilling man's man, he was by all accounts well-liked in the police force and in East London's white community generally.

Louis was also a ladies' man, marrying four times before being sent to prison at the age of 40. He met his second wife, English-speaking Beverley, in the Baysville Church of Christ when she was already married to someone else. A member of the congregation recalls: 'He would go on fishing trips with Bev's husband and then sneak away to be with her.' The couple wed in 1978 and set up home with Beverley's three young sons on a farm near East London, where their daughter Sabrina was born in November the following year.

A neighbour recalls that Van Schoor used to spend his weekends training the dogs of other smallholders, including his close friend Bazil Niemand, who was taken to court by an elderly farm worker, accused of unleashing a pack of German shepherds on the frightened man. Louis later helped Niemand campaign for election to Parliament beneath a poster featuring a snarling German shepherd and the slogan, 'I'll be your watchdog'.

According to Louis, he left the police in 1980 because he was tired of being forced to fight in Angola, where the South African army had intervened in a civil war. But Beverley, his wife at the time, who said Louis actually volunteered to go to 'the border', gave another reason. Beverley suspected him of being unfaithful and demanded that he spend more time at home. Van Schoor agreed and took a job at the carpet company where Beverley worked but it proved too mundane an occupation for a man who was not only attracted to danger but who enjoyed the adulation bestowed by whites on policemen and soldiers with dangerous reputations. With Beverley's blessing, he took a daytime security job. Still discontent, he filed an application to rejoin the police. Why he was rejected has never been explained, but this was a turning point in his life. Against his wife's protestations, he accepted a job working nights at Falcon Security, owned by former police major C J H Cloete, and the marriage collapsed.

Until the late Seventies, security companies using silent alarms had relied on the police to do their investigations. In 1978, when the police force decided too much of its time was being wasted on false alarms, Major Cloete and Louis van Schoor moved in to fill the gap. 'Van Schoor and I did this work because it paid well,' Cloete told a reporter after Louis' arrest. 'I know Van Schoor was the kind of bloke that liked to use his firearm. He had shot two dead at that stage; that I know because I killed one and he used to say, "Ha, I'm ahead of you".'

Louis and Beverley were divorced in 1983. Sabrina, not yet four at the time, later recalled in her teenage diary that '... not knowing what was going on around me except heartache and pain ... my mom fled to Queenstown ... because my dad threatened to kill her ... We built a life up from scratch. Seeing I no longer had a father to look after us, my mom took his place and proved to be a much better father in the long run ... I just had to adapt to it all.'

Louis then married Sabrina's nursery school teacher, Anne. Although her parents' marriage was on the rocks before Sabrina saw Louis kissing her teacher, it was she who related the incident to Beverley and thereafter blamed herself for the break-up. Louis had two daughters with Anne but she left him in 1988. Two years later, he proposed to Sandra Bing, daughter of a wealthy East London businessman. The hopes Louis is said to have nurtured of her social status rubbing off on him were dashed when her family failed to attend the wedding.

Sabrina got along well with Sandra, who was kind to Anne's two daughters as well as to Sabrina. Although she divorced Louis when he went to prison, Sandra helped him stay in touch with his three daughters by encouraging the younger girls, whose mother wanted nothing to do with Louis, to visit him and by arranging for Sabrina to see him whenever she was in East London. It was to Sandra that Sabrina turned in one of her darkest moments when, three months pregnant with Tatum and on the run from Beverley's wrath, she was staying in East London with a former boyfriend called Allan. She recalls: 'Dad accepted Allan as a coloured and cared for him deeply, and he was happy I was pregnant. Dad wanted me to stay in East London and leave Mom alone. I agreed I wanted to stay in East London but Mom threatened Allan's family and he decided that it was best I went back to Queenstown. I tried to phone my stepmother but I couldn't get hold of her. So I gave in and went back to Queenstown. I often wonder what would have happened if I had stayed in East London. I would have Tatum, Mom would be alive, and who knows what else could have come of it.'

A local journalist, commenting on Louis' four marriages, described his wives as 'either vulnerable, overweight or meek'. Family photograph albums show Beverley, for instance, as a slender beauty in her youth but very overweight by the time she divorced Louis and, according to her friend Maggie Riggien, deeply troubled by her obesity. It was perhaps Beverley's buried sense of inadequacy that caused a number of undesirable effects, including her bullying. As for her racism, it is hard to name a more obvious sign of negative self-esteem than the need to perceive some other group as inferior.

'It is a running theme in all (Louis') close relationships and even some distant associations (that) he has surrounded himself with those mentally weaker than himself,' continued the newspaper report on Louis' personality. 'Indeed, there lurks behind Van Schoor's stern facade and fearsome reputation a boyish innocence, a lively and unassuming nature. Perhaps that is part of his electrifying charm ... Van Schoor is a self-imposed loner – flippantly extrovert on the surface, but guarded on the inside. People who know him speak of him more as a subject than as a person. He reveals no public emotion ... He exhibits a strong affinity to children. The only time I have seen him display any real delight was during a conversation about his favourite (step) son, Shane. And while his wives may not pay him many compliments, they do concede that he was a good father. When he was around, that is.'

Sabrina's half-brother Allister van Schoor confirmed during an interview in Queenstown that Louis was good to him and his brothers while the marriage lasted. 'We had many fun times, playing rugby and cricket with Louis,' he said. 'He was like any other father figure. But what sticks in my mind about Louis was his abuse of my mom. He never abused us but we saw him hit her.'

When Allister was telling me that they had been 'just one big happy family', I remembered Louis saying during my first brief interview with him at Fort Glamorgan that his three stepsons had resented Sabrina when she was born, so I pressed Allister on this point. 'I did feel Louis favoured Sabrina,' he admitted. 'He had a very soft spot for her, but that was only natural, I suppose, because she was his own child. Shane, being younger than Lester and me, and maybe not seeing what we saw later on, took very well to Louis and continued to see him after he went to prison, regardless of what anyone told him about Louis.'

According to Maggie Riggien, Sabrina's two older half-brothers reacted to the news of Louis' arrest with indifference, saying they did not care if he went to prison because he was not their father. Beverley did not bother to disguise her approval of what she saw as payback time for her abusive ex-husband. 'Even in front of Sabrina, she said it was right that he goes and sits in jail, not only for the people he shot but for the way he treated everybody, especially her. That was how she saw it,' says Maggie. 'Sabrina was heartsore because she idolised her father. After Louis went to prison, I think she used it as a bit of an excuse, telling herself, "This is why I am no good".'

It is possible, given voluminous evidence showing how people tend to do to others what was done to them, that the whole Van Schoor family suffered from the effects of child abuse, especially in the form of low self-esteem. Prison evangelist John Stoltz told me that Louis' father bullied his son and withheld affection from him to the point of emotional abuse. Maggie Riggien recalls Beverley's account of her early life, in which her mother had been thrown out of the home by her lay-preacher father for having repeated extra-marital affairs, only to be replaced by a stepmother who was jealous of her three pretty stepdaughters and cut their hair so brutally short that they felt disfigured.

Allister, Lester and Shane van Schoor, in witnessing Louis hitting their mother and generally throwing his weight around, may themselves have transgressed into violence as children. Sabrina claimed in court during her bail application that her brothers used to beat her and throw knives, pliers and darts at her. 'My youngest brother even shot me with a pellet gun once,' she said. In response, Allister told the court that Sabrina was so big that she often got the better of him while playing, despite being ten years younger. 'She would hold me down so that I couldn't move,' he said. On Sabrina's claim that Beverley had beaten her, Allister testified that his mother was small and no match for Sabrina. 'If I can be blunt,' he said, 'I think it is utter nonsense.'

*

Trying to make sense of what had at first sounded like nonsense, *Daily Dispatch* journalist Andrew Austin decided to discuss Des Nish's allegation that Louis had shot 100 people with a few local businessmen. After numerous telephone calls in search of information about the guard's career in private security, he realised that he had stumbled on a closely kept secret. While some of the traders and police officers he spoke to acknowledged that they knew the security guard, no one was willing to talk about him. Even the police media liaison officer, Major Trevor Hayes, would go only as far as admitting that he knew a guard called Van Schoor.

Austin was about to leave South Africa for a year in Europe so he passed the story on to a newcomer at the paper, 24-year-old Patrick Goodenough, who initially thought the allegations were too outlandish to be true. Then, a few weeks after first hearing about Louis, Goodenough became suspicious when he read in a front-page report in May 1989 that two suspected burglars had been shot dead by a factory security guard.

The report did not identify the guard so Goodenough called the owner of the factory where the shootings had taken place and asked for the man's name: it was Louis van Schoor. Although he still did not know how much to believe of the extraordinary story his colleague Austin had related, Goodenough now knew that Van Schoor had killed two men, although this was not unusual in his line of work.

Ten days later, the trial of two housebreaking suspects gave Goodenough further evidence of Van Schoor's licence to kill. The State alleged that the two – Thanduxolo Tshana (28) and Simpiwe Tom (16) – had been caught breaking into a clothing shop. Tom testified that he had been asleep on the pavement outside a bakery when Van Schoor woke him and offered him a job. He accepted and they drove down East London's Oxford Street to Budget Buys. Inside the store, Tom told the magistrate, the guard shot him in the chest. When he fell, Van Schoor fired three more shots straight at him.

Tshana told the court that he was on his way to work at a beachfront hotel when Van Schoor suddenly came out of an alley and opened fire. He collapsed and the guard hauled him into a courtyard behind the building. When Van Schoor disappeared, Tshana dragged himself into an outdoor toilet. On his return, Van Schoor tried to kick down the door, and then fired two shots through it.

Tom and Tshana protested their innocence but the magistrate dismissed them as liars and sent them to prison. However, an encounter between a young woman reporter and Louis during the tea break shortly before sentencing left Goodenough in no doubt that he was on to an important story. The reporter, Sally Shaw, related how she had decided to act girlie when she spoke to Van Schoor outside the court.

'Your job must be quite dangerous. You must have shot quite a few people,' she ventured.

'Yes,' answered Van Schoor, revealing his arrogance. 'Off the record, it must be about a hundred now.'

Shaw included the chilling exchange in her report but the *Daily Dispatch* editors took it out on the grounds that it might have been an idle boast and that it was in any event an off the record remark. The following day, Patrick Goodenough combed through the *Dispatch*'s crime reports and found three more violent incidents involving Louis. One in August 1987 described Van Schoor shooting and wounding two suspects. Another in December said a Mr S van Schoor had shot and wounded an escaping burglar. The third, also in December, told of an unidentified man who had been shot dead while resisting arrest by Sybrand Jacobus Lodewickus van Schoor.

Goodenough was intrigued. Slim, fair-haired and earnest, he pressed on and found a dozen more cases which fitted Van Schoor's modus operandi, though none of them named the shooter. He rang Major Hayes, who again declined to provide details or to confirm Van Schoor's involvement. 'Why are you after this guy?' the police media officer asked. 'He does a lot of good work.'

Unable to confirm that the burly former policeman had killed at least three people and wounded four more, Goodenough discussed his suspicions about Louis with several security officials around the country, all of whom agreed that it was unusual for a guard to shoot that often over a short period. The reporter then wrote a story expressing concern about a local security guard with too many notches on his gun-belt. Included in his piece was the claim Van Schoor had made to Sally Shaw. The *Daily Dispatch*'s editors spiked it.

The next suspicious pointer was a call to Goodenough from an agitated local resident, insurance executive Ed McFarlane. He said he was calling the *Dispatch* as a last resort after failing to get the police to allow his domestic worker, Grace Sipolo, into the mortuary to confirm whether or not an 18-year-old youth who had been shot dead two nights earlier at Mike's Tavern was her missing son. Goodenough telephoned Major Hayes, who confirmed that there had been a shooting at the beachfront restaurant in which a security guard had killed two people, but the policeman refused to name the guard. Goodenough immediately called the restaurant's security company and asked to speak to Van Schoor.

Louis returned the call a few minutes later, sounding cheerful when he admitted his involvement but telling the journalist that any further comment had to come from the police. Goodenough called Cambridge Road police station to find out how he could gain entry to its mortuary. Because it was a public holiday, the duty officer said his request would have to wait, but he let slip that three people had been shot at Mike's Tavern, not two, the third having been wounded.

After work that evening, Patrick Goodenough went to Frere Hospital and searched the wards for a gunshot victim. He found Siyabonga Tom – who had been admitted on the night of the shooting at Mike's Tavern – wired to life support machines in the intensive care unit, too ill to receive visitors. In the meantime, McFarlane and Sipolo managed to get into the mortuary where they found Grace's son Steki, who had died from bullet wounds in the upper arm and chest.

Goodenough eventually interviewed Siyabonga in a general ward. He and two friends, Steki Sipolo and a youth he knew only as Patrick, had been looking for food in rubbish bins outside Mike's Tavern, he said. Patrick kept watch while Steki, who had found the back door unlocked, went into the kitchen. Suddenly, a gunshot rang out. The two ducked and scurried into hiding places. Siyabonga saw a tall white man with a long beard coming over the wall with a torch in one hand and a pistol in the other.

Van Schoor found Steki hiding behind the fridge and dragged the screaming youth out by his leg. 'I apologise, my baas, please don't shoot me, rather call the police,' Steki begged. Two shots rang out. Steki fell silent. Van Schoor swung around and saw Siyabonga inside a large rubbish bin, also begging not to be shot. The powerful security guard grabbed him and shot him in the back at point-blank range. As he fell, Siyabonga saw Louis climbing back on to the wall, speaking into his walkie-talkie.

The image of three poverty-stricken kids cowering in front of a murderer as he takes aim is enough to bring tears to the eyes of a stone statue, I thought one day while driving past the recently erected likeness of freedom fighter Steve Biko that towers above the traffic in East London. On an impulse, I turned back and drove around the statue distractedly seven or eight times, to the delight of a giggling group of schoolchildren standing nearby. I was wondering how this local hero – once known as the *swart gevaar*, meaning black danger, of white South Africa and now celebrated nationally as the founder of black consciousness, a political philosophy that inspired the famous Soweto students' uprising in 1976 – would have reacted to Louis van Schoor had he been alive in his hometown to witness the decline and fall of a man who, according to his stepchildren, got along so well with white kids.

Biko, who died in detention in Pretoria after being tortured and beaten by police, had been trying to empower poor black South Africans to shed the collective inferiority complex bequeathed to them by generations of white masters demanding subservience. Having sacrificed his hopes of studying medicine, Biko examined instead the psychological mechanism by which esteem operates between people, particularly the deeply ingrained way many white South Africans selectively switch off respect and sympathy. Biko would probably have acknowledged that the humane response sometimes crashed through defences supposedly constructed in concrete, a cause for hope in the country's agonising race relations.

I remember reading a newspaper report, around the time that Louis was on the rampage in East London, of a political demonstration in Durban to which the police were responding with their customary violence. A policeman was running after a black woman, intending to whip her with his sjambok. Suddenly, her shoe fell off and she stumbled. The brutalised cop was simultaneously a young Afrikaner with nice manners, who had been brought up to know that if a lady's shoe falls off you have to pick it up for her. As he did so and handed the shoe back, their eyes met fleetingly. His gesture had begun to restore the woman's dignity and so he had to walk away rather than whip her: cruelty was no longer an option.

Cruelty is a recurring theme in Sabrina's letters and among the subjects she had touched on when she wrote to me shortly before my June visit to East London. 'I wonder, if this whole thing hadn't happened, would my father and I ever have been as close as (we are) now?' she asked. 'How cruel it is to think that being arrested for my mother's murder has brought me closer to my father ... I also think of how different my life could have been if I had had a father in it full-time.'

In her own view, much of Sabrina's unhappiness during her teens stemmed from Beverley's arguably cruel efforts to prevent her from seeing Louis, who was a mass murderer and a racist of note but who apparently loved his daughter, at least to her satisfaction. Though withholding access to shared children is a common form of retribution between divorced parents, and is sometimes defended to the hilt by women struggling to raise kids without maintenance contributions from their former spouses, it is doubtful that a mother can justify keeping a child away from a father – assuming he poses no undue threat to his offspring and that the child wants a relationship with him – except in terms of her own anger and vengeance.

*

Anger of another kind was brewing up at the *Daily Dispatch*'s offices back in May 1989. Patrick Goodenough was about to write a story based on his interview at Siyabonga Tom's hospital bedside when he was interrupted by his news editor, who informed him that the youth had been charged with housebreaking and the case was now sub judice, meaning that Goodenough could not report Siyabonga's claims until he repeated them in court. Frustrated and annoyed, the reporter decided to ask a human rights organisation to arrange for a lawyer to represent Siyabonga.

He went to the Black Sash offices in Oxford Street, where he spoke to Mtelei Tobana, a young activist. In the privacy of an adjoining office, they discussed the reporter's growing suspicions about Louis van Schoor with the organisation's feisty advice coordinator, Sharlene Craige. When Goodenough had finished describing the factory shooting, Tom and Tshane's case, Van Schoor's claim to have shot a hundred people, the reports of similar shootings in the *Daily Dispatch* files, the police media officer's refusal to provide details and his own interview with Siyabonga, he noticed that Sharlene Craige seemed strangely excited as she handed him a document.

It was a statement she and Mtelei had taken a month earlier from a 26-year-old man called Vusumzi Gcaza. In it, he said he was on his way home in October 1988 after trying to get work at a bakery when a man in a bakkie asked him if he wanted a job. Gcaza said he climbed into the vehicle and the two drove a short way to the Turnbull Bowling Club, where the man, who said his name was Van Schoor, told him to wait outside the window on the left of the building. According to the statement, Van Schoor then disappeared and returned holding a gun. Without warning, he shot Gcaza twice, in the chest and in his left arm. When he was taken to hospital, Gcaza said, he was charged with housebreaking.

Vusumzi Gcaza's statement was the fourth account describing virtually identical incidents, each given independently and none yet revealed publicly. Sharlene Craige decided to contact David Pitman, a lawyer at the Legal Resources Centre in Grahamstown, who suggested getting sworn affidavits from Siyabonga and Gcaza in order to lay criminal charges as well as civil claims for damages.

'I drove to East London where I was joined by Sharlene Craige,' recalls Pitman. 'Accompanied by a relative of Siyabonga, we went directly to Frere Hospital where we found the victim with a bullet wound running from his abdomen clear through to his back ... A telling piece of evidence, collected from the custody of the hospital, was the clothing he had been wearing when he was shot, notably a synthetic fibre tracksuit. The tracksuit top had a gaping hole in front, with indications that the fibre had been burned in the vicinity of the hole, which would prove Siyabonga's allegation that he had been shot at point-blank range. Armed with Siyabonga's statement and his clothes in a plastic bag, we drove jauntily to the Fleet Street police station.

'At that point,' says Pitman, 'I knew that Louis van Schoor's life was going to dramatically change. The South African Police force was known to be partisan and duplicitous when it came to dealing with political opponents of the state. But when it came to ordinary crime, they were capable of being thoroughly businesslike and transparent. Louis van Schoor's crimes did not involve the political role of the police but were horrendous commercial crimes.' Less convinced of the police's capacity for transparency was opposition MP Andre de Wet, who noted that, when South Africa's police investigated an ordinary criminal allegation with racial connotations, as in the Van Schoor case, they tended to turn it into a political matter.

Shortly after Pitman had taken Siyabonga's statement, there was another shooting in East London. The police again refused to name the security guard involved. The Black Sash had by then notified a wide network of activists about Van Schoor's executions, among them a doctor who was able to confirm informally that Louis had pulled the trigger in the latest shooting.

This time the victim was Mntunzima Titi (24), a night-watchman, who told police that he was on his way home in the early hours of the morning when a tall, bearded man approached him in the road and shot him without saying a word. The gunman threw him into the back of a bakkie, where he passed out. When he woke up in hospital, the police were at his bedside to charge him with housebreaking.

Six weeks had now passed since the factory shooting that had encouraged Patrick Goodenough to stay on the trail of an alleged killer. The victims were piling up: at least five dead and seven wounded. He tried again to get the story published but his editors again spiked it. The reporter's frustration was becoming unbearable when, in June 1989, lawyer David Pitman filed attempted murder charges and civil damages suits against Louis van Schoor on behalf of Siyabonga and Gcaza. Obtaining copies of the victims' statements and Pitman's covering letters to the police, Goodenough handed them to his editor, Glynn Williams, feeling sure that the documents would finally convince the *Daily Dispatch* to print his story.

To the journalist's amazement, however, his news editor, Mike Chandler, emerged from an urgent editorial meeting repeating the sub judice rule: Goodenough would have to wait until each of the cases came to court before he could report on them. The next day Goodenough decided to file a brief factual report stating that police had confirmed that they were investigating two charges of attempted murder against a security guard called Sybrand 'Louis' van Schoor. To the reporter's fury, even this bland story was rejected by his newspaper at a time when Van Schoor was boasting on the phone to him: 'I'm in full production ... full production.'

A week later, Goodenough was tipped off by a court interpreter that Van Schoor was about to appear before an inquest into the death of a child, Liefie Peters, who had been shot dead at the Esplanade Wimpy Bar in June 1988. He rushed to the court to find that Van Schoor had just left and that the case had been postponed for two months. In the inquest docket, he found a statement by a boy called John Swartbooi. The teenager stated that he and Liefie had broken into the Wimpy to steal money. After entering through a smashed window, they saw a white man answering Van Schoor's description peering through the front window. They ran to hide in a toilet.

It is this sad story that leaps to mind whenever I think of Louis van Schoor and his tragic killing sprees. While staying in East London during my first research trip, I took to running on the beach each morning before sunrise. The Esplanade Wimpy Bar, where Louis shot Liefie and John, was a few hundred yards below my guest house, Dolphin View Lodge in Seaview Crescent, and the end point I chose for my daily run before strolling back up the steep hill for breakfast. The exercise reminded me of the human faces involved in Louis van Schoor's reign of terror and became my ritual memory jog each time I returned to the city.

Under a vanilla sky, witnessed by white-faced seagulls, I stood in front of the Wimpy recalling the inquest docket details and trying to imagine short, skinny 13-year-old Liefie and his friend John, whose chubby cheeks made him look younger than 15. Hiding in the dark restaurant on a winter's night, their eyes all over the place, hearts thumping, they watch as a huge figure looms through the glass, his greasy hair and wild beard visible in the dim glow of a street lamp. The kids are huddled together, barely breathing. Louis walks around outside the Wimpy, finds the broken window through which the boys have entered and hauls himself on to the ledge. Then he spots them in the gloom and fires. Seven shots. If they scream, their voices are drowned by the roar of the ocean. Standing astride their crumpled bodies like a giant, Van Schoor calmly radioes the police.

The image of Liefie and John lying at the feet of the monster was what haunted Patrick Goodenough, too. With certain knowledge of six people killed and nine wounded by Louis van Schoor's deadly hand, and the public none the wiser, he finally lost patience with the newspaper he had once been proud to represent. Considering that the *Daily Dispatch* had been hailed internationally during the turbulent Seventies when its editor Donald Woods bravely championed black rights in general and Steve Biko in particular, losing faith in his editors was as bleak a moment for Patrick Goodenough as it was for the reputation of South African journalism.

Having confirmed with police records that Louis had attended to 272 silent alarm calls where the perpetrators were still on the scene, Goodenough approached a colleague who had been assisting him with his research into the Van Schoor killings – 21-year-old Dominic Jones, who had just completed a cadetship at the *Daily Dispatch*. The two agreed that, because Goodenough risked dismissal at the start of his career if he filed for a rival newspaper, Jones would write the Van Schoor story for Durban's *Sunday Tribune*.

'He (Goodenough) had gathered enough for a detailed story, but one crucial aspect remained unsolved: had Van Schoor killed as many as he claimed?' Jones recalled. 'There was only one way to find out. I went to the courts and, after the usual stonewalling from officials, started going through the inquest files. I started with the boxes labelled 1987. I had no idea what I was looking for. I had never even seen an inquest docket, but I soon got the hang of it.

'On the face of each inquest docket was a covering sheet

listing the name of the dead person, the date of death, the most likely cause of death and whether or not anyone was responsible. On the reverse side was a list of witnesses, at the top of which was the name of the person thought to be immediately responsible for the death. I found a docket that had 'bullet wound to the chest' as the cause of death. I flipped to the back of the cover sheet and at the top of the list of witnesses was the name S J L van Schoor.'

Jones noted the name of the deceased: Zola Sotyhifa (27), shot dead on November 15, 1987. Then he found another: Sidwell Bomba Koboka (37), shot in the abdomen on June 17, 1987. And another: Khululekile Nxego, shot in the head and stomach in 1987. The list grew steadily longer. Inquest files from earlier years were kept in a vault beneath the Magistrate's Court building, and Jones had to obtain special authorisation from the chief magistrate to continue his search underground. After four hours amid the dusty files, he left with the names of 22 people who had been killed by Louis van Schoor. 'The evidence of Van Schoor's bloody reign had been there all the time, gathering dust,' he commented. 'It seemed incredible that so many were dead and yet no one had ever raised the alarm.'

All the inquests had been held in private. Van Schoor was never called to account for himself in court, all his statements being coldly factual, vague in detail and carefully constructed to comply with the law. A trivial item was always missing from the premises he was guarding, he always shouted a warning before opening fire, and he invariably fired 'in the direction' of the suspects. Most died of bullet wounds to the upper body, often three or more. Although Louis maintained that he had not meant to kill the men, the fact that he often fired up to twelve shots at them without aiming at a non-lethal part of their bodies told a different story.

The prevailing law, subsequently changed as a direct result

of Louis van Schoor's bloody excesses, enabled a magistrate to close an inquest without a finding if he concluded that a hearing with live witnesses would not throw further light on the facts, and that the facts did not indicate a crime had been committed. As Van Schoor was often the only witness left alive at the end of one of his interventions, and as he was an ex-policeman who understood the law, his affidavits reporting a killing always included the allegation that he had been attacked while investigating a burglary, and that he had fired on the assailant in self-defence. Inquests in the majority of these cases were all summarily closed without a hearing or a finding. In a few instances, when a witness had been left alive, criminal trials had followed in which the witness/victim was the accused. Van Schoor was able to prove that a triggered alarm had called him to business premises and that the shootings had taken place on these premises. His facts would point damningly to the shooting victim as a burglar whose credibility, from the magistrate's point of view, was consequently zero when he complained that he had been shot at close range while surrendering. In one instance, a magistrate had sensed that something was wrong with Van Schoor's evidence and had recommended further investigation by the police, which never happened.

'I never fire warning shots because they could injure innocent people,' Van Schoor told an inquest court in 1988, knowing that the law required him only to shout a warning and claiming that he always did so. However, in 1990, Louis admitted that, even knowing the shouts were useless, he still failed to fire warning shots. He told a magistrate named Dicker: 'Previously, when I have shouted warnings at people, I have not had one stop.' As Mr Dicker poignantly noted: 'A warning shot remains the same thing in any language … To the two deceased, the silent, charging figure of Mr van Schoor coming at them out of the light must have been, to say the least, terrifying. It was only natural that they would turn and run.'

None of the people Louis claimed had attacked him was armed with anything more than a knife, whereas he carried a 9mm Parabellum, sometimes loaded with lethal hollow-point bullets. The important element of surprise was always on his side since the alarms he monitored sent a silent radio signal to his control room while the intruder remained unaware that he had been detected.

As the picture of Louis' ferocious progression grew clearer, Dominic Jones kept asking himself the same question: why was none of this damning evidence enough to attract official curiosity? He could safely have guessed the answer: because Van Schoor was white and all of his victims were black. The criminal justice system was dominated by whites who either did not care or actively supported the killer guard.

Jones gave Patrick Goodenough the list of inquest victims with which to make a last-ditch attempt to publish details of the Van Schoor murders in his own paper. When the *Daily Dispatch*'s editors again declined it, the *Sunday Tribune* ran the story on its front page alongside dramatic photographs of Van Schoor copied from the inquest files. Finally, the public had been informed of Louis' death patrols.

Police officers nationwide were suddenly bombarded with outraged enquiries. The story sparked what police head-quarters in Pretoria called 'a general polemic'. Van Schoor's actions became the subject of intense public and media interest at home and abroad. Lawyers called for a revision of Section 49 of the Criminal Procedures Act, which, in effect, permitted the killing of a child running away with a stolen apple. The disclosures put the criminal justice system and its attempts to protect Van Schoor under the spotlight at a time when the police spokesman on the matter, Colonel Steve van Rooyen, was still referring to Louis as 'just a bloody efficient security guard'.

During the week following the Sunday exposé, an opposition Member of Parliament, Jan van Eck, demanded to know from the Minister of Justice how it was possible for the inquest magistrate in East London to summarily close 35 inquest dockets, in which one man had been implicated in each killing, without a single hearing taking place. Lawyer David Pitman recalls: 'The next thing we heard was that the state prosecutor was filing an indictment. The Minister apparently saw this as an opportunity to allow the police to be seen doing a proper investigation so as to take the focus off the political violence that they were otherwise so clearly engaged in at the time.'

The Black Sash's East London office was inundated with information, mainly from township dwellers who had had near-death experiences with Louis but also from doctors, policemen, members of the Van Schoor family, as well as ordinary citizens. The investigating journalists and activists spoke to hundreds of people and read scores of court transcripts. A massive dossier began to grow against the man whose callous exploits read like a scene from a Dirty Harry script. He ran across roofs, entered dark buildings alone and unafraid with his gun clasped in both hands, arrogantly admitting in court documents that he fired seven, eight or even ten shots at a time.

To everyone's surprise, Van Schoor himself contributed to the dragnet that was closing in around him after he heard on the radio that investigators believed he had killed at least 34 people. At around 12.00 one night, three days after shooting his latest – and last – victim dead, Louis telephoned Dominic Jones to set the record straight. 'Number 39, pal,' was all he said to the reporter.

'This behaviour, at a time of mounting public calls for a full investigation of his actions, is indicative of the extreme confidence and bravado that dominate his outward persona,' wrote Dominic Jones after Louis' arrest. 'To his everyday acquaintances – policemen, court officials and local businessmen, many of whom hold him in awe – he plays constantly on the role of protector. Every action, from the striding walk to the macho grip on his Chesterfield cigarette, exudes absolute sureness. At times it is almost condescending.' Louis' behaviour mirrored that of the state, which presented itself as the omnipotent protector of whites. No show of strength was considered excessive if it was seen to be in the interests of individual and collective security of the white community.

Incredibly, Van Schoor had gone on killing despite the mounting allegations and the public outcry. He was shooting at someone almost every week; one person on average was being killed by him every three weeks. With 38 people already murdered by him, he was cleared of the death of Liefie Peters following an inquest in which he was questioned for the first time in open court.

By November 1989, the relentless press coverage and human rights campaign against Van Schoor prompted the Eastern Cape Attorney General to order an inquiry into all Louis' shootings. The decision marked an unprecedented moment in the history of white South African rule: an act of self-evaluation, doubtless with ulterior motives as David Pitman had suggested, but nevertheless a willingness by the state to put itself and East London's white community on trial. If Van Schoor was found guilty, the system that gave rise to him, encouraged him to maim and kill, and protected him, would be guilty, too.

It was the biggest murder investigation the country had ever seen. A senior lawyer and a couple of able police investigators worked tirelessly for nearly two years to amass the evidence needed to charge Van Schoor. So much time had passed since he began his killing career that a lot of hard evidence had been destroyed and some important witnesses had died. Vital files and documents had mysteriously vanished, while many of Louis' police colleagues were either reluctant to cooperate in solving crimes in which they had been involved or loath to give evidence against a man they continued to believe had been acting in the public interest.

Finally, after examining scores of shootings, the investigators believed that Van Schoor had shot over 100 people, 39 of them dead, but there was adequate evidence to convict him on only 19 counts of murder, 21 of attempted murder and three counts of assault. Louis was arrested and charged. Almost three years had passed since estate agent Des Nish called the *Daily Dispatch* with his unbelievable story. The killing was over at last.

Dominic Jones, covering the trial for various newspapers, described the opening scene. 'There was something of a crowd outside the East London Supreme Court at 9.00am on August 19, 1991. Lawyers, policemen, journalists, witnesses and family members mingled, smoked and chatted. The chatter stopped when somebody said: "Here he is". He was smiling – a big broad grin that pulled at the laughter lines next to his eyes. He wore a conservative dark grey suit, black grasshoppers, under his left arm he had a bundle of bright red and orange files, and his beard (was) respectably trimmed. "Morning, morning," he waved, gliding past the crowd and into the courtroom, oblivious of the cold stare from the old woman looking up from the wooden bench next to the door.'

The prosecution set about trying to prove that in 13 of the charges, Van Schoor had gunned down his victims after securing their arrests; that in 15 cases independent medical, ballistic or eyewitness accounts contradicted Van Schoor's version of events; that on one occasion he attempted to murder a totally innocent bystander; and that in at least three cases he used excessive and unjustifiable force. The state's case was compromised, however, by the fact that the police and magistrates had hardly ever asked questions of Louis – even when he said he had shot a 'fleeing' suspect in the chest because the man was running backwards. Pathologists' reports of shots fired within inches of the victims allegedly escaping arrest had ignited no greater interest among the magistrates. In a single inquest in 1989, for example, Van Schoor was found to have justifiably killed 25 of his victims. When the local MP had demanded that Louis' gun licence be revoked, the police had argued that they could not take away a man's livelihood.

Dominic Jones wrote: 'Many of the state's witnesses were not all that credible. Some were prisoners, others experienced criminals. They admitted lying under oath at previous court cases, saying they had done so to avoid imprisonment. For many, it was the first time they had told their stories to anyone in authority. And the obvious question was why they had not spoken up earlier. A subliminal case was being made for their part in some underhand and sinister plot, a malicious vendetta instigated by the slimy liberal press. But the fact was that they came and told their stories – and all were so similar.

'Van Schoor's counsel went into a no-holds-barred cross-examination, questioning witnesses at length and launching stinging attacks on their credibility,' recalled Jones. 'Often the questioning was condescending. Nearly every complainant was asked the same volley of questions: How old are you? When were you born? Did you go to school? What standard did you pass? Do you work? And, on one occasion: What is the time on the courtroom clock?'

For a man with all the credentials of a monster, Louis cut a convincing figure in the dock. With years of courtroom experience, he spoke clearly, looked straight at the judge and said 'My Lord' before or after his explanations. Although sometimes vague on detail, he stuck to his original stories. Steadfastly denying that he would shoot rather than arrest, or stage break-ins, or lie under oath, his defence counsel led him through an interminable list of shootings and killings, each punctuated with the same questions.

Were your actions criticised by the magistrate in that case? No.

Did any official in the criminal justice system ever accuse you of recklessness? No.

In all your contacts with the police, did any officer ever caution you? No.

In an interview with the London *Sunday Times*, Van Schoor had claimed that the only reason other security guards did not have high death tolls was because they were not doing their jobs properly. Testifying at the trial, alarm technician Leo van der Schyff said Louis had told him after being injured in an incident at a butchery that he was 'not going to try and arrest them any more'. The conversation, said the technician, took place in early 1986 – around the time the killings began.

On April 9, 1992, Mr Justice Lionel Melunsky found Louis van Schoor guilty of seven murders and two attempted murders. Sentencing him to a total of 91 years in jail, of which he would serve an effective prison term of 20 years, the judge said he had been given the benefit of the doubt even when the court was not convinced that he was telling the truth, and he was lucky to get off so lightly.

In a magazine article Dominic Jones wrote shortly after Louis began his sentence, the journalist asked: 'How is it possible that a ruthless, cold-blooded murderer can commit his deeds without fear of prosecution for almost three years? Why did none of the police or court officials who knew Van

As a young child before her parents' divorce, Sabrina was pampered by her father. She was 12 years old when she heard on a lunchtime news broadcast during the dying days of apartheid that Louis – the man she liked to describe as her 'knight in shining armour' – was in fact a triggerhappy killer.

An aunt described the young Sabrina as 'quite serious but sweet-natured. I never saw anything wrong with her although she used to talk a lot, such a lot, as if nobody ever listened to her.'

Sabrina at home in happier days with her father and two of her half-brothers. Although Louis van Schoor was known in East London as a man who got along well with kids, he did not hesitate to shoot two black teenagers in 1988.

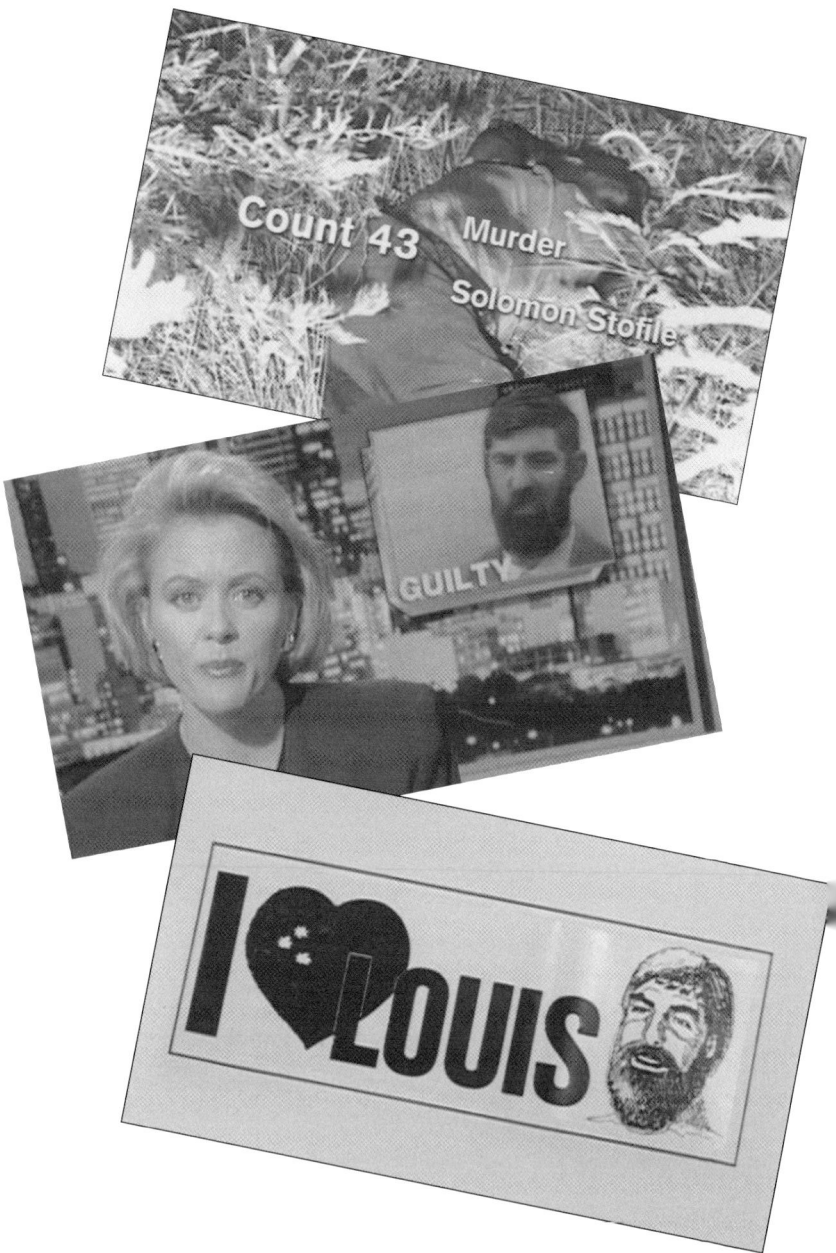

Supporters of Louis van Schoor's killing spree in East London – who awarded him three-quarters of the town's private security business – displayed bumper stickers decorated with three bullet holes through a heart.

Under cross-examination by the prosecutor, bullet wound in the leg. Mr Swartbooi in the left buttock and chest aft... Mr Van Schoor shot ... lung. Mr Alfonso Hallingh, Prof Schwär testified

Van Schoor trial: State calls for guilty verdict

10 MAR 1992

Daily Dispatch Reporter

EAST LONDON — Mr Sebrand Louis

dence of state witnesses, and ceded not all evidence could be ... at face value.

---

killing machine

Sentence details, more reports page 2

Van Schoor sentenced to 91 years in prison

17 JUN 1992

Daily Dispatch Reporter

EAST LONDON — Sentence was passed on multiple

● Count 17. The murder of Mr Thembesile Sambato: 15 years imprisonment ...

● Count 25. The killing of Mr Mbulelo Ma... siza: 12 years' imprison... The judge ... though ...

Why was Van Schoor allowed to go on killing?

3 intruders shot dead

Louis van Schoor has been convicted on seven counts of murder and two of attempted murder. PATRICK GOOD-ENOUGH looks back over the drawn-out investigation into East London's killer security guard and asks whether he alone is to blame.

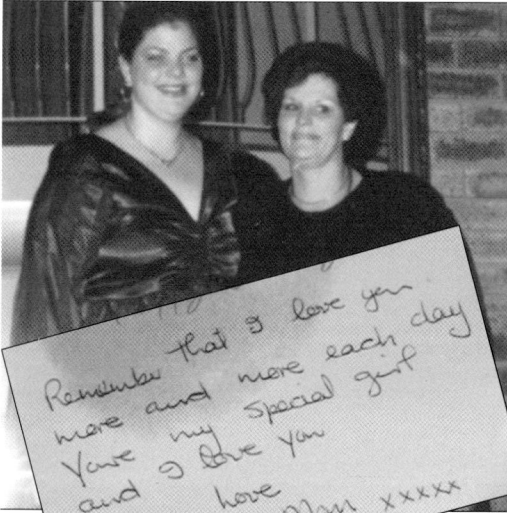

Sabrina poses with her mother and baby Tatum. The portrait of three generations of Van Schoors was taken shortly before Beverley's murder: the handwriting is part of Beverley's message to Sabrina on her 22nd birthday in November 2001, just four months before the killing.

Remember that I love you more and more each day. You're my special girl and I love you. Love Mom xxxxx

Businesswoman murdered

By Sonja Raasch

QUEENSTOWN — Prominent Queenstown businesswoman Beverley van Schoor, 48, was stabbed to death at her home here yesterday, police said.

Van Schoor was the owner of the Curly B florist and coffee shop, a hairdressing salon and the franchise of Golding Estates in the town.

Superintendent Bubandzwa Dada said Van Schoor's daughter, Sabrina, was at work when she received three phone calls at about 7.15am.

The calls kept disconnecting and Sabrina decided to return home to check on her mother.

At the house, she was confronted by a man armed with a knife. He demanded the keys to her Golf.

As the man drove off, Sabrina entered the house and found her mother dead.

Dada said the car was found abandoned later outside town.

The motive for the killing is not known. Police have offered a R20 000 reward for information. Det-Insp Stephen Sanders can be called on 083 262 1167.

BEVERLEY VAN SCHOOR

JOHANNESBURG — Even when Lance Klusener was threatening to tear the Australian attack apart at the Wanderers yesterday, Ricky Ponting was confident that his side would pull off the victory.

This Australia defy achieved by 19 runs, but at one stage it looked likely that Klusener would smash South Africa to an unlikely win with a 77-ball 83.

"I suppose it was a bit more exciting..."

HARARE — Political violence dogs Zimbabwe, where backers of re-elected President Robert Mugabe are engaged in "uproots witchhunting" against suspected opposition supporters, human rights activists said yesterday.

"There's a lot of retribution against individuals and poll observers seen as sympathetic to Mugabe's main rival Morgan Tsvangirai," said Frances Lovemore of Amani Trust, which funds medical care for victims of political violence.

"There's serious witchhunting going..."

Feza Mdutshane entered Beverley's house with Sabrina's help and took a knife from the kitchen dresser to slit the throat of a woman he had never even seen before. His motive was money; the crime was a reflection of the chillingly violent nature of South African society.

Gladys Nontombi (below) was the woman to whom Sabrina turned for mothering because Beverley spent more time at work than at home and the mother-daughter relationship was strained. When Sabrina played 'ladies' as a small child, it was in the dingy quarters of the domestic worker in the backyard of the family home that she clattered about in Beverley's handed-down high-heels, not in her mother's luxurious bedroom inside the house.

South Africa's most notorious mass murderer went to prison in 1991 for randomly shooting black people on the pretext of combating crime. Eleven years later, Louis van Schoor's daughter Sabrina joined him behind bars at Fort Glamorgan, East London, after she hired a hitman to slaughter her mother.

Louis' influence on Sabrina, who adores her father, has been disastrous over the years. While still at school, she was given a project to study one person who had left an evil mark on history. Deciding initially to write about her father, she later changed her mind because her friends were blacks and coloureds and she feared they might think she was glorifying Louis. So she chose Hitler as her subject instead.

Schoor say anything? How is it possible that 39 people were dead by the hand of one man and the only concern came from a handful of private citizens?

'The police and Department of Justice continue to sidestep the issue,' Jones wrote in July 1992. 'How do they explain it? They can't. Not unless they're prepared to admit that certain of their members and officials were guilty of racism; that prejudice from years under apartheid so clouded their judgement that they were unable to distinguish right from wrong.'

The answers to many of Dominic Jones' questions lie in the idea of necessary evil – accepting the unacceptable – that some societies embrace in response to fear. Just as most white South Africans approved of Louis van Schoor's killings on the grounds that he was protecting them from the evils of crime, much the same belief has begun to spread in post-9/11 America. The idea in both countries is that whatever it takes to protect one's family is justified. A recent award-winning US television show called *24*, about counterterrorist agent Jack Bauer and his quest to save a presidential candidate from assassination by preventing, among other catastrophes, a nuclear bomb from detonating in Los Angeles, explores ominous ethical questions. Subtly making the case for the necessity of evil in the pursuit of good, *24* presents Jack Bauer in a world devoid of an overarching pre-9/11 moral framework: all that matters now is protecting one's own. Freed of ethical restraints, how bad can Jack Bauer or Louis van Schoor become and still be seen as the good guy?

According to criminologist Irma Labuschagne, who pleaded leniency for Louis during his trial, distinguishing right from wrong and good from evil was never his problem. She argued that his confusion came from a society that supported murder. She claimed that, in effect '... Louis went to the prosecutors and said, "I realise I am shooting many people. Is it wrong?"' They allowed him to carry on killing by not stopping him. According to Labuschagne, Louis was so popular in his community that the prosecutor in his case had to have an armed guard during the trial because he received so many threats from angry white East Londoners.

While Labuschagne and most whites in East London believe that Louis killed because he believed he was serving his community, blacks in the town have a different view. When I visited Louis at Fort Glamorgan in June 2003, I was waiting in line to sign a visitor's application when the only other white in the reception area, a young woman who was attempting to jump the queue on the muttered grounds that she had to visit her husband early or be late for work, asked me who I had come to see. On hearing Louis' name, the person immediately ahead of me, an old man with greying hair wearing a sagging pinstriped suit that looked incongruous among the humbly dressed visitors, swung around and asked me: 'The one who killed in East London?' I answered yes and added, 'He shot 101 people in just three years.' The young white woman shuffled and sighed theatrically. I could feel the irritation radiating from her though I looked straight ahead, as did the man in front. Then she remarked sarcastically, 'It's funny how people remember only the bad things you do, never the good.'

Later, I spotted the elderly man walking ahead of me out of the male prison grounds as I was on my way to visit Sabrina next door. Catching up with him, I explained my writing project and he told me how much the people in the townships of East London hated the man they had bizarrely nicknamed Jesus, even though he destroyed lives rather than saving them. 'There was a plan to kill him. He was lucky to get arrested before he, too, was murdered.' Aware of the circumstances surrounding Sabrina's case, the man continued angrily, 'There is never a reason to kill your mother. The Van Schoors are cruel people, both of them. Evil blood is in them.'

*

During my visit with Louis, I had tried to discuss the grim irony of white South Africa's hypocrisy in his case. First they adopted the mechanism of denial to enable a regime founded on greed and violence to thrive. Then they employed denial to avoid having to face responsibility for the past. Many observers have noted over recent years how difficult it is to find whites who admit to having supported apartheid, Louis van Schoor being among a handful who is unable to deny his past.

If Louis has something to say on the subject, he is keeping it to himself, or perhaps waiting to publish it in the book he says he intends writing when he gets out of jail. He is hell-bent on impressing the parole board; nothing much else seems to matter to him. Deflecting questions about his deathwatch on East London's streets, he insists to me that he has found God and is a reformed character. It is obvious that his experience of journalists has made him fear the power of the pen.

What he is prepared to tell me is that he is engaged to be married as soon as he is free. It will be his fifth marriage, this time to a Cape Town lawyer who was interested in his case and began writing him letters some years ago. I wonder briefly what makes a woman fall for a man behind bars – his gratitude, his longing perhaps, as in poet John Keats' image on a Grecian urn of a snogging couple whose unconsummated love he describes as 'forever warm and still to be enjoyed' – before remembering guiltily that what I should be surprised at is the notion of a woman falling for a racist murderer.

Louis tells me that he and his father will be moving from East London to a farm his fiancée has bought in the Cape. Which is more than Sabrina knows. She continues to believe that Louis will adopt Tatum the minute he is free, as he publicly claimed at her trial. She assumes that Louis will bring Tatum to visit her at weekends so that mother and daughter know each other well by the time she, too, has served her debt to society. Where access to her beloved father is concerned, Sabrina is not only behind bars but completely in the dark about his motives.

Louis is permitted to visit Sabrina twice a month, though she told me in one of our interviews that, because she once attempted to commit suicide in her cell, she is allowed to see him more often if she is particularly depressed. While we are on the subject of Sabrina, Louis points out that some of the difficulties she is having adjusting to prison life are of her own creation. She likes to be known as a rich girl, he says. 'If she pretends to have money, prisoners will try to get favours from her. It is better to admit she has none.'

Louis' comment on his daughter's pretensions to wealth rings a bell: in her diary written when she was 14, Sabrina begins grandly: 'Everyone thinks life is such a breeze because I am rich and well known in the town I live in. They are wrong. I have had a hell of a life and I haven't even reached a quarter of a century.' Later, in a letter to her father, she admits to loathing Queenstown because of her notoriety there. 'You wouldn't know how much I hate this town,' she writes. 'They all look down on me because I am friends with different races.'

At the end of our interview at Fort Glamorgan, Louis sighs dejectedly. 'To be quite honest,' he says, 'I am finding Sabrina difficult at the moment. I don't think I am giving her the support she feels I should because I am spelling out to her the realities of life in prison. She has been spoilt in the past in the sense that she is used to getting her own way.'

The visiting hour is almost up. As I prepare to leave, Louis suddenly leans towards me and I recoil involuntarily. Smiling wearily, he confides: 'I have achieved everything I ever wanted to achieve in life. I have nothing left to prove.'

Chapter Five

Sabrina was closer to her grandmother than to Beverley as a young child, and closer still to her black mother, the family's domestic worker Gladys Nontombi, during the rest of her youth. After her grandmother's death it was invariably to Gladys that Sabrina turned for comfort and advice, partly because Beverley spent more time at the office than at home and partly because the mother-daughter relationship was strained. When Sabrina was six, Gladys recalls, it was in the dingy maids' quarters in the backyard of the Van Schoors' home that Sabrina played 'ladies', rather than in Beverley's luxurious bedroom inside the house. In a drab space not much bigger than the family car, which typifies much of the accommodation provided for live-in domestic workers in South Africa, Sabrina would dress up in Gladys' threadbare clothes and clatter about in her shoes, most of which were hand-downs from Beverley. She didn't want to play in her mother's room, according to Gladys.

Sabrina nicknamed Gladys 'Fatty' to differentiate her from another maid, also called Gladys but known as Thinny, who worked in Beverley's home. Compared to Beverley and

Sabrina, Gladys Nontombi was hardly fat but the name did not bother her. 'I want to be fat,' she explained when I asked her about an epithet that some would consider insensitive. 'I want to have a lot to eat,' she insisted.

The issue of names is a fraught one for employers who try to present themselves favourably in master-servant relations. The official term for an employee in this sector is domestic worker, though most white South Africans employ 'maids'. Foreigners on short-term contracts in the country, at once embarrassed to employ a domestic worker yet eager for the resultant leisured lifestyle, prefer 'housekeeper'. While hiking the maid's salary a little to justify neutralising the language that describes the job, expatriates seldom make much effort to dignify the job itself. Nor do they bother to find out that, according to Muzi Kuzwayo in his book *Marketing Through Mud and Dust,* domestic workers themselves prefer to be called 'helpers'.

Language is a prickly issue in South Africa. In some respects, the country lags 50 years behind the West, especially in gender politics and various social mores, including politically correct speech. Many South Africans have not yet learnt to couch their conversation in phrases designed to conceal their true feelings on contentious subjects. Indeed, some whites have not even learnt to identify which issues – notably race – are red-hot buttons signalling extreme caution and, at the very least, neutral terminology. Visitors to the country are constantly astonished to hear racially inflammatory comments delivered with aplomb by white South Africans, which is interpreted as defiance or evidence of enduring evil when it is often simply ignorance of Western norms. This isn't to say that white South Africans need only learn to mask their bigotry rather than conquer it, any more than it is an acknowledgement that Westerners in general are as innocent of racism as they sound. South Africa might be the headquarters of racism but is far from its only site.

I had been wondering why Gladys understood absolutely no English – or so she indicated in a series of shrugs, blank looks and furrowed brows – considering that she had worked in the home of the English-speaking Van Schoor family for so many years. On a previous research trip, I had interviewed her clumsily at Longview Lodge, with my host Justina Mashiya translating the questions into Xhosa and Gladys' answers into English. I subsequently asked an African languages professor in Johannesburg to transcribe and translate Gladys' taped answers so as to stay true to her idiom.

Much of this tedium goes out of the window soon after Gladys gets into my car for the drive to East London, however. I go to fetch her early one Friday in August 2003 at the home of the Queenstown woman who employs her part-time. The plan is to take Gladys back to Longview Lodge for tea with Justina while I complete my business. When I arrive, Gladys is standing at the gate. She is wearing a patchwork apron over a beige tartan skirt, a navy pullover on top of two other jerseys, a maroon knitted cap. On her feet, she wears white socks and trainers. She also wears a half-smile on her pleasant face, as if enjoying a mild joke.

Fortunately, Justina has come with me to translate if necessary, though I am expecting simply to fetch Gladys. A long discussion ensues between the two, from which I can tell there is a problem. When Justina explains that Gladys hasn't brought appropriate clothing for the journey to East London despite the arrangements having been confirmed several times over several weeks, I swear inwardly and consider abandoning my plan to reunite Sabrina and Gladys. I still have someone to see in Queenstown and an appointment on arrival in East London, which leaves little time to take Gladys back to the township for her overnight stuff. Seeing my impatience, Justina offers to drive Gladys home in her own car after I drop the two of them off at Longview Lodge before my next appointment.

Justina's plan works perfectly and we draw up outside Longview Lodge simultaneously. When Gladys opens the passenger door to get into my car, I notice she still has no luggage, only her handbag. I query this with Justina, who shrugs and waves us cheerfully onward, telling me to go quickly before Gladys changes her mind. She has been threatening to stay behind since becoming concerned about her young employer, who had been ill the last time Gladys saw her and who had failed to sleep in her own bed the previous night, according to Justina. 'Gladys is a person who cares about others,' Justina says, still urging me to drive away.

Gladys sits silently beside me, now wearing a calf-length dress with a purple, black and blue abstract design reminiscent of various wildlife prints, possibly leopard and zebra. As we get onto the open road for the two-hour run to the coast, I remark: 'That's a nice dress you're wearing, Gladys.' She replies, 'It's Beverley's dress,' which throws me for a while as I take on board not only the fact that she understands English after all but that she will be wearing the dead mother's garment when she goes into the prison to see Sabrina for the first time since her arrest eighteen months earlier. The bizarre coincidence of this is not, of course, squandered on the writer in me as I ask cautiously about the yellow cardigan she is wearing over the dress.

And the jersey?

'Beverley gave it to me.'

Then, perhaps because we are alone and Gladys feels she has nothing to lose by shedding her shyness, she starts to tell me how I can help her. I can find her a job in Johannesburg since she is willing to move there with two of her children, she suggests. I shake my head firmly, saying she is better off in Queenstown where she already has a job: it is very difficult to find work in Johannesburg, let alone accommodation. She considers this information and then suggests I collect second-hand clothing from my friends in Johannesburg and bring this to her in boxes each time I come to Queenstown. She will sell the clothing to augment her income, she tells me. I explain that I will not be coming to the Eastern Cape for much longer and that, in any case, I fly from Johannesburg and cannot bring boxes of clothing on the aeroplane. This she considers for a long time before advancing a third plan: if I buy her a commercial telephone, 'with the hole (slot) for the money', she can set up a business in Queenstown. One of her friends has been successful in such a venture, she says. I laugh at her persistence and agree to consider the suggestion.

We talk about her life. She was born in 1953. This trip is the first time she has ever been outside Queenstown. One of seven kids, she never went to school because her father absconded when she was a baby and her mother was permitted to stay on the farm where he had been employed as a labourer only on condition that she and the children worked for their basic board and lodging. She has five grown-up children. Two of them, whose ages she does not recall, work on farms near Port Elizabeth in the Eastern Cape. They telephone her occasionally. One sent her a cellular phone but she does not have the money to pay for call cards. The other three, aged 26, 29 and 30, have always stayed with their father's family in a local township because Gladys' successive live-in jobs as a domestic worker provided only single quarters.

She cannot tell the time or left from right. Most of her children are illiterate. The accommodation she lived in when she worked for Beverley was the best she had ever had, even though it was so small that the shower was directly above the toilet and there was no space for a wardrobe so she kept her clothes under the bed. The worst day of her life, she tells me, was when Allister van Schoor informed her that the family was terminating her employment because Beverley was dead, Sabrina had been arrested and baby Tatum, who had been Gladys' charge since birth, was going into foster care.

We drive along in silence. I try to imagine how someone who cannot read or write negotiates the world: about nine million South Africans are functionally illiterate. In all likelihood, school-going Sabrina's relationship with Gladys – who would have been absolutely confident nurturing, controlling and caring for the young Sabrina – changed once the child discovered that she knew more than the adult. It is a moment of separation that comes to many parents, usually when the child hits puberty, but it would have bedevilled Gladys' relationship with Sabrina much earlier. Perhaps Sabrina lost respect for Gladys at that point and tried to turn to Beverley for help with her homework, only to find that her mother remained otherwise engaged.

There would probably have been a number of shifts in the power relationship between Gladys and Sabrina thereafter, most acutely during Sabrina's early teens when the schoolgirl was entering arenas where the surrogate mother could not go. Did Gladys feel humiliated and powerless? Did she find creative ways to counter the growing gap between herself and Sabrina, as Dali Mpofu, a well-known Johannesburg lawyer who heads the South African Broadcasting Corporation, remembers his illiterate domestic worker mother doing? Mrs Mpofu asked her employer, who read the news over breakfast, if she could take the paper home to Dali at the end of each day. He then read it aloud to her and they discussed the stories.

A small town called Cathcart appears ahead and I tell Gladys we will be stopping there to fill the petrol tank. She rubs her stomach and says 'food'. There is a teashop adjoining the service station, where I took a break on the incoming journey. Not wanting to repeat the experience of sitting next to a deafening generator in a shop with a few tins of pilchards, packets of biscuits and detergent spaced across otherwise empty shelves, waiting ages for a pot of tea without the lid, milk in a cracked cup and sugar in a saucer, I proffer some money and invite Gladys to go in and buy herself a mid-morning snack while I tend to the car. She shakes her head resolutely, continuing to rub her stomach, and I have the familiar suspicion that she is testing to see how far she can exploit the guilt that many whites in Africa feel. On the other hand, maybe she is hungry but doesn't want to go into the shop any more than I do. I shrug, putting the money back into my purse as Gladys rubs her stomach some more. When I take no notice of the gesture, she says 'food' again, very loudly.

There is a crude saying in South Africa that when a white person sees a black person approaching, he thinks, 'Here comes trouble', but when a black person sees a white approaching, he thinks, 'Here comes opportunity'. It expresses not only the acute imbalance of resources between the two racial groups but the improbity that characterises poor people everywhere. Even after more than ten years of representative democracy and the growth of the black middle class from 4 per cent to 20 per cent, unemployment in South Africa hovers around 40 per cent. Poverty seems to be growing. Trash bags left by householders for weekly collection on Johannesburg's leafy streets have invariably been searched repeatedly before daybreak by penniless rubbish raiders from surrounding townships. If you are unable to find a job in a capitalist economy, you must either starve, steal or beg. There is more welfare available to needy South Africans today than ever before but nowhere near enough to enable the destitute to live decently.

I go into the shop to buy Gladys a sandwich, which is

what she has requested. Realising that it is going to take too long to prepare, I pick up a pre-wrapped portion of cake instead. When I hand this to Gladys with a bottle of fruit juice, assuring her we will have lunch in East London, she takes it without a word and places it at her feet in the car.

The Amatola mountains loom ruggedly beautiful up ahead. It is strange to think of Gladys living in their midst all her life yet never seeing their dramatic escarpments and valleys. We pass fields of sunburned straw and the occasional solitary farmhouse protected from cattle and perhaps thieves of a gentler era by a prickly pear border. Water sparkles on a pond next to the house, with uniformly patterned brown and white cows lazing on its banks.

We talk about Gladys' job as domestic worker to a young woman called Loreka, the daughter of Beverley's friend, Maggie Riggien. She starts her chores at 7.30 each morning except Sundays and works a three-and-a-half hour day, cleaning the house and doing the laundry for R400 a month, of which she pays R3 a day in taxi fare, leaving her with R340 – less than US$50 a month. Gladys is fond of Loreka despite the paltry wages. While the relationship between domestic workers and their employers is a conspicuous microcosm of the exploitation on which the country's social order is still based, there is more love between people engaged in this alliance than you would expect to find. And more hatred.

Nothing exemplifies the universally reviled politics of exploitation and disrespect more readily than the typical South African maid-madam relationship. Straddling the love-hate fault line uneasily, it is at once intimate yet distant; caring yet callous. Double standards abound, shifting like desert sands in the windy moods of the day. Though regarding her maid as a potential thief from the moment she walks through the door, the employer nevertheless entrusts the care of her children to the domestic worker.

When I grew up, maids were less common in white homes than men, known as houseboys. Because our staff were expected to be silent and virtually invisible, I do not recall the names or faces of any of the people employed by my parents to look after us, except a cook who wore a tall, starched chef's hat. I only remember him because he used to squash spiders dead on the dining room wall with his thumb while we were eating. We communicated in a makeshift language known as *chilapalapa* in Zimbabwe and *fanagalo* in South Africa – a language based on Zulu which contained only words and phrases of instruction, having been developed to serve the mining industry.

You don't have to look far in South Africa for signs of the lack of empathy that most whites continue to exhibit towards their domestic staff. On some formerly whites-only beaches, for example, you can still see the enclosures that were erected to contain maids and nannies while their employers and charges frolicked in the waves. They were expected to be out of sight until their madams yelled for them to spring into action, perhaps to pacify a screaming child, to remove a soiled diaper or to gather up the family's belongings at the end of a day's play. It was not uncommon to see a maid in a floral uniform with matching lace-trimmed apron staggering along the beach with a heavy picnic hamper balanced on her head, holding a white child by the hand, while the madam strolled ahead in her bikini.

The domestic worker, often referred to as 'the girl', is still viewed as a child by many South African employers, just as gardeners are still called 'boys'. These analogies, reeking of inequality, originated in nineteenth-century Britain where domestic workers suffered the same acute class discrimination, later amplified in South Africa by apartheid. A key concern among employers of domestic staff in Victorian England was to inculcate attitudes of subservience. In speaking to her betters, the servant was expected to keep her voice low and respectful and never to reply without saying madam or master. Under the influence of such strictures defining appropriate behaviour, the recognition of a common humanity was difficult. Servants were regarded as members of an entirely separate category of people, whose only contact with their superiors was through their daily chores. By the 1950s, live-in domestic service was virtually non-existent in the United Kingdom but these attitudes persisted in South Africa, where the sector is today dominated by black women who languish at the base of the racial, gender and class hierarchies. While the intimacy of the relationship between maid and madam does sometimes yield insights into a shared motherhood, it is amazing how seldom it breaks down stereotypes.

We drive on in silence until we round a bend and Gladys gasps as the sea appears before her for the first time. Spotting the cityscape on the horizon, she is overwhelmed at buildings taller than she has ever imagined – and so many of them. 'Ahhhhhh,' she breathes, 'ahhhh.' Then the long, empty beach of an upmarket area called Nahoon sprawls ahead of us, the lacy edges of the waves unusually white, and Gladys is ecstatic, squealing with delight.

At our destination in East London, Dolphin View Lodge, we settle into our rooms on the waterfront. I have a date with a policeman who knew Louis, after which my plan is to track down one of Sabrina's friends, Sonja Botha, whose evidence at the trial was intended to show what a regular person Sabrina was in the days when she used to visit her father in East London. Sonja has eluded me on each of my previous trips, despite numerous attempts to pin her down in order to collect copies of letters and birthday cards originally sent by Beverley to Sabrina, in which, according to both Sabrina and Sonja, Beverley frequently apologised for her ill-treatment of her daughter. Having obtained Sabrina's permission to see and record them, and Sabrina having duly told Sonja that I have permission to do so, it is puzzling to find Sonja once again stringing me along. I call her and she tells me she'll be home in half an hour, when she'll ring me to drive over and collect the copies. She does not ring. An hour later, I tell her not to worry about copies; I'll settle for sight of the letters and cards. She says she's on the highway and will call from her office. No call. And so it goes on all afternoon.

Having waited for Sonja's call as long as possible before East London's shops are due to close, I rush out to buy supplies for Sabrina as I am planning to get to the prison with Gladys the following morning at 8.00am, which is visitors' opening time at Fort Glamorgan. The early start, particularly so for a Saturday morning, is a precaution against the possibility that Sabrina, who is allowed a fixed number of visits each month, might exhaust her quota before we arrive. Although I have ascertained in a phone call to the prison before setting forth with Gladys from Queenstown that Sabrina still has visitation credits, I do not want to take any chances.

Piling a range of toiletries into a trolley at a nearby super-market, I scan the letter Sabrina sent me several months earlier to see if there are any other reasonable requests to add to my purchases. It reads in part: 'Thank you very much for taking time out to see me and show an interest in me. It means a lot because the only people who visit me or send me stuff are you and Isa (the Cape Town film-maker who is researching a documentary about Sabrina) and I thank you profoundly for that. But I would like to ask a big favour. I don't like doing this because I like being independent but I am in prison and I have to ask if I get a chance. If you can, could you please send me a parcel. The thing is, it is winter and no one to help me and I also have no money. If you can, I would really appreciate it tremendously.'

Her wish list follows: winter pyjamas, XL, '. . . 'cause it is cold and I only possess a short sleeveless summer nightie and I can't sleep 'cause it is cold'; one pair of socks; a long-sleeve shirt or polo neck, white, XL; '. . . a flask so I can drink coffee 'cause I don't eat the food here. Then I want to ask if you could send me some pens and pencils, paper and envelopes so I don't have to borrow other people's stuff 'cause that causes fights in prison.

'Lastly – this I know is wrong – but if you could send me some money so that I could buy stuff from the shop eg sugar, coffee, porridge, and stuff to put on bread 'cause that is all I eat. That would help a lot. Sorry but if you could include some toiletries, shampoo and maybe a blonde hair dye I would be deeply grateful.

'I am ashamed to have asked this from you but there is no one else. Everyone has practically turned their backs on me. My doctor said ask, all they can do is say yes or no. He is treating me for depression 'cause I tried to slit my wrists. But it looks better and I feel better as well now.'

Returning to Dolphin View Lodge, I hear from the proprietor that Gladys has been delivered into the care of the staff – at her own suggestion – who have shown her around and invited her to eat with them in their lodgings alongside the guest house. Having ascertained that buses run constantly to Queenstown from a terminus very near the lodge, I find Gladys relaxing in the comfortable staff quarters and explain that she can either go home after the prison visit on Saturday or stay another night and return to Queenstown on Sunday if she wants to see Sabrina again.

Saturday dawns perfectly. I watch the light spread slowly over the ocean while waiting for the kettle to boil and then go back to bed with tea and a book. An hour later, dolphins are leaping in the sparkling sea below my window. Over breakfast, I chat with other guests, one of whom is from

East London and still proclaiming Louis van Schoor's right to have 'kept them under control'. It occurs to me, a few months after America, Britain and their allies invaded Iraq on a foolish pretext, that vigilance sometimes becomes a morbid obsession in the face of the fear of spectacular violence. Louis' readiness to shoot alleged criminals earned him 75 per cent of the security contracts in East London at a time when whites, propagandised by their leaders, had become paranoid about lawlessness. Following the events of September 11 in New York in 2001, anti-terrorism and the newfound terror in the American psyche have become the animating principles of nearly every aspect of America's public policy. It was similar fears among white South Africans of black rule and post-colonial revenge that drove them to pursue the folly of apartheid.

I find Gladys waiting next to my car, still wearing Beverley's dress and yellow cardigan. We drive to Fort Glamorgan, sign in, and queue for the bus. I sit next to the driver, an Afrikaner, who tells me he has been working in the prison service for many years. He likes his job, he says, because it follows the same routine every day and people are friendly in a tight community. Is it ever dangerous? 'Sometimes a warder gets stabbed,' he admits. 'But that's just because the prisoners have to draw blood to get rank in the gangs, not because they're trying to escape. Some people like being in prison. At least they get three meals a day.'

We have brought magazines, white shirts and the bag of toiletries for Sabrina. Gladys, carrying the glossies, is searched ahead of me in one of the security huts just inside the perimeter fence by a female warder, who flicks through *Marie Claire, Elle* and *Cosmo*, pausing to read the intro of an article that interests her, before continuing to turn each page carefully. What is she looking for? Money, she says, chewing furiously on something that has left her lips shiny with grease. The bag of toiletries gets a cursory glance as I hold it open for inspection. 'Next,' she yells above the din of a drill working nearby.

We sit together on a bench in the waiting room until a warder calls our names and shows us into the visitors' cubicles. I wait for Gladys to go in front as I am planning to observe her and Sabrina as unobtrusively as possible. She is hesitant and I guide her forward, my hand on her shoulder. Sabrina is already there peering at the approaching visitors through the glass, bending forward to make sure her eyes are not deceiving her. When she realises it is Gladys, she lets out a long, mournful sob. Gladys begins to cry, too, silently, taking a checked handkerchief from her pocket to mop her tears.

Sabrina wipes the corners of her eyes with the tips of her fingers, trying not to smudge the mascara. The tears continue to well up until she can no longer hold them back. Her shoulders sag and she starts to wail; loud, sad sounds that bring a warder to the door briefly to make sure nothing untoward is going on. The two cry helplessly for a while. Sabrina is repeating, 'I love you, Fatty,' between sobs. 'You don't know how much I love you, Fatty.'

'I love you, too, Sabrina.'

Silence, just sobbing, and then Gladys asks: 'Why?'

When Sabrina does not answer, Gladys repeats the question, her voice shrill: 'Why?'

Sabrina replies hurriedly, first in Xhosa before switching to English: 'I'm sorry, Fatty. I am so, so sorry.' They continue to cry quietly, Gladys burying her face in her hands. When she lifts her head and gazes back through the glass at Sabrina, she asks again, 'Why?'

Sabrina shakes her head, staring with glazed eyes as if in a trance. 'I can't tell you properly, Fatty. I wish I could ... I just don't know, really. It seems like a dream. But Fatty, I know I hurt you and I'm so sorry, you know I am ... but at least you have a job.'

Standing beside Gladys' chair, I see her stiffen and adjust her posture, sitting very upright. Sabrina notices the change and watches, a quizzical look crossing her streaked face. 'You have a job, Fatty,' she says, half-questioning.

'No.'

'But you were working for Loreka ...'

'No.'

Sabrina is frowning and looking stricken. 'I thought you were working for Loreka ...'

'No.'

'I was sure you were ...'

'No.'

'I'm so sorry, Fatty,' Sabrina gulps, tears again spilling down her face. 'It's all my fault. If I hadn't killed Mom, you'd still have your job. I'm so sorry, Fatty.'

Gladys nods, looking unblinkingly through the glass, her backbone rigid. She does not utter a sound as Sabrina stares back, waiting for forgiveness.

'Fatty ...?' she ventures.

There is no response. Then Sabrina has an idea, delivered with a sudden grin. 'Dad will give you a job,' she says, sighing. 'He's coming out on parole next year – probably – and I'll tell him to give you a job, Fatty. Okay? Is that okay?' She is leaning forward, scanning Gladys' face.

Gladys nods and gives Sabrina one of her secretive half-smiles. Then she turns to me and states, 'I want to go now.' I tell her very quietly that she does not have to leave yet; almost half the visiting hour remains. She shakes her head firmly, pushes back her chair and repeats without looking at Sabrina, 'I want to go.'

Sabrina, in obvious distress, tries to delay her departure. 'Wait, please, Fatty,' she implores again and again. When she realises that Gladys is determined to leave, she calls a passing warder and asks in Xhosa and English if she might be permitted a brief moment of physical contact with Gladys, 'to kiss her, please, please'. When the warder does not respond, Sabrina seems to panic, bolting out of sight. We hear her calling out in Xhosa behind the scenes.

I am by now struggling with my own tears but Gladys seems resolute. Back in the corridor, we walk towards the reception, where the vast doors leading into the cells are standing open. There, in front of us, stands Sabrina, arms above her head, clutching the black steel bars just inside the entrance, sobbing noisily. Gladys turns away. Confused, I ask Sabrina, 'Are they going to let you out?' and she shakes her head, looking desolate.

'Bye-bye, Fatty,' she calls after us, but Gladys does not turn around. She clearly has no intention of walking up to the bars to hold Sabrina through them, as she could have done; as the waiting warder who has opened the forbidding doors seems to have intended. I catch up with her as she walks out of the entrance, away from the haunting image of Sabrina behind us. Glancing at her inscrutable face, I try to understand why she is so intent on leaving so quickly. She is not crying, or even looking particularly upset. She is just walking away. I don't get it, but decide to mind my own business. No doubt she has her own unfinished business with Sabrina. However, by the time we reach the car, I am feeling annoyed with Gladys for lying about her job, to Sabrina's obvious distress, and for terminating the visit so abruptly for no apparent reason, and for failing to register Sabrina clinging to the bars imploringly in the hope of a kiss from her surrogate mother.

So I confront Gladys: 'Why did you lie to Sabrina about your job?' She gives me a blank look and I repeat the question. When she shrugs and frowns as if she doesn't understand a word I'm saying, I tell her firmly that I know she speaks English perfectly well because she has proposed a number of ways for me to help her during the journey from Queenstown. Would she please explain why she has just lied to Sabrina about her job. To my surprise, Gladys giggles, a light-hearted, girlish gurgle, while folding her hands together in her lap and staring straight ahead. The matter is evidently closed as far as she is concerned. I guess that, if you are constantly treated like a child, you can be forgiven for behaving like a child. Or perhaps Gladys has shut down in the time-honoured tradition of domestic service, where it is better to say nothing than risk the unpredictable wrath of the madam.

We drive along in silence. I am crosser than I should be and Gladys is more peaceful than you'd expect in the circumstances, though she shoots me a couple of searching glances. If the mutual incomprehension hangs heavily between us, it is not because it is a new experience. Figuring out each others' motives is a lifelong preoccupation in post-colonial Africa. Why did Gladys tell Sabrina she was unemployed when I was standing right there beside her, knowing without any doubt that she has a job because I have seen her in the house where she works? Is it just an index of her powerlessness that she considers white Sabrina, albeit locked up in prison, to be more empowered than black Gladys? Is she so desperate that she must grab Sabrina's sympathy by dishonest means on the off-chance that the prisoner can do something for her, seeing she can do so little for herself? Is it at some level, perhaps only half-consciously, payback time for Gladys, whose relationship with Sabrina must have been affected by the dehumanising master-servant norm in South Africa; a little bit of revenge for a lifetime of humiliation in the service of whites? Or is Gladys conveying to Sabrina that her loyalty, the only commodity she has to trade, remains with the Van Schoor family, despite what has happened: so how could she have a new job?

We stop at East London's central police station in Fleet

Street for Gladys to sign an interview release, the publisher's document which I have already asked her, via Justina, to endorse. Because Gladys is illiterate she gives her thumbprint instead of a written signature, a procedure conducted by a senior police officer called from an inner office by the counter staff. There are a lot of people milling around us on both sides of the counter and I watch Gladys closely. She stares straight ahead while a black policeman explains the wording of the interview release to her in Xhosa. Is she embarrassed, I wonder. There is no way of knowing. When the presiding white officer grabs her hand roughly in order to press her thumb into the inkpad, she still looks unconcerned.

Gladys' muteness throughout what looks to me like an embarrassing process is reminiscent of the state to which domestic workers are often relegated by their employers in South Africa. Like Victorian children, they must be seen but not heard. The idea that the maid has an opinion is vaguely ridiculous; her voicing of an opinion is 'cheeky' and possibly punishable. She is expected to be so discreet, so efficient, so smiley, contented and grateful for her job, so obedient and dedicated to her tasks that she might as well be invisible; an automaton.

In my sister's home in KwaZulu-Natal one Christmas, I watched day after day as eight-year-old Thulani – the son of the family's domestic worker – sat on a stool at the counter dividing an open-plan kitchen-cum-living room. He was watching the crowded household go about its business, studying everything they did as if engrossed in live television. Nobody spoke to him or he to them – for days on end. What does it feel like to be that insignificant? Most of us know how humiliating it is to be openly discounted by people who consider themselves superior yet when I put the question to a black journalist friend, his answer flawed me. Underlining yet again the gulf between black and white perceptions, he said amiably, 'That child may be learning a lot by watching the white family. It's a lesson every bit as important to him as history or geography. The world is run by white people and he may be able to use the information he gets from watching whites to his advantage later on.'

The social distance between maids and madams is partly the result of fear. While living outwardly affluent and complacent lives, white South Africans' homes are elaborately protected by steel gates, alarm systems, electrified fences and vicious guard dogs. There is something of the siege mentality in every town and city; an atmosphere in which black household staff are often viewed with suspicion by their white employers. Yet the mutual dependence persists. The ill-educated 'girl' has little choice but to find employment in the domestic sector. The madam, for all her complaints, is too accustomed to freedom from housework to go it alone.

Several African writers, including Es'kia Mphahlele, have focused on the image of 'the menacing servant', pointing out that whites live in 'fat feudal comfort' but at a heavy price: their humaneness. 'A kind of moral corrosion has set in in this privileged society ... they are never sure, by virtue of their master-servant relationship, what goes on in the mind of this seeming automaton ... But it is a menacing automaton.'

I remember a vivid scene in a book by Daphne Anderson called *The Toe-Rags: A Memoir*, in which three impoverished white children are wandering through the Zimbabwe bush with their trusted teenage servant Jim who is climbing trees in search of *mohobohobos* for them to eat. One of the kids remembers her mother's friend's description of the massacre of three white children by 'their boy' while they were looking for berries in the bush. The frightened child – citing a sharpened piece of iron with which Jim is peeling the tough-skinned *mohobohobos* as his possible murder weapon – whispers her fear of Jim to her sister before running home. The other girl, contemplating the charge incredulously, watches her little brother, '... so trustingly following the boy who looked after us, who dressed us and fed us, and who had so recently taken care of us when my mother had not returned from the city.' Suddenly, overwhelmed by the bigotry of her upbringing, she too sees Jim as a savage murderer, an uncivilised criminal filled with hate and evil, his cheerful face a mask for his true intentions. She also flees, clutching her baby brother. Later, when Jim comments on the unnamed fear that made her run away, telling her she need never be frightened if he is there to look after her, the white child contemplates her shame, her empirical knowledge of Jim's kindness having once again overcome the irrational, racial fear she has learnt from her community.

*

When Gladys and I get back to Dolphin View Lodge, I am drained and cranky. Gladys rubs her stomach theatrically as I am parking the car and I tell her: 'The staff will give you lunch. Please go and find them.' I lie on my bed trying to concentrate on the novel I am reading but I remain upset for no reason good enough to grapple with and decide to walk on the beach. Near the rocks beside the Wimpy where Louis murdered Liefie, I see Gladys making her way up the steps from the seashore. She is carrying two large plastic bottles that once held detergent, which are now filled with seawater, one in each hand, and she looks happy.

South Africans living inland are wont to take seawater home from the coast in the traditional belief that it contains medicinal properties. Or, as some believe, the seawater sprinkled around the perimeter of the homestead will chase away the *thokoloshe*, an amorous little man with one buttock and an extraordinarily long penis slung over his shoulder, who not only tempts women to break their marriage vows but causes his victims to commit mayhem and is to African courts what the failed memory – 'everything went blank' – is to jurors elsewhere.

I walk towards Gladys, smiling when she sees me. Putting down the water bottles, she mops her brow and doesn't answer when I ask lightly, 'How are you?' I then ask her if she had a nice lunch and she shakes her head dolefully. By now I am vaguely amused by her fibs, knowing that she has eaten a hearty meal at midday with Dolphin View Lodge's staff. While victimhood is understandable in the circumstances of someone like Gladys in a country like South Africa, I am struck, as I watch her diminish from the jaunty figure I saw approaching a few seconds earlier, by the thought that victimhood may be inevitable but it is also regrettable for reasons beyond the pity of poverty. It cannot be good for a person to feel sorry for herself even in the midst of unexpected bounty, however brief. Gladys' trip to East London must rank among the greatest adventures of her life but, in a pointless gesture of disempowerment, she cannot admit to enjoying it. Or is she simply baffled by me – a stranger who appears from nowhere to ask her endless questions and reward her for answering them? Maybe she has learnt to be so careful not to say the wrong thing at the wrong time that silence seems her best bet.

Sitting on a rock overlooking the sea, I try to imagine how Gladys views me: perhaps as just another white woman who she might once have worked for. Few white South Africans have noticed that the outer perimeter of humanity and humaneness has been extended in prosperous nations over the last fifty years. In every way of life, especially race relations, people are expected to listen to each other and treat each other with respect, though it was not always so. Back in the 1930s, when a Canadian mother gave birth to the country's first known quintuplets, her babies were taken into care and exhibited around the country in what was seen as a harmless show. The two surviving siblings, now old ladies, recently won a damages claim against the state for abuse of their human rights those many years ago. Even chimpanzees are accorded human rights in New Zealand today, making it illegal to keep them in captivity when they have not done anything to warrant imprisonment.

I take Gladys to the bus station later in the day, giving her money to buy food during the journey back to Queenstown. She climbs on board without a backward glance, immediately engaging with a woman sitting in the front row of seats. I watch her animated face through the window until the bus moves off. Seeing the excitement she is prepared to convey to a black stranger but not to me, and knowing we would have enjoyed each other more if we had been fluent in the same language, I leave feeling puzzled.

My flight to Johannesburg is at 10.00am on Sunday morning, giving me time to visit Sabrina again on the way to the airport. She thanks me repeatedly for bringing Gladys. I tell her that Gladys is, in fact, employed, albeit part-time and at very low wages. Sabrina says she is nevertheless going to ask her father as soon as she sees him to give Gladys a job once he is out of prison. It is clear that all Sabrina's hopes are pinned on Louis and equally clear that she does not know he is planning to live in Cape Town rather than East London after his release. I feel I ought to break this bad news to Sabrina, especially seeing I have informed her that Gladys does, in fact, have a job, but the thought of her distress makes me chicken out.

We talk about Gladys' visit. When I ask Sabrina why she thinks Gladys lied about having a job, she replies without hesitation: 'She's punishing me.' I can see she is close to crying and I don't want to upset her further but I have to ask how she felt seeing Gladys in her dead mother's clothes. Closing her eyes, she shakes her head, unable to speak. Tears start to spill down the sides of her nose and I wonder if I should leave. Then she looks at me, still shaking her head, and says, 'Shame, ag shame,' and shuts her eyes again. I stand up to go but she leans forward with her hand up so I sit down again. Speaking in an unsteady voice, Sabrina tells me how much it meant to her to see Gladys. 'She will forgive me but she needs time and I understand that,' she says, beginning to cry again.

Back in Johannesburg, the tapes of my earlier interview with Gladys have been transcribed and translated from Xhosa to English by an African languages professor. He has written a number of comments for my benefit, including the observation that Gladys is 'very honest and good natured. She basically trusts everybody and she does not criticise or speak badly about anyone.'

He points out that Gladys grew up on a farm in Tarkastad, near Queenstown, speaking Afrikaans, which is reflected in her use of English in such words as 'tjommie,' meaning friend, derived from 'chum' but pronounced in an Afrikaans accent. 'She repeats a lot when telling stories,' the professor's notes continue. 'It is as if she ponders on these matters in her own mind ... She has an astonishing insight on matters relating to the raising of children.'

I am a little nonplussed to see that, according to the professor's transcript, my first question, as translated from me to Gladys by Justina, goes straight for the jugular: Was Sabrina a violent child? Unable to see myself being quite so insensitive, I listen to the beginning of the tape again, discovering that the question I actually asked Justina to ask Gladys at the outset was: What type of a person was Sabrina as a child? It is a reminder of how meanings get lost in translation.

Gladys answers: 'Sabrina did not want anything that was wrong. If her mother scolded me, she would cry. And if her mother scolded her, I would cry ... Sometimes, when I would be working in the house, I would see her playing and then suddenly not see her any more. When I went to look for her, there she was asleep in my bed. Sometimes all my belongings would be on the floor, where she was playing with them. Then I would just stare at her if she was awake; fold my arms and stare.'

She didn't play in her mother's room?

'Hayi' (meaning no, emphatically, notes the translator).

'When we went shopping, if she had no money, I would give her my money to buy sweets. Then when her mother arrived home, she would tell her that she took my money and her mother would give it to her to give back to me.

'I often think about the things Sabrina used to do. When we were sitting, just the two of us, she would switch on the TV for me. Lying like this on my side, she would sit here on top of me. She had a cat, and she would take that cat of hers and sit here beside me and it (the cat) would also sit here. Then she would get up and sit on me and take the cat and put it on her lap. And we would sit like that, all three of us. Once she said: "Even if we are to die, Gladys, we ought to die together, the three of us." '

I recall a sudden smile spreading across Gladys' face when she told me during the interview that she taught Sabrina to speak Xhosa. Then she began to sing an old English nursery rhyme called *London's Burning* in Xhosa. The tragedy the song celebrates, a terrible fire in England, seemed ridiculous coming from a black woman in Africa with so many of her own tragedies to commemorate that I started to laugh, as did Justina. When Gladys finished the song, we clapped playfully and she doubled up, slapping her sides.

'If I said hayi, no, Sabrina understood. She often wanted

146

to help me in the house and I would not let her because she would have burnt herself on the high stove. I remember, when I was busy, she would say, "Ha, Fatty, I'm hungry. I want food." If I had finished roasting a chicken, I would cut her two slices of bread and dip them in the hot chicken fat and put them on a plate and give it to her. She would not eat supper that day.

'But I would put her supper away. I kept it for her because I know her; she is someone who likes food. Then at about 9.00pm, I took out her food and she ate it. The older children would not have come home yet – we would be waiting for them.

'She would give me all the old toys to give to my children. Even if you were annoyed, Sabrina had joy. She laughed all the time. And if she saw that you did not want to talk to her, she would cry.

'She used to call me *mama wam* (Xhosa for mother of mine). She never failed to say I was her mother. She knew that I was her mother. She would *terega* (from the Afrikaans for tease) me as a joke. And I would forgive her saying "Go away, little child. You have a lot to learn" and she would laugh.'

When I asked if Beverley helped Sabrina with her home-work, Gladys replied: 'Hawu, her mother was not there. She was constantly not there. The mother of Sabrina did not come home; she worked. This business that your child is constantly without you, it can be okay, but sometimes you have to be there. Whenever there is a special occasion for the child, you, as a mother, should be there.'

I asked Gladys if she remembered Sabrina and her mother laughing sometimes and having a nice time together. 'Hayi, they would not laugh,' she replied. 'Her mother would be in her sulky mood all the time. And a child does not want that. A child must have the opportunity to converse with you and you should sit down peacefully. When Sabrina spoke to her, she quarrelled. A child does not want that: it gets confused.

'Sabrina had no tjommie. Over weekends she would simply sit in her room. There was no tjommie to visit her. She watched TV, but you cannot talk to the TV. When she was alone, she was thinking quite a lot …

'Her mother did not want my friends to visit me either. I was supposed to live there without seeing anyone apart from Sabrina. I worked there for years but nobody was allowed to visit me, even to inform me about something important relating to my family. She (Beverley) would say: "Niks visits!" If something serious happened in my family, I heard about it late because the person bringing the news had to wait until I *tshayisa* (went off duty).'

Was Beverley a racist?

'Sabrina's mother did not like black people but she had her own people (blacks whom she liked) with whom she laughed, although I don't know how she felt in her heart. She did not want me to be sulky. She did not want me not to look happy. If something worried or annoyed me, she would look me in the face and say, "Gladys, what's wrong." I would say, "There is niks, m'am." And she would say, "Ah, Gladys, I know you …"

'In some ways, she was like a mother to me. When I left Tarkastad, I had only one dress. I worked at her house for some time and then, one Saturday, I said, "M'am, you should give me some clothes. I have no clothes. You know, late at night I have to wash my only dress, hang it up and dry it and then, the next day, I have to iron it and wear it again." So she gave me some dresses.'

How was Sabrina towards black people?

'Eyi, she liked black people. Even if you didn't know her, if you asked Sabrina for money she would not say no. She would give it to you. Even when she was still small, she did not want you not to be eating when she was eating. When her mother brought her something, she would ask, "Where is Gladys', Mom?" Even when her mother arrived late and brought something for all four children, Sabrina would not eat hers if Gladys' was not there. Even over a weekend when I was off, if ma'am, their mother, had brought them biscuits or ice cream, Sabrina would not eat hers if mine was not there. She would put hers away and give it to me.'

Gladys' job in the Van Schoor household was arduous, to say the least. Up every morning at 5.00am, she prepared breakfast for the family before Beverley drove the children to school. They came home at midday for lunch, after which Gladys would sometimes walk Sabrina back to school for afternoon sport – on the occasions when Beverley allowed her to participate in extramural activities – and return later in the afternoon to fetch her. 'After I had washed the lunch dishes, I would start cooking supper for them. In the evening, I dished up the supper for them and put their mother's food in the oven. Then I would wash those dishes and sit. Sometimes Allister would say, "Fatty, you can go now: it is late." I would excuse myself and go to sleep in my room. Or I would wait until their mother came home.'

Once a month, Gladys was given a weekend off. 'I would leave the family on the Saturday and go home. Sabrina's mother would then be with the children over the weekend. But I worried about Sabrina. I missed her. Even if she is a white man's child, I also have children and she is also a child just like those of mine. She is just like my own child.

'I used to talk to my friends about Sabrina, my child. They knew how it was with me and Sabrina. When they finished work and *tshayisa*, I did not go off. I would still be looking after Sabrina. And it was Sabrina who would see them at the gate, waiting to speak to me, and announce them. She would say, "Gladys, here is Melody, your tjommie." I would then go out to the gate and talk, even though the mother did not want my friends to come to me, and Sabrina would stand next to me.'

Gladys confirmed in our interview that Sabrina and Beverley quarrelled constantly. 'Eee, she fought with her mother all the time when she became a teenager because her mother did not want her to have coloured boyfriends. Ja, they quarrelled. There was tension all the time.'

Confirming that Sabrina ran away from home on discovering that she was pregnant for the second time, Gladys recalled that Beverley was distraught. 'Hey, then the mother goes and looks for Sabrina. She turns at that corner, crying, at another corner, crying, and then she says, "Gladys, where was Sabrina going?" I replied, "Mom of Sabrina, she did not tell me where she was going." (Sabrina had, in fact, told me where she was going.) Then the mother asked me if Sabrina had told me not to tell her mother and I replied, "Yes, she told me not to tell her mother." '

According to Gladys, Beverley angrily accused her of causing trouble by keeping secrets, and threatened her with dismissal. Soon afterwards, Beverley found out that Sabrina was staying with friends in East London and persuaded her to come home.

I asked Gladys what she thought of Sabrina's coloured boyfriend, Shaun Ortell, the likely father of Tatum, and she replied: 'He was loved by her. She was loved by him and she was having a child by him. What can I say about that? It's her life.'

The relationship between mother and daughter did not improve after Sabrina's return from East London, Gladys told me. When Sabrina went into labour, Beverley was on tenterhooks, as any mother would be, though she was not only anxious about the birth: her prayers were also for a light-skinned baby. 'When the child came out,' Gladys recalled, 'her mother just sat down and cried. Sabrina really loved her child right from the outset but not so the grandmother.'

Gladys said Beverley barely gave Sabrina time to recover from the birth or to bond with her baby before ordering her back to work. 'She told her to go straight to the office now that the child was born. Even if Sabrina was inclined to be lazy, she did need time to relax and be with her baby but her mother forced her to work so hard. She did not get the chance to rest due to her mother.'

Gladys' daughter Lettie was hired to work in Beverley's house while Gladys, at Sabrina's insistence, went to the office every day to take care of Tatum. Beverley had tried to insist that Tatum remain at home, said Gladys, but Sabrina flatly refused to leave her baby behind. At first, Beverley was so embarrassed by the presence of her dark-skinned granddaughter that she quietly told Gladys to push the baby carriage at the back of the shop rather than out front in the street. After a while, Gladys ignored the instruction. When reprimanded by Beverley, Gladys told me she retorted angrily. 'I told her if she didn't want the child, she must give it to me.'

When I asked Gladys why Sabrina did not leave Beverley's home, she replied with her head on one side, a sorrowful expression on her face. 'Sabrina asked her mother so nicely: "Mom, I have a child now. Find me a flat and let me live there on my own." But her mother said that if Sabrina left, she would take the child away. She said that when I was present.'

How bothered was Sabrina by the fact that she was very tall for a girl, and very fat?

Gladys appeared not to understand the question, possibly because obesity is not an issue for her. Answering what she thought I had asked her or possibly the question she thought I should have asked or perhaps deflecting the whole issue of Sabrina's size – which seems to me a contributing cause

of her plight – Gladys replied that, as Sabrina got older, '…
she did not hear any more. I would just keep quiet and look
at her.'

Confirming Sabrina's account of Danie Nel assaulting
Beverley, Gladys said: 'Sabrina told me at the time that he hit
ma'am, and she (Sabrina) then hit him.' Gladys also confirmed
that Danie Nel added to the tension between Sabrina and
Beverley by reporting back to the mother whenever Sabrina
was seen around Queenstown with black or coloured friends
by members of the police force.

Gladys told me she was devastated when she heard,
shortly after Sabrina's arrest, that the daughter had murdered
the mother. 'It hurt me, but then, my pain could not help
me in any way; it had already happened.' Although Gladys
insisted that Sabrina had not wanted to see her while she
was in prison in Queenstown awaiting the outcome of her
bail application, she went on to explain how she had hoped
and expected to adopt Tatum because, she said, Sabrina
had asked her to take care of the child and it was clear to
her that Sabrina's brothers did not want Tatum. According
to Gladys, Allister discussed the future care of Tatum with
her but, shortly afterwards, the baby was taken away by a
social worker bearing a court order. 'I thought they (Sabrina's
brothers) meant me to look after the child until the mother
came out of prison. I don't know where the court came in
because, if the brothers had said there is someone to look after
the child, then the court would not have said anything.'

I asked Gladys if she had forgiven Sabrina. Looking
suddenly irritated, she bared her irregular, yellowing teeth in
a grimace, sighed deeply and considered the question before
answering. 'She made me suffer. I am struggling while she,
on the other hand, is in jail, eating. I am eating smoke.'

At the end of the interview, when I pointed out that neither
the judge nor the psychologist in Sabrina's case could decide

with any certainty why she hired a hitman to murder her mother, Gladys nodded vigorously. 'I don't know either,' she said. 'Many judges would be perplexed. Nobody knows the answer to that question.'

Chapter Six

Half a dozen possible motives for Sabrina's matricide have now come to light, apart from the reason argued by her defence attorney, Siphiwo Burwana, who tried to convince the court that Beverley's racism caused the killing. An abusive mother-daughter relationship that grew out of the punishing emotional climate of Sabrina's childhood undoubtedly contributed to Beverley's murder. In particular, the mother's failure to believe her daughter's allegations of sexual abuse at a time when Sabrina was experiencing hurt and shame might have festered in Sabrina's mind over the years, turning to anger at Beverley's betrayal – a common response in the circumstances – and eventually to the murderous rage that Freud identified in unacknowledged victims of sexual abuse.

Other contributing motives may have included the severance of Sabrina's relationship with her father, for which she blamed Beverley. There was also the possible cause cited by both the investigating officer and the public prosecutor: Sabrina's imminent detection as the thief of a large sum of money missing from Beverley's trust account. Another possibility is that Sabrina, immature at 22 and therefore still a child emotionally, could have been copying her murderous father, thus identifying with the aggressor as is common in abusive families. Then, on top of Sabrina's other reasons for wanting Beverley out of the way, came the powerfully provocative threat by her mother to gain custody of baby Tatum if Sabrina persisted in her attempts to get out of Beverley's way by leaving home.

I arrive on my fourth visit to Queenstown with some ideas to bounce off Sabrina's lawyer in respect of his defence of racism. Even before I meet Siphiwo Burwana, however, it becomes obvious that he is not the same character I interviewed a year ago. His law practice was then situated in the town's smartest office sector, not far from the Van Schoor brothers' Red Guard headquarters in ritzy Ebden Street. Now, he is working from down-at-heel Bushell Street. I wait a long time for him there amid April's ever-whirling dust in an area crammed with Queenstown's ubiquitous motor spares businesses. His neighbours, no longer offering discreet accountancy, security and funerary services, are flogging suppressed ignition cables, steering racks and cv joints.

At first, I don't realise that the house with bolted doors at 27 Bushell Street is not, in fact, where he works. It is the address he gave me himself over the telephone when I rang from Johannesburg only a few days earlier to confirm our appointment prior to booking my air ticket. After waiting an hour for somebody to show up, I go to the back door and find a notice handwritten on a pink card, instructing those who need to consult with lawyers to 'go to the back'.

There does not seem to be anything remotely resembling a law office at the back, which is a scrapyard belonging to BF Panel Beaters. I walk among the wrecked vehicles through a tangle of weeds and discarded plastic bags. The sound of children's voices singing *He's got the whole world in his hands* drifts over the wall surrounding the warehouse next door. It turns out that a sagging corrugated iron workshop behind the wrecks is where Siphiwo Burwana now dispenses his legal counsel.

His pretty secretary is sitting there with three young lawyers in an incongruous setting described by one of them as 'a people's practice'. There are several rows of empty chairs, presumably awaiting clients. The floor comprises slabs of cracked concrete; a makeshift door creaks on its hinges in the gale blowing outside. As I wait and wait for Siphiwo, whose progress is being monitored by his secretary on a cellphone, a few dishevelled people traipse in and sit alongside me to await legal redress. Apparently the three lawyers present cannot help any of them. They fiddle with piles of pink case files and talk quietly among themselves. It is hot in the shed with no ceiling. The darting eyes of the clientele suggest desperation and make me feel jumpy. One of the lawyers cannot stop yawning and I find myself constantly gulping for air, too. After a while, one of them returns to his desk behind me and starts to sing 'Money can't buy you love' to an improvised tune, over and over.

When Siphiwo Burwana arrives, two hours late for our appointment, it is clear that he feels inclined to attend to his clients before me so I lose patience and reschedule. Next day, when I arrive for my second date at 10.00am, the beautifully groomed young lawyer in a yellow shirt and matching tie, whose desk faces the entrance, is peacefully asleep in his chair. There is no sign of Siphiwo. When he turns up, another two hours late but unhurried, a few desperadoes are again waiting to consult him. I jump up as he enters the shed, clasp his arm firmly and suggest we go to a restaurant because I cannot wait in line any longer.

He gives me a swiftly calculating glance and then nods, requesting a ride to his smallholding in order to collect his car before our interview. We drive down Cathcart Street and turn left into farmland. Sunflowers are waving in the wind amid other crops that have long gone to seed. Siphiwo suddenly tells me to turn right and we bounce past a sign announcing a conference centre and guest house, down a curling dirt track to a bungalow which, like just about everything else in Queenstown except some of the manicured white properties, is tumbledown and uninviting. 'I'm still building this business up,' he admits. As we stop alongside scaffolding and a hungry-looking black dog, he is describing big plans for the property as well as for another of his businesses, the panel beating yard in Bushell Street. 'If only I had the money to proceed,' he grumbles. Getting out of my car clumsily, he climbs slowly into his own gleaming, gold, top-of-the-range Mercedes Benz C180 Compressor and drives off to the restaurant with me following.

The Parlour in Ebden Street is dark and dreary except for fresh roses on each table. I have heard that it serves delicious peri-peri prawns, which I order while Siphiwo requests a burger. We sit beneath an amateurish painting of an outsized nude gazing at herself in a handmirror. He removes his trendy sunglasses to reveal multiple rivers of blood in the whites of his eyes. He looks so unwell that I ask if he is okay, to which he shakes his head. His life is a mess, he confesses. 'Sabrina's case left me with a lot of enemies, especially on the side of white people, to such an extent that I encounter a lot of problems. I no longer have the working relationship I had before with some white law firms around Queenstown. We used to exchange clients but not any more and I can tell by the attitudes that Sabrina's case is behind it all.'

He says he expected hostility from the controversial case '... but now that the chickens are roosting, I realise that I must pay for being the first black attorney, not only in Queenstown but the whole of South Africa, to defend a white person on

157

such a criminal charge. I don't regret it; not at all. A lot of journalists and magistrates, even judges, congratulated me, blacks and whites. They phoned and said, well done.'

This generous endorsement of his own performance is interesting because my suspicion, backed up by a couple of experienced and fair-minded legal friends to whom I have shown the transcript of Sabrina's bail application, is that Siphiwo Burwana may well have weakened Sabrina's defence by highlighting the racial aspects.

I begin to examine the questionable parts of the proceedings with Burwana by suggesting we cast our minds back to the Regional Court in Queenstown on 29 April, 2002, reminding him that it is just over a month after Beverley's murder, when Sabrina is applying for bail. At the front of the stark, carpeted room in a new building devoid of memorable features sits the prosecutor, Advocate Malherbe Marais, alongside the investigating officer, Inspector Stephen Rheeders. The magistrate is Mr Pondo Makaula, recently appointed and acutely conscious of the media attention focused on his courtroom. Representing the defendants are Siphiwo Burwana for first applicant Sabrina van Schoor and Livingstone Ceyane for second applicant Feza Mdutshane.

Malherbe Marais is a wiry figure in a black gown and lacy white legal bib, his hair greying, large moustache neatly clipped. His presence dominates the courtroom. He is well known in the local legal fraternity for his precision, and the black-robed magistrate eyes him warily as the proceedings get under way. The public benches are full, occupied mainly by black and coloured people from the townships around Queenstown, as well as by members of the Van Schoor family and some of their closest friends.

An emotional Sabrina, who has confessed her involvement in the murder to the police, tells the court that physical abuse by her family, sexual abuse by three of their acquaintances and rejection of her non-white friends by her mother drove her to organise the contract killing. After she tells the magistrate that her only motive was 'to liberate myself', her lawyer's voice rises as he begins to emphasise what he considers to be her best defence.

'Was your mother a racist?' Siphiwo Burwana asks Sabrina.

'Yes.'

'Am I correct if I'm saying to this honourable court, you'd been kept captive by your own mother?'

'Yes.'

'Am I correct if I'm saying to this honourable court, by doing this (matricide) you were trying to liberate yourself from this monster?'

'Yes.'

A premeditated, preplanned murder, to which the accused has confessed, is the least likely category of crime to achieve bail in South Africa. This leaves the defence few options in the way of the 'exceptional circumstances' that govern bail. Nevertheless, Siphiwo Burwana returns again and again to legally irrelevant explanations and accusations of racism in an attempt to portray Sabrina's murder of her mother not only as politically desirable but fully exculpatory.

'Your Worship,' he tells the exasperated magistrate, 'apartheid has to be blamed. The mother was the victim of apartheid.' Quoting an inflammatory political speech by liberation leader Oliver Tambo, wherein '... the oppressed people ... must and will settle accounts with their oppressors by any method and means open to them ...' he compares Sabrina's situation to that of a freedom fighter: 'It's (a case of) whether she wanted to liberate herself from this monster or remain in bondage for the rest of her life,' he claims.

Having introduced all the evidence that is relevant to mitigation of sentence rather than to bail, Siphiwo Burwana finally adds the issues that he ought to be dealing with at the bail application stage. Sabrina duly explains to the court that she needs to be out of prison pending her trial for the benefit of her child and so that she can return to the business she claims to co-own with her late mother, Lady B, to raise funds for her defence. She also tells the magistrate that she wants to seek psychiatric counselling.

Then the proceedings go awry again. Inspector Stephen Rheeders' opposition to bail on the grounds that Sabrina and her co-accused Feza Mdutshane are a threat to the community provokes both Siphiwo Burwana and Feza's counsel to debate what the investigating officer means when he refers to 'the community'. The two black lawyers try repeatedly to get Inspector Rheeders to concede that his concern is only for white community interests. They accuse Rheeders of having snatched the Beverley van Schoor murder case away from the black policemen who were first in line to investigate it.

In his attempts to prove that racism governs the criminal justice system, Burwana repeatedly cites a case in Queenstown in which a white accused was granted bail even though he had killed three blacks. The proceedings border on farce as tempers flare on both sides of a growing racial divide in which two white men are prosecuting the case while two black men are representing the defendants – not an unusual legal situation except in the minds of Siphiwo Burwana and Feza's lawyer, Livingstone Ceyane. What is unusual is the spectacle of two ambitious lawyers waging their own wars at their clients' expense. Such might be the price of victimhood, though Burwana's paranoid belief that he is the target of constant discrimination is understandable in South Africa.

The unseemly racial clash is fuelled by prosecutor Malherbe Marais' constant prompting and correction of the court's decisions on procedural matters, though magistrate

Pondo Makaula himself seems to accept the guidance graciously. When the prosecutor refers to parts of the defence's argument as 'nonsense', Siphiwo Burwana loses his composure. 'I am expecting to be reprimanded by this court,' he tells the magistrate, 'but not by my colleague ... The reason he is doing that (is because) he is a white man.'

Stephen Rheeders' obvious contempt for Burwana's outbursts and inexperience feeds the latter's indignation. 'Are you not even sympathetic to the fact that (Sabrina) has been oppressed, ill treated and molested by her mother and the family and rejected by them?' Burwana demands of Rheeders, who directs his reply to the magistrate rather than to Burwana. 'Yes, I am, Your Worship,' he says, 'but I still think she's a murderer.'

Burwana persists: 'But you can concur with me that an incident like this is not happening for the first time in this country. The freedom fighters went out and fought for their liberation. In the process they maimed and killed people and they were indemnified because they were fighting for liberation, is that correct?' To which Rheeders retorts, 'Well, I don't know, Your Worship. I was never a freedom fighter myself.'

With black and coloured people packed into the public gallery, both defence attorneys begin to argue that their community supports the granting of bail for the two killers who eliminated one racist. It is a populist stance patently devoid of judicial or moral validity, as both the magistrate and the public prosecutor are at pains to point out. Burwana goes on relentlessly. 'Your Worship, in addressing this honourable court on the relevant facts, I assure this honourable court that half of the people who are here are from the (black) community. They are not in this court for anything other than to show their support for the first applicant ... If these people right in this court could be asked, (they would say) the applicant deserves an award, to be regarded as a heroine, (because) she liberated herself.' To the magistrate's horror, Burwana goes so far as to call for a show of hands from the public gallery.

I ask Siphiwo Burwana, sitting opposite me with his food untouched in The Parlour, to comment on his unsuccessful defence. Sabrina had already signed a confession so his technical incompetence – as Burwana's courtroom performance was described to me by two legal experts with no apparent axe to grind – did not rise to the level of unnecessarily admitting guilt at the bail application stage. But he presumably believed that his political tactics were going to get her out on bail, whereas they simply confirmed her guilt and foreclosed any chance of her receiving bail.

He shrugs and looks back at me without comment or any apparent discomfort so I remind him of the magistrate's words at the end of the judgment: 'The contention by Mr Burwana that first applicant wanted to liberate herself from the monster, that is the deceased; that first applicant deserves an award and can be regarded as a hero (because) she liberated herself ... was a most unfortunate statement to be advanced in court and on behalf of the accused person. There is no basis for such a statement. And surely, it did not advance the case of the applicant any further ...'

I wait again for Burwana to comment but he stares calmly back at me. Feeling uncomfortable at his unexpected indifference to my provocation, I read out some of the prosecutor's admonishing words, scribbled in my notebook while studying the court transcript the night before.

'I ask Your Worship not to allow this to be converted into a political issue,' said Malherbe Marais. 'That is absolutely, with due respect, ... nonsense. We are not dealing with an indemnity application. If those circumstances are proved to be true, they are valid circumstances that will be considered in relation to sentence and sentence only. And to submit that, rather than being incarcerated, (Sabrina van Schoor) should be labelled a hero – that is, with respect, absolute nonsense. And that's not the sort of thing that should be advocated by a professional person in a court of law. We know the principles. The public may be gullible, but we know the legal principles. And it is irresponsible to make that sort of submission where the accused has hired the services of another to have a murder committed.'

Suddenly Burwana looks annoyed, pushes his hamburger aside and laughs humourlessly. 'It is strange that the Jewish people, even 50 years after the Holocaust, are expected to still feel bitter about what happened to them in Germany,' he says with a sneer. 'It is not a problem for them to keep reminding the world of that outrage. But here in South Africa, we black people are told to keep quiet about what happened to us. If we show that we are still angry and hurt and wanting explanations, we are told to move on; that is all in the past now. Forgive and forget.

'I was a policeman before I became a lawyer. I was a secret member of the African National Congress (while) in the SAP (South African Police). I watched how people like Stephen Rheeders treated blacks in their custody and also how they treated the blacks who were working with the white cops. Nothing happened without fists and abuse, verbal and also physical. If you hear them in the courtroom telling me to obey the law of the courts, don't say this or that, you will think they are very law-abiding citizens but they are not. They will do anything they want to represent whites only, their people, the white community.'

I decide not to argue with him. What he says is undoubtedly true of the apartheid era. As an undercover political activist witnessing torture and torment in the police force, his anger is understandable. What I want to know from him, though, is whether he really believed he was acting in Sabrina's best interests by raising the racism defence so aggressively or whether, as Stephen Rheeders believes, he was hoping to benefit from the media attention his political handling of the case added to an already sensational crime.

He nods. Unsure of what he is assenting to, I ask if he thought he was going to make a name for himself.

'Yes,' he says disarmingly. 'It was the first time a black man had defended a white murderer against racism in South Africa. It was a political event.'

I realise that Siphiwo Burwana's experience of racism and his resultant sense of victimisation, so apparent during the court proceedings, might have overwhelmed his legal judgement in this case. He is as much prey to bigotry, racial hatred and irrational fear as the people he accuses of those sins. Tragically, his life, as surely as Sabrina's, has been ruined by the evils of racism. He seems to have internalised apartheid and become hopelessly one-dimensional on the subject, seeing the scourge everywhere and demanding random redress. As a lawyer, he is guilty of the cardinal sin of bringing his own emotions to bear, possibly adversely, on his client's case.

I want to discuss with him my belief that exposure to a racist society gives rise to a form of mental illness in which life is pervaded not only by colour differentiation but by the constant threat of violence. Sabrina made an attempt to escape the culture of racism that dominated the Eastern Cape and the whole country but she had become trapped by the psychology of violence to which her father had succumbed so dramatically a decade earlier. The attempt by her lawyer to argue that Sabrina was trying to escape racism failed to acknowledge that racism and violence are part of the same social malady: her attempt to escape was a total failure.

Racism is not a simple event on which South Africans

can pontificate and then turn their backs. It is a virus of the mind that affects all who are exposed to it for a long, long time because it reaches so deep. Some, whites as well as blacks, got a bad dose; others were able to hold it in check and move on. Only their children who grow up in a relatively race-free environment will be able to walk away from it with ease.

I want to identify with Siphiwo Burwana's burden and share my own guilt by telling him about my own exposure and how difficult it has been for me to recover from the racist attitudes inherited from my parents and the society that shaped me. My Swiss mother recounts a story of me, aged three, embarrassing her during my first visit to my grandparents in Zurich. They had given me a doll's house as a gift and, because I was an African child, they had sat two little dolls together on the sofa, one of them black and the other white. As soon as I lifted the roof to reveal the rooms underneath, I removed the black doll from the sofa, sitting her firmly on the floor. In my South African world, it was an unthinkable gaffe for the two to be sharing the sofa, or indeed for the black doll to be sitting anywhere but on the floor.

I would like to talk honestly to this troubled man but he is looking at me so irritably that I lose my nerve. Then he picks up his car keys and prepares to leave. While I pay the bill and he shuffles restlessly beside me, glancing constantly at his watch, I reflect on the fact that today is South Africa's national election day, 14 April, 2004, marking ten years into a fledgling democracy. There has been much discussion in the media at home and abroad about the country's miraculous escape from what seemed in 1990 to be an inescapable spiral of mutual destruction. Did South Africans, in fact, escape? I wonder. How did they escape? Is it possible to escape?

Next day, when the banks reopen after being closed on election day, an event held on the tenth anniversary of the birth of what Archbishop Desmond Tutu dubbed 'the rainbow nation', I intend to slip quickly into the high street to send some money to a relative but I find the Standard Bank in Cathcart Street crammed so tightly with people pushing towards the counters that there is barely room for one more. An air of noisy excitement fills the normally hushed business chamber and I ask a woman who is standing on my toes what is going on. 'Cheques from the IEC,' she shrieks, referring to the Independent Electoral Commission. Several hundred local election monitors are clearly wasting no time in collecting their payment, which will bring a rare mid-month bonanza to Queenstown's traders. I join a short, exclusively white queue standing in front of a counter marked Business Accounts, knowing that I will be served ahead of the crowd. As soon as I stand behind her, the woman in front turns around and confides, 'Like ants, aren't they?'

The election has been declared a big success by most observers. Although little more than half the electorate voted, perhaps indicating disenchantment with the hard-won democratic process, the ruling African National Congress scored its biggest majority. This has given rise to euphoria on the streets of Queenstown as taxis displaying ANC flags toot their horns and pedestrians respond with the raised fist salute of the liberation movement. I join in the hooting and get a frosty look from a white woman waiting alongside me at the traffic lights. When I call in to say hello to Sabrina's schoolfriend Cherie van Heerden in the office she shares with the bookkeeper of a company selling exhaust pipes, she tells me indignantly that taxis have been seen driving fast through town with white coffins on their roof carriers.

White coffins?

'Ja, white for us whites. We're dead now as far as they are concerned.'

There is no sign of this bitter rebuff to white South Africans while I wander the streets, however. I ask several people if they have seen taxis bearing white coffins and they all look mystified. Nor is there any sign in Queenstown that those who are no longer European but not yet African are debating their whiteness. I spend a couple of hours talking politics to every white resident I can engage and discover that their integrity seems to be beyond interrogation: whiteness avoids self-examination. One woman tells me angrily that, because the election result proves the country is a one-party state, she will consider emigrating.

Many whites in South Africa exhibit forms of psychological emigration, such as retreating into self-contained villages behind tall walls. They feel displaced yet unable to express nostalgia for the past because the ANC's acclaimed Truth and Reconciliation Commission, which exposed the deeds of perpetrators while validating victims' experiences of state-sponsored violence, revealed white complicity and complacency about apartheid. 'Many don't want to simply hanker over the past because they now know it was wrong,' said Liese van der Watt, an academic at the University of Cape Town. It is only through increased activism around whiteness that people will gain insight into their position and privilege.

It is only when whiteness is deconstructed that '... the quest for a new white humanity will begin to emerge from a voluntary engagement by those caught in the culture of whiteness of their own making,' said writer Njabulo Ndebele during the inaugural Steve Biko Memorial Lecture in 2000. A new white humanity is unlikely to emerge if prominent white people are unable to be magnanimous in the face of the sort of inexperience exhibited by the defence during Beverley's trial, although the legal profession cannot be expected to indulge incompetence either.

At the end of Sabrina's bail application – a few days after the magistrate pointed out that the case was no longer about the merits of the murder, to which the accused had confessed, but about sentence in the High Court – the plea entry proceedings in State vs Van Schoor took place at Queenstown's Regional Court. In a colourful exchange, Advocate Marais took the opportunity to compel Sabrina's counsel to apologise on the record for calling the prosecutor 'a white male racist' in a meeting off the record. 'My learned friend has apologised to me and he has withdrawn such statement and he is prepared to confirm it in open court,' Marais told the magistrate. 'And if he does so, Your Worship, I will accept the retraction and I will accept the apology.'

Burwana then apologised. The exchange, obviously embarrassing for him, showed an officer of the court suddenly discovering that he was not free to dish out insults as he might have been on the street. The criminal justice system was able to compel a higher standard of conduct. Unfortunately, though, his apology to the cocky prosecutor was likely to reinforce Siphiwo Burwana's lifelong aversion to white authority and his insecurity about his role in the world. His retraction also exposed the futility of Sabrina's legal explanation that everyone who stood in her way was a racist.

This is not to say that racism – both in Beverley's conduct and in the values of Queenstown's white community – was not prominent among the causes of Beverley's death. Siphiwo Burwana clearly believed this to be true when he prepared Sabrina's defence but when I talk to him again briefly the day after our lunch, specifically about Sabrina's motive, he tells me that neither he nor the court were able to establish why she killed her mother. 'I would say there was severe provocation,' he ventures. 'Sabrina told me repeatedly that she and her mother were always quarrelling and I checked this out among people who were close to the family, including the servants who worked for them and who saw what was happening between Sabrina and her mother. There was a lot of hatred.

'Those brothers of hers are running the show in Queenstown. The boyfriend of the mother is running the police.' I stop Siphiwo to point out that Beverley's boyfriend Danie Nel is not the most senior policeman in Queenstown and that, according to Sabrina's brother Allister, the family merely knew the investigating officer rather than being friends with him. He laughs. 'No, there is a black man in the top job but he is doing what Danie Nel tells him. The high-ranking black policemen are only warming the seats.

'There was a lot of hatred in the Van Schoor family,' Burwana continues. 'I had the impression that part of the reason Beverley hated Sabrina was because she was the daughter of Louis, who had made Beverley's life miserable. I tried to pursue this in court but, when Sabrina was giving evidence, she sometimes disregarded what she had told me. When we consulted, she would say her mother didn't love her and tell me how Beverley treated her and her baby so badly. But in the dock, she changed her whole story and said, "My mother loved me. She loved my kid." '

Burwana is at a loss to explain why Sabrina, who he describes as highly intelligent, could not see that she was shooting herself in the foot by contradicting her own defence. 'I think she regretted what she had done and she wanted to try and make it all sound a bit better,' he believes. 'It was really frustrating for me but there was nothing I could do about the answers she gave which were not in her best interests. In all the discussions I had with Sabrina, she gave me the impression that, from early childhood, she felt that she was isolated and she felt neglected. She was longing for love and acceptance. She said to me that she was very comfortable when she was with coloureds and blacks. She felt accepted by them whereas her mother used to insult her even about her body, about how she was built, and such things that a mother should not accuse her own child.'

This is a matter that has been bothering me since my first visit to Queenstown, when I already knew from newspaper reports of Maggie Riggien's evidence that Beverley had taunted Sabrina about her size. It was on my initial research trip that I first noticed in the police file pictures of the murder how fat Beverley was herself. A few days later in Lady B Florist and Bridal Boutique, I studied a large colour photograph of Beverley that was displayed in the shop on the first anniversary of her death. She was smiling, not a young woman but a good-looking one, with sculptured facial bones and striking blue eyes. The portrait was cut off at the shoulders but not soon enough to conceal an obese body beneath the attractive face.

What makes a mother torment her child in such a cruel way? Was Beverley so embarrassed, so deep in denial about her own obesity that she couldn't bear to tolerate it in Sabrina? Many of us project our own unresolved emotional issues onto our children. It's all too human to decry in others the things we dislike in ourselves but the process sometimes makes hypocrites of us. Beverley could not control her own weight yet she felt free to ridicule Sabrina for being fat. Her daughter became the target of her own bad feelings.

After my final discussion with Siphiwo Burwana, I phone my contacts in Queenstown in search of Navin Neermul, a young coloured man who was Sabrina's boyfriend for eighteen months while she was still at school. He gave evidence in her defence at the bail application, describing to the magistrate his own experience of Beverley's racism.

Nobody seems to know how to contact Navin Neermul. I eventually track him down via Maggie Riggien's sister, who had met him two years earlier outside the Regional Court after Maggie had given her evidence in Sabrina's favour at the bail hearing. I follow her directions through cut-price shops with short names like Jet, Snip and Pep on the outskirts of Queenstown to Mlungisi township, where the respected Neermul family runs a number of businesses including a pub called The Black Ball.

The area is dusty and teeming with pedestrians. A lot of dilapidated taxis are parked in front of The Black Ball, a small building painted bright yellow. Several women with baskets of bananas balanced on their heads are standing together laughing. A naive artist, possibly a child, has painted a fish and a packet of chips on the wall next to the entrance. Inside is a bar, where a man is drinking beer at 9.00am. A pool table stands alongside a cluster of dining tables and chairs. The music throbs so loudly that I cannot introduce myself to Navin's father. He points to a tiny office at the back and closes the door behind us. When I tell him I'm looking for Navin, he immediately claims his son is out of town. Where? I ask quickly, sensing that he is fibbing, and he flounders before saying 'Durban'.

Once I explain my mission, he lightens up and gives me his son's mobile phone number. I call it straight away and arrange to meet Navin at The Parlour in half an hour. On my way out of The Black Ball, Navin's father introduces me to his wife, Pushaka, who is standing behind a takeaway counter that specialises in cooked chicken's feet. These, piled high on a tray in front of me, are a worrying orangey colour, hopefully the result of exotic spices. It is evidently Navin's mother's car I have noticed parked outside with the unusual licence plate PUSH 1 EC. I comment on it, knowing this will go down well in a town where the vehicle one drives accounts for a hefty proportion of one's prestige, or lack thereof.

Pushaka shakes her head at the mention of Sabrina. 'You can't control the kids of today,' she says. 'Sabrina was a very friendly girl but she had problems with her own people; her

171

own mother. You've got to live within your own culture or terrible things can happen.'

At The Parlour, Neermul rushes in to greet me, a well-built young man with a wide grin, who apologises for being in a hurry: he says he has to drive to Johannesburg but has managed to squeeze me into his schedule. We settle beneath the narcissistic nude and I get straight to the point. How was it possible, in racially segregated Queenstown, for Sabrina to have so many relationships with non-whites? How did he negotiate his relationship with her?

'I have a sister, who was a junior at Queenstown Girls' High when Sabrina was in her last year there. All these schools had become racially mixed, as you know. They had a system of mothering the newcomers and Sabrina was my sister's mum. She looked after my sister. That's how Sabrina and I met. At lunchtime, I would visit her and my sister at school, take lunch for them, and we'd chat. After school, we'd chat again before the driver came to take Sabrina home. She was studying for exams and I sometimes sat and studied with her. We were friends at first but then I realised that she was head-over-heels in love with me.'

They began to meet outside the schoolyard after Sabrina took to accompanying one or other of her brothers when they were called to attend to crises at Red Guard's offices over weekends. Once in the city centre, she would call Neermul and arrange to meet him on a street corner while her brothers were busy in their security business at all hours of the day and night. 'We'd walk a few yards, usually to The Parlour if it was still open, have a drink, hold hands so nobody could see, that sort of thing. Then she would go back to Red Guard and I'd go home.'

Beverley's purchase of the Action Quicket business provided opportunities for the two to start dating and having sex, according to Neermul. Although Sabrina was seventeen and still at school when they met, he was only a year older, having dropped out before his final exams. 'The mother got to hear about it. She arrived at my house in a red Isuzu 4x4 double cab. Beverley was sitting left hand side front, one of the brothers was driving and another was sitting on the back seat. I was busy cleaning a pump-action firearm in the garage at my home, with the door standing open to the street. They swept into the driveway and I stood up, holding the gun, to see who had arrived. They all jumped out and started yelling, warning me that if they catch me next to Sabrina they are going to kill me.'

According to Neermul, when he saw Sabrina the next day and described the confrontation, she told him that 'she had got a terrible hiding the night before'.

Who hit her?

'I don't remember exactly – maybe one of the brothers or the mother. Beverley's boyfriend, the policeman, used to hit her, too. That's what she told me.'

Did you believe her?

'Oh yes. I know it was true because by that time we were intimate and I used to see the marks and bruises on her body. Once, while I was talking to Sabrina on the phone, I heard her mother start to shout at her and then, when the phone fell out of her hands, I could hear the sound of hitting, the foul language from Beverley and Sabrina crying for help. She had already run away from home once by then, before she got pregnant for the first time. Her mother went to fetch her in East London. You should have seen her feet when she came back, cracked and bleeding: she walked and walked to get away from her family. I said to her, "Why didn't you call me to help you", and she replied that she didn't want anything to happen to me because of my relationship with her. She said her brothers had told her that they would hire someone to kill me if we continued to see each other.'

The reason Sabrina might have taken her brothers' death threats seriously is because life is still so cheap in South Africa following 40 years of state-sponsored violence and assassinations that it is possible, according to newspaper and police reports, to hire a killer for as little as R10 000 (less than 1000 pounds). Domestic murders are regularly committed by impoverished individuals on behalf of wealthier people, including whites, who, as in all other aspects of life, delegate their dirty work to poor blacks.

Neermul's recollection of Sabrina's bleeding feet reminds me of her account, both to the magistrate during the bail hearing and again to me when I interviewed her in prison, of the occasion when she, as a teenager, was riding pillion with her brother Allister and got her heel trapped in his motorbike. The resultant wound was so severe that Beverley rushed her to hospital in East London, where she remained for several days. Beverley drove daily from Queenstown to visit her daughter, spending more time with Sabrina than she had ever done before. It might have proved an opportunity for the two to bridge the divide between them but Beverley returned to her old critical and dismissive ways once Sabrina was released from hospital. Sabrina remembers trying hard to recapture the closeness they had shared while Beverley was worried about her foot, but to no avail. For a while, Sabrina says, she even resorted to opening up the wound on her heel deliberately in the hope that the blood flowing from self-mutilation would kindle her mother's love.

Navin Neermul confirms that Sabrina told him about the heel she deliberately cut open in her desperate attempts to win Beverley's affection. He then tells me a story to illustrate Beverley's racism. He and his cousin and another coloured man had gone to the café adjoining Lady B, which was run by Beverley some of the time and by Sabrina when she was not at school. He says he left the payment for the meal on the table in the bill folder presented to them by the waitress but Beverley was so prejudiced against them as coloureds that she convinced herself that they would leave without paying. 'Without even bothering to check, she chased after us when we left, demanding that we pay and shouting insults.'

He and Sabrina were careful to conceal their sexual relationship, says Neermul, and it continued until he heard she was pregnant by another man. 'I was shocked and asked her: "How can this be when you are going out with me?" And she said, "I'm sorry, my love. It was like this and like that …" I realised the girl didn't know what she wanted in life. Her family's corrupt and they're corrupting this poor kid. I decided to keep my distance; to be her friend and that's it.'

Promiscuity is a well-documented symptom of low self-esteem among young women, as are eating disorders like obesity. Cherie van Heerden believes Sabrina slept around indiscriminately in an attempt to find the affection she lacked at home. Navin Neermul agrees. Cherie also thinks her old school friend was unusually immature, citing a letter she received soon after Sabrina went to prison. 'She asked me to check with one of her boyfriends "if we are still going out together". The whole letter was very childish.'

I suggest to Neermul that the public prosecutor had put him under considerable pressure during the bail hearing to concede that Beverley's threatening behaviour towards him was understandable in the circumstances. 'Malherbe Marais was tough but okay,' replies Neermul. 'The problem was not him but the investigating officer, Stephen Rheeders.' Neermul insists, like Burwana, that Rheeders was a friend of Sabrina's brothers and therefore not an entirely impartial law enforcement officer in the case.

Our time is up but, having forgotten to bring an interview release form for Neermul to sign, I ask him to swing by Longview Lodge. He follows me in his own car. Justina greets him like a long-lost friend even though she had earlier claimed not to know Neermul when I asked if she could help me to contact him. She explains later that she knows him by another name and that she often hires buses and other forms of transport from him, both for tourists staying in her guest house and for the political rallies that she still sometimes organises on behalf of the ruling party. Navin is a good guy,' she confirms, '... a straightforward, honest businessman.'

Justina and I go out for dinner that evening, once more into The Parlour seeing its food is so much better than in Queenstown's other eateries. We talk about South Africa's achievements over the past decade and the changes in Justina's own life during that time. We both get teary remembering Nelson Mandela with his fist raised high as he walked out of prison after 27 years, and at the memory of black South Africans patiently lining up in endless queues to vote for the first time in 1994. We discuss the fact that the economy and the intellectual capital of the country remain largely white, a legacy of apartheid that will challenge the ANC for a long time to come. 'People now need to benefit from democracy,' says Justina. 'Not only the political elite but also the poor.'

She has travelled much further economically than most South Africans during the last decade. For many years a political activist, along with the rest of her family, she says she can assemble an AK47 assault rifle in record time. She recalls the sorrow of saying goodbye to two of her brothers when they left the country for military training abroad, knowing they might never return.

Her career in the hospitality industry began as a waitress in a hotel in Queenstown, where the young white man training the staff would whack them on the bum with a plank each time they made a mistake. 'I knew that was not right but what could I do? I wanted the job. We were so exploited. We were employed to do one job but if somebody was off sick or late for work, they would say, "Now you do the cooking or the housekeeping or even the gardening." It taught me a lot, at least. By the time I opened my own guest house in 2000, I knew everything about hotels.'

As we chat, Justina tells me disapprovingly, 'Queenstown is a place where everybody knows everybody else's business.' Yet she is clearly a free-ranging gossip herself. When I comment on this, she laughs and explains: 'Throughout the struggle years, listening in on private conversations became a political tool. A lot of intelligence was passed on by the staff employed in the homes of white policemen, soldiers and politicians. Activists made it their business to talk to maids, nannies and gardeners about their employers.'

The habit has evidently persisted in Justina's case. I have recently gleaned a lot of insights, particularly into Beverley's oppressive behaviour as an employer, via Justina's underground networks. She tells me: 'I discovered that one of the black women who worked first for Beverley and now for the brothers in the florist shop has set her daughter up in a rival florist shop in the centre of Queenstown. It is a secret but already some of the Van Schoors' clients are going to her daughter's shop because it is cheaper than Lady B. When that employee decides the moment is right to leave Lady B, quite soon now, she will go. The funny thing is that, because there is so little contact between whites and blacks, it will be years before the Van Schoors realise, even in tiny Queenstown, that it was their own employee who took their clients away by quietly offering them discounts. After years of being underpaid and obliged to work overtime for no pay, she has no loyalty to them.'

The next person I hope to interview is Ursula Tromp. Both Allister van Schoor and Stephen Rheeders have told me that Beverley 'gave' her hairdressing business to Tromp, a coloured woman. Both of them have made this claim in an attempt to counter accusations of racism against Beverley: if she gave her hairdressing business to a coloured, how could she have been a racist?

I walk through the Pick 'n Pay Mall into the tiny hairdressing salon which used to belong to Beverley. Four clients are sitting inside, one under a dryer, another at the basin having her hair washed by a young assistant. A handsome woman with glowing brown skin and closely cropped black hair stops snipping at a schoolgirl's blonde mane and stares at me as I enter. She is wearing a stylish brown and beige dress with zebra skin mules on her feet.

Ursula?

She nods and puts the scissors down slowly without shifting her gaze off my face. I have the feeling she already knows who I am and is not pleased to see me. Strangers stick out in Queenstown and the word has doubtless gone out by now that a nosy writer is asking questions about Beverley van Schoor's murder. As I introduce myself, speaking as softly as I can, four pairs of eyes bore into me. Tromp walks in my direction, staring at me. I take a few steps backward into the entrance foyer where she asks me very, very quietly to come back later.

Four thirty?

She nods and scurries back to her clients. I return to my room at Longview Lodge to answer emails and think about Tromp's salon full of hostility. Perhaps the word doing the rounds is that I am sympathetic to Sabrina or, at any rate, not sympathetic enough to Beverley and the Van Schoor brothers. Perhaps the stony stares are just signs of small town paranoia. Or frank curiosity. My lunches and dinners with black people will certainly not have gone unnoticed. If I was spotted going into The Black Ball, an unseemly dive by white standards, I might even be considered subversive. In the old apartheid days, such a visit could have been enough to attract the attention of the security police. Nowadays, Queenstown's former rulers can do little more than whisper their suspicions among themselves. What a giddy time they must have had speculating about Sabrina and her dark-skinned lovers: how they must have hated her for blurring the bedroom boundaries so publicly.

When I arrive for our appointment, Tromp steers me into the empty tearoom next door. It is another of the businesses Beverley set up, which Tromp took over from Beverley with the hairdressing shop. She looks so uncomfortable sitting with me that it is a wonder she has agreed to the meeting. When I ask if it is true that Beverley 'gave' her the salon, she looks indignant and explains. 'I paid her for it over one year. She said if I couldn't afford the payment one month, I could leave it until the next month. That was nice of her but she *gave* me nothing. I had been doing her hair for many years, even before I worked for her and did it almost every day. We agreed she could carry on having her hair done three times a week once I owned the salon instead of me paying her interest on the money outstanding. That was our deal. It was Allister who told Bev to give me first option when she decided to sell the shop, and she decided to sell it in the first place because she was not a hairdresser herself so this business didn't pay her well enough.'

After a while, Tromp relaxes and tells me how well she knew the Van Schoors. 'I first met Bev and Sabrina the day they arrived in Queenstown, when Sabrina was about four. The first thing Bev did was come to the salon where I was working to have her hair done. We became friends. She used to talk to me about everything, including Sabrina. I was fond of Sabrina and her brothers. I also knew the guys Sabrina dated. When Sabrina ran away to East London, Bev asked me to phone her and persuade her to come home.

'Sabrina was even in love with my son, who worked with Allister and them at Red Guard. When Bev was complaining about Sabrina's coloured boyfriends once and I told her that, she looked at me and said, "Ursh, if only your son was the father of her child, I would be happy." '

And you believed her?

'I did, yes, because there's nothing wrong with my son.'

I point out that there is nothing wrong with Navin Neermul either. Tromp does not answer. We move on. She recalls the morning of the murder, a busy Friday in the shop. 'My cousin phoned to tell me that Bev was dead. I phoned Lady B to confirm it was true. I was so heartsore. I couldn't believe it, and I still can't believe it sometimes. I think of Bev whenever I see her grandchildren. She used to tease me because I was a grandmother before her. She didn't want Sabrina's baby in the beginning but then she loved that child very much.

'What really makes me heartsore,' says Tromp, 'is the thought that Bev knew Sabrina was there in the house on the morning of the murder. She screamed for help but Sabrina didn't come ...'

When I try to find out how Beverley treated Tromp as an employee, she looks wary and dodges the question. Then, to prove how often she still thinks about the dead woman, she tells me revealingly: 'I dreamt recently that I had such a fight with Bev because she told me that I was making the milkshakes wrong.' Another of Beverley's former employees, Cherie van Heerden, who used to work as a waitress in the tearoom, had told me earlier how critical Beverley was of all her staff. 'Only she knew how things were done,' according to Cherie. 'She was constantly telling me how to do things, including how to run my own life. She was a complete control freak.'

Interestingly, controlling individuals present as know-alls who never tire of indicating that they are better and best, yet psychologists invariably find that such people suffer from anxiety, depression, inadequacy or insecurity. Constantly worried about lack of control in their own lives, they project their fears onto others. As Freud told us, there's a lot going on in the unconscious: the way we feel about ourselves all too often governs the way we behave towards others. We may never know exactly why Beverley rejected Sabrina so early in her only daughter's life. Was it because Sabrina was an ugly baby perhaps? All mothers believe they will love their babies, no matter what they look like, but this is not always true. Or was it because Sabrina reminded Beverley of her unhappy marriage to an abusive ex-husband?

Tromp provides no further insights into Beverley's character. When I ask her why she thinks Sabrina murdered her mother, she shrugs and shakes her head. 'Don't ask me,' she says. Then she describes going to Allister's house to offer her condolences on the Friday of the murder and telling her cousin afterwards: 'You know, Sabrina didn't look heartsore ...' Despite a vague suspicion that Sabrina might have had something to do with Beverley's murder, Tromp confesses that, when Allister implored her to give evidence for the prosecution in support of Beverley's good name, she declined because she felt sorry for Sabrina. 'What I told Allister was that I couldn't do it because I had nobody to look after my shop.'

Over a year after Sabrina went to jail, in September 2003, Tromp was startled to see Sabrina sitting outside Pick 'n Pay Mall in a prison vehicle. She had been brought to Queenstown to defend herself against fraud charges laid by her brothers in respect of R170 000 missing from one of Beverley's businesses at the time of her death. 'I went to the window and saw that she was handcuffed and her legs were manacled,' says the hairdresser. 'I could see she was upset but she reassured me that she was fine.' On the same occasion, Sabrina persuaded the prison guards who drove her to Queenstown to drop in on another of her coloured friends at the realty business known in Beverley's day as Pam Golding Properties, which the Van Schoor brothers have renamed Rainbow Estates, an interesting choice in post-apartheid South Africa.

Back in Johannesburg, I study the translation from Afrikaans into English of the testimony that most damaged the state's case against Sabrina – Maggie Riggien's evidence. Describing her relationship with the deceased, Maggie told the court: 'Eighteen years ago, we became best friends. We were very young at the time. And still beautiful. And we decided to live together because we did not have money in those years. We loved each other more than we loved our sisters.'

With the credibility of a virtual family member, Maggie wholeheartedly corroborated Sabrina's evidence about the dysfunctional mother-daughter relationship. Prosecutor Malherbe Marais tried to discredit Maggie by ridiculing her educational pretensions. 'The less said about the witness Riggien the better,' Marais told the court. 'Had she sought to convince us that she majored in drama, I would have been more inclined to believe her. I submit that she was grossly guilty of exaggerating and the most I can say about her performance is that it was entertaining. And I submit that we should take whatever she has said with a grain of salt.'

When I had earlier asked Siphiwo Burwana to comment on what Maggie had told the court, explaining to him that Stephen Rheeders believed she had 'made a fool of herself', he disagreed. In Burwana's view, Maggie was brave to stand up in front of Beverley's family and Queenstown's outraged white community and pronounce her deceased friend a cruel mother. 'She was adamant to tell the truth and it was painful for her to do it,' according to Burwana. 'She did not make a fool of herself, not at all. You see, Stephen Rheeders and all the whites in Queenstown didn't like the fact that Maggie testified. No matter what she told the court, they would have said it was nonsense.'

While it is true that Maggie Riggien has a theatrical personal style characterised by deeply despairing sighs and exaggerated facial grimaces, she has seemed to me in several meetings to have been not only genuinely distraught over the circumstances of her friend's death but sincerely determined to tell the truth about Sabrina's ill-treatment by Beverley. Virtually everything revealed to the court by Maggie Riggien has been independently endorsed in my interviews with Cherie van Heerden or Gladys Nontombi, both of whom had intimate knowledge of the Van Schoor family. I believe, like Siphiwo Burwana, that Maggie deserved a pat on the back for having the courage to risk alienating Queenstown's white community by speaking out on Sabrina's behalf: she certainly did not deserve Malherbe Marais' ridicule. Apart from a lapse into *LA Law* mode, when she cheekily addressed the whites in the public gallery in an attempt to bolster her claims that Beverley would have expected her to tell the truth about the mother-daughter relationship and to try to help Sabrina, Maggie Riggien's evidence was appropriate, respectful and trustworthy.

In response, Malherbe Marais was well within his professional rights to try by all possible means to discredit Maggie Riggien as a witness. Nevertheless, several of the journalists who covered the bail application and trial have told me that they found him particularly hostile towards both Sabrina and Maggie in the briefings and interviews he conducted on and off the record with the media. Perhaps the case – and especially the issues it raised about racism – touched an exposed nerve in the public prosecutor, as surely as it unsettled, albeit briefly, most of the white South Africans who heard about Beverley van Schoor's murder.

Chapter Seven

'Our knowledge of ourselves and the unfair world we live in has been corrupted by our inadequate insight into the belief system that formed us,' said an earnest psychology student while we drove together from Port Elizabeth, the Eastern Cape capital, to her university in Grahamstown. We had met by chance one Sunday in August 2004 when she sat beside me on the plane from Johannesburg and we talked about the Van Schoor murders. After she accepted my offer of a ride to Grahamstown, our discussion turned to the stigmatisation Sabrina had inevitably endured following her choice of black and coloured friends in bigoted Queenstown. Having spent some of her formative years in Queenstown, my companion knew quite a lot about Beverley's murder although she did not know the Van Schoor family. As we drove through bushveld, green pastures and mountains ablaze with aloes, she bemoaned the continuing intolerance not only in her hometown but among young people at Rhodes University.

White students were irritated by the ongoing hurt expressed by black students and often resisted discussing apartheid history, she told me. They seemed unaware of the extent to which so many South Africans, including themselves, had been dehumanised by apartheid. Psychologically, she felt, many of her acquaintances had become emotionally retarded by apartheid. They had never been encouraged to embrace black rule and so they continued to blame it rather than themselves or their parents for ongoing social ills such as crime. 'The Van Schoor murders reflect that immaturity. Louis killed blacks to prove he was a big man, however futile a gesture that had become by the end of apartheid; Sabrina killed her mother because she was hurt and angry and frustrated. When things don't go their way, white South Africans blame somebody. Look at their aggressive response to defeat even in rugby games.'

When we arrived in Grahamstown, the legal and educational centre of the region, we parked the car but carried on talking. She was a pretty young woman, dauntingly smart and eager to share her insights, though she pleaded not to be quoted by name. 'When asked to take on board the effects apartheid had on us and on our fellow blacks, we go into denial. We will have to conquer our defensiveness before it becomes possible to listen. You can't possibly hear another person's point of view if you are busy arguing your own.'

Impressed by such perceptive analysis, I commended her for it, saying jokingly that if psychologists like her were on their case, the former rulers would have a good chance of rehabilitation. She laughed and replied: 'I reckon I might need a bit of help because the whole country is crying out for prolonged therapy, not just the whites.'

After settling into a hotel in the town that celebrates its colonial architecture – where I have come to discuss Beverley's murder with the public prosecutor and the psychologist who helped him present the state's case against Sabrina – I wander through wide, empty streets. Grahamstown's history began in 1811 when a British army officer named Graham sat down to rest in the shade of a giant mimosa tree. He was so pleased with the circle of hills protecting the valley around him, as well as with the abundant water supply from several sources of the Blaauwkranz River, that he decided to establish a permanent military base there.

Grahamstown's most beautiful landmark and the country's oldest church, the Cathedral of St Michael and St George, was built thirteen years later on precisely the spot where the mimosa tree had once flourished. The white community subsequently spread in every direction around this classically English stone-walled place of worship until, a decade after holding its first service, the cathedral became a refuge for women and children during frontier wars lasting until 1850.

Today, Grahamstown is part of the municipality of Makana, recently renamed after a Xhosa prophet who led an attack on the town. The same mimosa tree that shaded Colonel Graham and then gave way to the cathedral crops up in Makana's history, too, having earlier marked the Great Place of the Xhosa chief, Ndlambe. Following his ruthless expulsion by British forces, thousands of warriors in battle array are said to have poured over the hills intending to drive away the British soldiers who had stolen the Xhosas' land. Despite their numerical strength, however, they were forced to retreat, leaving behind hundreds of dead and dying men. Makana was captured and, like Nelson Mandela over a century later, imprisoned on Robben Island. Near the base of Makana's Hill in Grahamstown on a site known as Egazini, meaning place of blood, is a monument to those involved in the battle. It is dedicated to reconciliation.

After a while, I notice that I am being followed at an un-threatening distance by two young black men, who both hold out their hands when I turn around. As soon as I proffer coins, another two skinny youths appear and gaze at me imploringly. Shaking my head at the newcomers, I walk on, wondering how kindness can prosper among those who are always pushing away the hands that beg for food. What damage do we incur as human beings by constantly saying no to the needy?

These are uneasy thoughts considering that I have been feeling unsettled since passing the turn-off to Motherwell, the site of an apartheid-era atrocity, on the incoming journey. My student companion and I had spent some time discussing recent extensive news coverage of the amnesty re-hearing of a case known as the Motherwell Four, in which former security policeman Gideon Nieuwoudt blew a few of his many victims to bits in a car bomb explosion. Like Louis van Schoor, Nieuwoudt is a reminder not only of the state that sponsored murder but of the citizens who condoned his actions.

As the afternoon fades, Grahamstown's cathedral spire stretches ahead into darkening sky like an exclamation mark lit by the sepia glow. I pass sweet-smelling frangipanis and a pair of howling hadedas near the church's entrance, and decide on an impulse to go inside for evensong. Although no longer formally religious, I have always loved the aesthetics of religion. While it is certainly true that violent faiths have much mayhem to answer for, I wonder sometimes how those of us with secular ethics can remain humane without a God or a moral law external to us. This thought occurs to me again on the way down the aisle, when I suddenly feel that I have been searching all my life for an alternative to God; for some other extraordinary spiritual idea to believe in. Like American philosopher Cornel West, who preaches social justice in the United States, I wonder about the spiritual impoverishment of 'market culture run amok', where the emphasis is on stimulation and titillation rather than intangible non-commercial values like compassion. The capacity to see the good in people is often promoted by Archbishop Desmond Tutu, too. He has for many years expressed his dismay at the capacity of church-going white South Africans to sacrifice their souls in order to secure their physical and material well-being.

Sliding onto an ornately carved pew at the front of the church, I watch two white women priests performing their rituals. 'Almighty God, forgive us all that is past,' says one of them, head bowed and eyes closed, a serene look on her face. The walls behind the cathedral's towering Gothic arches bear frescos etched in gold. Gorgeous tapestries of two saints, Michael and George, hang on either side of the altar. 'God bless Africa,' sings the all-white choir.

The sermon, about guilt and forgiveness, is given by a professor from Rhodes University, one of the many educational institutions in Grahamstown. It is dedicated to prisoners countrywide and the authorities who tend to them. 'Lies, corruption and even murder can be forgiven,' declares the lay preacher, a white man. I think of imprisoned Sabrina, who recently sent me a letter asking when I would next be coming to Fort Glamorgan because she had something urgent to discuss with me. Most of the problems she has complained about lately have involved abuse of power by the head of the prison. There is no evidence that prisons in South Africa today are any better than they were under apartheid, which is partly because those who try to make a better society will themselves bear the marks of the old system.

As the preacher quotes scriptures, my mind goes back to Gideon Nieuwoudt and the awesome significance of what some people expect others to forgive. Nieuwoudt's lawyer even argued in court that '... he believes what he did was the Christian thing to do. In his Bible, it is there.' I recall a documentary in which a television camera followed Nieuwoudt into the house of one of his victims, where he made a lame apology to the family. The son of the dead man picked up a vase and smashed it over Nieuwoudt's head, fracturing his skull. One critic noted that it was only in the brief moment after he was hit that viewers finally saw some humanity in the killer's eyes. Nieuwoudt was suddenly being addressed in the language he understood – violence.

How do people become as depraved as Nieuwoudt and Van Schoor? How do they become so blindly racist that they can kill with little or no provocation? Inadequate gun controls, protracted border, colonial and civil wars on the continent, a 'wild west' tradition in rural areas where white farmers feel exposed and entitled to radical forms of self-protection, incessant propaganda and the bureaucratisation of killing are all partial answers. Another explanation is fear. The many South Africans who carry guns for self-defence on their persons and in their vehicles reveal not only bravura and aggression but also fear. Outnumbered 9:1 by black people, whites were always defensive, believing that suppression of the majority would ensure their dominance. Because they could never face the politics of compromise, their collective morality became increasingly callous.

Differences between nations in their human rights records lie in their situations rather than their intrinsic moral qualities. Apartheid could perhaps have happened, or still happen, in other culturally diverse societies, given sufficient fear and the historically defeated psyche of the Afrikaners to tip the balance. As Alexander Solzhenitsyn warned in *The Gulag Archipelago*, '... the line dividing good and evil cuts through the heart of every human being ...'

Our human inclination to show respect for someone else's dignity or to show disgust at another's humiliation are powerful restraints on cruelty except in situations where 'the other' is considered subhuman, as in South Africa. This is the low point at which whites became so deeply racist that they were universally reviled for being on the wrong side of world history in pursuing racist policies at a time – post-Nazism – when Western nations were identifying increasingly with human rights ideology.

Most of the people involved in Beverley's murder, its prosecution and in giving evidence to me about the Van Schoor family are ill-educated, psychologically tormented or poverty-stricken individuals whose various misjudgements are a reflection of the racial policies to which they have been subjected by their society. Sabrina's lawyer, persecuted all his life, sees discrimination under every bush; her friend Cherie van Heerden anticipates black revenge at every turn; Sabrina's surrogate mother Gladys Nontombi is powerless to the point of annihilation. Less obviously prejudiced are the wise men of the case, the middle-class, middle-aged, privileged professionals: public prosecutor Advocate Malherbe Marais, clinical psychologist Professor Mark Welman and his assistant Mike Earl-Taylor, who have all agreed to talk to me about Sabrina, the mother-killer.

After lunch next day, I have an appointment with Malherbe Marais in the elegant building of the Ministry of Justice. Arriving early, I meet one of the state advocates in his office downstairs from Marais' chambers to discuss, on condition of anonymity, the legal situation regarding Sabrina's two accomplices. He begins by expressing disgust at Sabrina's crime. 'To kill your own mother and to be there right in the next room – that's a hell of a thing, even by the standards of what we see in this job.'

Then he explains the state's attitude towards Gino Redcliffe and Kello Nieuwenhys, the shady characters to whom Sabrina turned for assistance when she first considered murdering her mother. 'When there is a shortage of evidence, the police may pull in an accessory or accomplice who may incriminate himself in exchange for indemnity from prosecution, which is contingent on his telling the truth to the satisfaction of the judge,' he explains. 'In this case, the judge has recently given his findings with regard to Gino and Kello, saying he relied on their evidence but he was not convinced that they answered all questions frankly and honestly. He made it clear in his judgment that it was not necessary for the state to now pursue a case against these two. I doubt any further action will be taken against them.' He pauses, then continues a little apologetically, perhaps because he realises how unfair the law looks to a layperson when it allows a lowlife like Gino – who planned Beverley's murder and tried himself to commit it – to go free without any form of censure. 'We, who must catch the killers, have to consider the lesser of two evils. If we didn't make these deals, we wouldn't get anyone to give evidence against criminals.'

I still have time to kill before my appointment upstairs so he and I talk about crime and South African modes of immorality. When I tell him that Queenstown reeks to me of unsavoury secrets, he laughs uproariously. A few years ago, he confides, there were a number of burglaries in wealthy homes all over Queenstown. A lot of expensive electronic equipment was stolen. The police were unable to find the culprits for some time, although they were convinced the break-ins were linked. One suspect led to another until the investigating officer eventually raided the house of the ringleader. Amongst the loot, the police found a pile of morally incriminating photographs. They were pictures, stolen unwittingly, of some of Queenstown's leading citizens – including Beverley van Schoor – cavorting naked in an extravagant orgy. When word got out that the unseemly images were in the possession of the police, most of the outstanding theft charges were quietly dropped. Although much of the missing equipment was located by the police, Queenstown's blushing residents declined to claim it.

When I meet Malherbe Marais, he greets me warmly

and seems eager to talk about Sabrina's case. He tells me he is an Afrikaner originally from Cape Town who lives in an elegant Victorian house in Grahamstown with his quiet, bookish wife with whom he lunches on the stoep at home every day. Although he enjoys a comfortable life as deputy director of public prosecutions for the Eastern Cape in the region's prettiest outpost, he makes no secret of his frustration at finding himself on the wrong side of history. A pale male in his mid-forties, Marais can no longer get onto the fast career track: he could have expected to become a judge before long under the apartheid government. If he is bitter about the turnaround, it shows only as wry resignation; the odd crack at a criminal justice system characterised by inexperienced legal practitioners; a cruel laugh here and there at the incompetence he witnesses among his new peers. He says he remains passionate about justice and his own contribution towards it. He takes a pride in his work and does not hesitate to correct colleagues if their knowledge of procedure or precedent is deficient or their standards of conduct inappropriate.

'It is so much against human nature for a child to kill a parent that I think Sabrina must have derived some moral authority or permission from her father's shocking crimes,' he says. 'Her dad was her role model. The idea that you can solve your problems with violence must have come to Sabrina from her father, who used to assault her mother. Louis' logo at his security company consisted of a round white circle with a red heart in the middle, two bullet holes in the heart and blood dripping from the holes.' He draws the gory emblem, which attracted three-quarters of East London's security business to Van Schoor, on a sheet of paper as he speaks.

'The murder of Beverley van Schoor wasn't done in a moment of rage. This was a carefully orchestrated and well-planned crime, which hurts even more. It was orchestrated to the extent that Sabrina was the mentor while the black man who committed the killing was the agent. She even covered for him, to make sure he got into the premises and got away with her car.'

I ask to what extent he sees racism as a feature of the case. Marais considers the question carefully before answering. 'Our predisposition and our bias in terms of race come from our parental role models,' he says. 'Bearing in mind that a person's personality or character, according to psychologists, is formed by the age of five years, you can see what happened in Sabrina's case. She felt comfortable amongst so-called coloured people and that's what turned her family against her, according to her testimony – and there is definitely some corroboration for it.

'It is a tragedy but also a case in which the red light must flash for all of us, in the sense that we must be careful what examples we set for our children. Sabrina's case was not only about racism but about negativity towards other people, whether black or coloured or just poor people. The message that we bring across (as parents) is that they (black people) are of a lesser breed; that we look down upon them.

'For example, in this particular case, there's a portion of the record in the bail proceedings where Sabrina has the shock absorbers on her car repaired by her mother's boyfriend, the policeman.' Paging through a copy of the transcript on his desk, Marais murmurs while searching for the relevant passage: 'This somehow had the ring of truth ...' When he finds the quote, he adds before translating Sabrina's words from Afrikaans: 'This is very blunt but I'm going to say it just like it is here.'

He translates the segment from the court record in which Beverley's boyfriend, Danie Nel, tells Sabrina that the shock absorbers in her car are broken 'because you have been fucking coloureds in the back of your car'. Closing the transcript and gazing out of the window for a moment, Marais continues: 'It is not only a coarse way for a man of 52 to talk to a child of 22 but also a nasty thing to say to a person who is very overweight.'

What it is really about is disrespect, I suggest. Marais seizes this, his voice rising. 'Exactly. When I first heard that Sabrina was responsible for the murder of her mother, I thought there must be something more to it than meets the mind. The case was about the dignity of other people, all of them, and the dignity of your own children. You can greet people with a smile on your face but if you don't let them come close to you, if you keep people safely at a distance – whether we are talking about Beverley's attitude towards her daughter or about racism generally – that is also a way of offending people's dignity.'

I ask the public prosecutor how the complex case was as swiftly resolved as it had been: South African murder cases usually last a lot longer than the seven months it took for Sabrina to become a sentenced prisoner. He explains that the investigating officer's use of police listening devices to trap Sabrina was irregular in some respects, necessitating his own intervention. 'My reaction when I heard about the case was that I should go and attend to it immediately because, being in charge of traps and undercover operations in the Eastern Cape, I know that there are certain prerequisites when approving a trap. In this instance, the police used the killer as bait to trap Sabrina. Normally, when that happens, one would give the trapper something in return. To use the co-accused against the other person implies that you're going to use him as a witness and indemnify him. That was not the case here. They just used him to trap her and then arrested him as well, which was not the correct procedure. That's why I got involved from the word go, at the bail proceedings stage, in order to do it thoroughly. Once they (the murderers) had admitted everything in the bail proceedings, there was very little left to go on trial.'

He explains that he asked the court to sentence Sabrina to life imprisonment, despite her youth, because of the grossly aggravating features of the crime. 'The premeditated planning, the fact that she took someone from a lesser background and corrupted that person's mind by offering Feza a reward for killing Beverley – a woman he had never seen before. In offering someone from a poor background over R100 000 to commit a contract killing, you must realise that person is going to be desperate for money and is going to commit even murder for monetary gain. Bearing in mind this country's history, it is also easier in South Africa to find someone from across the colour barrier to commit such an atrocious crime because of feelings of racial resentment. So Sabrina's crime perpetuates the evils of the past in a lot of respects, not only the sins of the father.'

When I ask Advocate Marais what part in the murder he attributes to Beverley's threat to keep the baby Tatum, in the event that Sabrina left home, he tells me that Sabrina was so immature emotionally that her mother believed her incapable of looking after the child. He backs this argument by reminding me that Sabrina spent every evening drinking in a nightclub rather than staying home with Tatum.

I point out that Action Quicket was her mother's nightclub, a business Beverley had asked Sabrina to run while she, rather than her daughter, stayed home with the baby. 'Well, yes,' he concedes, 'it may not have been all that healthy to expose Sabrina to all those influences, knowing what happens in a nightclub, especially in view of the fact that Sabrina was emotionally immature and looking desperately for acceptance.'

When we discuss Sabrina's motive for murder, Malherbe Marais says he believes, like the investigating officer Stephen

Rheeders, that Sabrina had stolen a large sum of money from her mother's property business and was about to be found out on the morning of the murder. 'The theory was that she used that money to buy drinks for her coloured friends at the nightclub in an attempt to gain social acceptance. That, to me, is not at all far fetched as the likely motive.'

Except that Sabrina was recently acquitted on those theft charges, I tell him. The case was thrown out for lack of evidence in October 2003. This information, verified by me a fortnight earlier with the police officer who investigated the theft case brought by her brothers against Sabrina, is evidently news to Advocate Marais. He looks blank and says nothing. He probably does not know either that, shortly before coming to Grahamstown, I rang a Port Elizabeth attorney to confirm that Beverley sought legal advice about a grievance she had against two of her sons, Allister and Lester. In preliminary papers drawn up by the lawyer, Beverley claimed that her sons had accepted her offer of ownership of her security business on condition that they paid their mother's insurance premiums and gave her a monthly allowance. When these payments stopped abruptly and her sons refused to resume them, Beverley decided to reclaim ownership of Red Guard.

I ask Malherbe Marais if he is aware that Beverley was considering legal action against her own sons at the time of the murder. He looks disconcerted and shakes his head, saying he recalls some mention of Beverley suing them but can't remember the details. He clearly does not want to dwell on the questionable integrity of Beverley's family, having portrayed them in court as dear and sweet. Throughout our discussion, he has been quick to blame Louis while trying to modify the sins of the mother by insisting that Beverley did her best as a parent. This may be true within the sad context of a mother-daughter relationship that had been severely strained since Sabrina's early childhood.

His defence of Beverley's intentions reminds me of the birthday card she sent Sabrina on 8th November, 2001 – just four months before the murder – which highlights Beverley's aspirations but alludes also to the real state of their relationship. 'To my darling daughter,' it read in Beverley's handwriting. 'Our lives have not been easy but I would not change you for any other person. I love you and I know I don't tell you often enough. Please remember that you can do anything that you tell yourself you can do. You are very special to me. My life would be empty without you in it. Also, thank you for all the hard work that you do. I know it is not easy to do your work and look after Tatum at the same time. I hope that we both grow closer and put all our indifferences [sic] away and forget the past and live for the future and look forward to the best years still to come.' The message goes on: 'Sorry I can't be with you all day today. But you will be in my thoughts the whole day. Enjoy your day. You are 22 years old today. Remember that I love you more and more each day. You're my special girl and I love you.' It is signed Mom.

Later in the afternoon, I ask Professor Mark Welman similar questions to those put to Marais after he, too, assures me that Sabrina's motive for matricide was her imminent capture for stealing money from Beverley's property business. Like Marais, he does not seem to be aware either that the fraud case against Sabrina has been dismissed or that Beverley was intending to take legal action against her sons. The information does not seem to interest him at all.

Mark Welman's attractive wife offers me tea while he answers one of many calls on a mobile phone. Among the callers is the father of a 21-year-old Johannesburg student, a kidnap victim who was murdered after her family had paid part of the ransom. Until her corpse was found naked in the veld, Mark Welman's public profile soared when he was quoted regularly in national newspapers, advising the family on how to deal with the young woman's captors and building up a psychological profile of the kidnapper.

The profile Professor Welman presented at Sabrina's trial in consideration of her sentence stated that she had no psychotic symptoms, that she appreciated the wrongfulness of her actions, and that the remorse she exhibited was related to the consequences of her crime rather than the crime itself. '... there is no conclusive sign that she has gained sufficient insight into her actions so that if faced with a similar situation she would proceed differently. In this regard it is important to make a distinction between accepting that one's actions were fundamentally wrong (ie an evolution towards mature moral judgement) and accepting that they were incorrect simply because one "got caught". It is my considered opinion that the defendant's present mental state is such that it is the latter rather than the former reality that is present, and that considerable counselling will be required for there to be a meaningful shift from the one to the other.'

Listing Sabrina's salient personality traits, Mark Welman told the court that she suffered from low self-esteem, that she believed she did not really 'belong' in her family, and that she mixed with and felt an affinity for 'persons who might be described as living at best on the margins of good citizenship'. When I point out during our interview that virtually all the black and coloured residents of Queenstown were obliged to live on the margins of good citizenship, it being the stated objective of apartheid to prevent black people from becoming regular citizens, he simply shrugs.

Professor Welman gives the impression of mild boredom throughout our interview. Wearing an electric blue shirt, he lounges on a leather sofa in his home, which is overflowing with children. He has a lot of curly greying hair, the beard, moustache and unshaven bits of his face merging untidily. He is an associate professor of psychology at Rhodes University, a registered clinical psychologist and a leading South African expert in the understanding and prediction of criminal behaviour. He conducts himself with the air of a man who expects his opinions to go unchallenged which, considering that the profession he represents is the least exact of sciences, seems to me to be surprisingly rigid. If I am looking forward to kicking around ideas about Freudians who see sex at every turn or psychoanalysts who spot unempathetic mothers in each case, I am quickly disappointed. I don't even get the opportunity to crack the usual jokes about analysts being sicker than their patients. Perhaps he is bored by my questions because there is so much violence in South Africa that blood and gore conversations have invaded everyday discourse, becoming the norm.

Professor Welman told the court that Sabrina's lack of maternal love and affection during her formative years 'may have been the breeding ground for later conflict, as it is possible that to some extent (her) choice of friends and sexual partners was motivated by the realisation that one way to gain the attention of her mother was to provoke clashes with her in this way. For a needy child, negative attention is a better option than no attention.'

He gave examples of Sabrina's dependency and attention-seeking behaviour, including a suicide attempt shortly before her mother's murder. He said her 'willingness to stand up in court and plead responsibility for her actions, and the submissive posture that she sometimes exhibits, are manifestations of a need to be liked and accepted'.

Welman went on to describe Sabrina's tendency 'to present things in such a way that they may become exaggerated or dramatised. This may be described by some as deliberate lying, but it is more likely a further indication of a need for attention – the more dramatic one's situation, the more attention it is likely to attract. There are two dangers associated with this tendency and both may have played a role in this case. Firstly, exaggeration of reality tends to lead to polarisation of differences and conflicts. Evidence of this is the portrayal by the defendant of her mother as an extreme racist.

'Secondly, it occasionally happens that the critical distinction between actual and portrayed reality becomes blurred, and in this case the possibility cannot be ruled out that the defendant exaggerated the tensions and conflicts between her mother and herself to such an extent that it impacted on her capacity to cope with the situation. In essence, she may have become the victim of her own exaggerations.'

Although the telltale symptoms of psychopathy, such as lack of remorse, premeditation and attention-seeking, appear in Mark Welman's report, the word psychopath does not. I ask him why he told me on the telephone that Sabrina was 'a classic psychopath' when he did not use this damning term – or its updated though lesser known alternative, antisocial personality disorder – in court. He replies that he considers it best to avoid labels that might be challenged in court.

I then ask him why he was engaged to write his report on Sabrina for both the defence and the prosecution. He explains that he was called in by Malherbe Marais, who told him 'the defence was in trouble'. He goes on: 'The public prosecutor is a fair man who wanted to avoid the possibility of anyone saying that Sabrina had not been properly evaluated. As it turned out, my report was more beneficial to the prosecution than to the defence.' He claims it was preferable for the court to get a single evaluation because, had he been brought in by the defence, he would have felt under pressure to be sympathetic to Sabrina. When I interpret this to mean that psychologists' evidence is of little value, he does not agree.

Regarding Sabrina's motive, I ask Professor Welman why he

did not give more weight to the fact that Beverley threatened to keep the baby if Sabrina carried out her intention to set up house on her own with her child. His first reply, a little irritably, is that, as he was not paid to write the report, the two days it took him to research Sabrina's personality was not enough time for a fuller assessment. When I ask if this means he wrote an inadequate evaluation of Sabrina, he disagrees.

I persist with the question of whether Beverley's threat to claim custody of the baby might not have been Sabrina's missing motive for matricide, reminding Mark Welman that his report confirmed that Sabrina had consulted a social worker about her mother's rights in this regard. To my surprise, he denies that his profile on Sabrina confirmed any such thing.

Disconcerted at having got this important fact wrong, and not having his report to hand to check it, I rest my case. Once back in my hotel room, however, I consult the official criminal profile he wrote for the court and there the assertion appears quite clearly: 'The defendant's claim that the murder was further motivated by a fear that her mother might pursue threats to have her child removed from her care may have some substance given that *the defendant did seek advice in this regard from a social worker*. However, it is more likely that this threat merely exacerbated existing tensions between (Sabrina) and her mother to a point where the defendant's hostility towards her mother reached, literally, a murderous pitch.'

More inclined to see Sabrina's state of mind as a response to the wounds of infancy than evidence of psychopathy is a colleague of Mark Welman's at Rhodes University, Mike Earl-Taylor. In preparation of Welman's criminal profile, he was delegated to interview Louis van Schoor to test some of the allegations Sabrina had made against her family, especially her claim of sexual abuse by one of Beverley's boyfriends and two others. Louis told Earl-Taylor that Sabrina had confided the rape charges to him a long time before Beverley's murder. He also confirmed Sabrina's insistence that Beverley was prone to physical violence and severe verbal abuse.

Earl-Taylor, an American, is a social worker and former journalist who teaches investigative psychology as well as conducting research in the Psychology Department at Rhodes University. With his ravaged middle-aged face, his hair pulled back into a ponytail and his tendency to delve into the deeper emotional reasons for criminal behaviour, he is known as 'Granny' by male colleagues like Malherbe Marais and Mark Welman. Although more sympathetic to Sabrina than Mark Welman, he, too, believes she is a psychopath.

'Look at the premeditation involved in the crime,' he says. 'If it had been a spur of the moment thing, I'd have said no, she meets the criteria but she may not be a psychopath. It was the planning that sank her. It was a cold-blooded crime, like her father's murders.'

What about the readiness with which she confessed? Psychopaths never admit their guilt. Was there a pattern of antisocial behaviour? Psychopathy is about a history, not a single episode.

'How much remorse did you see in her?' he counters. 'Was she truly sorry or just crying because she had been caught?' These are impossible questions to answer definitively, he admits. 'We're left with conjecture. None of us knew what her motive was. She wasn't able to say herself. Judge Leach questioned her at length, asking repeatedly: "Why did you do it?" She answered so vaguely that the court never knew why.

'It may have been the most hideous act of revenge for those years of perceived mistreatment and lack of love,' he speculates. 'That was the key to me. I saw a child crying out for affection, who never received it from a very young age. If we don't know love, we can't give it. Without it, you can't know empathy. That young woman lacked empathy to a pathological degree. And I'm stating the obvious there because she couldn't have done what she did to her mother if she had had empathy.

'I don't think Sabrina really had a chance from the start. She couldn't develop properly with her mother throwing material things at her while withholding affection. There seems to have been a huge emotional absence for that child in that family. I found the three brothers very puzzling in court. The disdain they displayed towards Sabrina was chilling. I felt instinctively that it predated the murder. Their hostility not only to Sabrina but towards anyone willing to give her a hearing was strange. They were even hostile to me, for example.'

Earl-Taylor says he finds it difficult to imagine a more dysfunctional family than the Van Schoors. 'The things she was alleging about her childhood were horrific and I don't doubt that at least some of them happened just as she claimed. She didn't turn out like she was without some of it happening to her. If we look at this case objectively, there were two victims – Beverley and Sabrina. Sabrina was the victim of a very poor childhood. Her problems did not start when she was a teenager, dating people her mother considered undesirable. Sabrina's tragedy goes right back to her early childhood.

'All societies are unique but South Africa is unique in a particular way in terms of its social engineering and its violent history. In terms of damage to the psyche, the country has a lot of very twisted people – members of the Van Schoor family among them.

'I think Sabrina may have become so overwhelmed by her circumstances within her family, a situation she considered inescapable, that she succumbed to a fantastical type of

thinking: "If I do this, the end result will be that – I'll be free."
That's why she could not articulate her motive.'

Driving along the road leading from Grahamstown to Port Elizabeth for the evening flight home, I catch a glimpse of the shacks where poor people survive on bare essentials within sight of the affluent suburbs. Rose bushes and clipped hedges soon give way to wild euphorbias and kiepersols as the town's encircling hills fold into the mighty Amatolas. There are signs on the roadside pointing to Kenton-on-Sea and Port Alfred, two fashionable holiday retreats. I recall a news item in *The Herald* that morning of three alleged rapists being 'necklaced' – covered in petrol and set alight – by an angry mob of 350 accusers. The men were piled on top of each other in a pyre of death, said the report. A rubber car tyre was set alight in a bizarre South African ritual designed to ensure that the victims burn beyond recognition. It was not clear to the police which individuals had been responsible for placing the tyre, pouring the petrol or striking the match.

Few stories illustrate South Africa's culture of violence as graphically as another item in the same newspaper – the arrest in a small room in Port Elizabeth of an Eastern Cape football referee who shot dead a coach and injured two players during a match at Kenton-on-Sea. Such a bizarre event, which would rate headlines in England, is buried in a few paragraphs in South African papers.

Beyond Kenton-on-Sea is a little place called Salem, where 'at the end of a winding track some miles outside town' is the setting of harrowing scenes in J M Coetzee's novel, *Disgrace*. A bleak story with disturbing implications, it is told amid 'red hills dotted with sparse, bleached grass' where the reality of shifting power unfolds in 'a sprawling farmhouse painted yellow, with a galvanised-iron roof and a covered stoep'.

Novels like *Disgrace* expose the deepest fears of whites in Africa; unspeakable fears that not only underpin racism but, paradoxically, challenge apparently unassailable notions of superiority. The rape of the white woman in Coetzee's story feeds into the mythology of the sexual prowess of black men as well as the visceral anxiety lodged somewhere in the mind of many white Africans: How long can we go on dominating these people before we become 'the other' and experience retribution?

For most white South Africans living under apartheid, such fears served only to strengthen the merits of suppression. Occasionally, though, dealing with contamination of thought, like bigotry and racism, was not so much a moral effort as a glaringly obvious fact of life. As a child, I remember my father's abiding prohibition against self-pity. I was the only one among my four siblings who whined for a 'bought' dress, 'one with a label', instead of the clothes my mother sewed for us. Complaining often about this and other imagined deprivations, I was periodically summoned by my father to follow him to 'the compound', where the farm labourers lived with their families. He would stride ahead, irritated with me, and then stand watching my reaction as I surveyed the scene: kids in tattered clothes with swollen kwashiorkor bellies, snot spilling from their noses, flies everywhere.

Although it was my father's intention to make me thankful for what I had, he inadvertently politicised me. He made me aware of poverty and what it meant to kids like me. He gave me empathy, the inclination to put myself in 'their' shoes, from an early age. I recall asking once, to my father's astonishment, why the cook worked in our kitchen on a Sunday instead of taking his children to church. From then on, he and I argued interminably about racism and abuse of power.

*

Arriving at Port Elizabeth airport with time to spare, I am impatient to get home. The first thing I do back in Johannesburg is listen to a tape given to me by Malherbe Marais. Having expected resistance from the public prosecutor to my request to hear conversations recorded by Inspector Rheeders between Sabrina and the man who slit her mother's throat, Feza Mdutshane, I am eager to hear what Sabrina had to say immediately after her arrest. Although Feza knew the conversation was being recorded, Sabrina had no idea that there was a police microphone hidden in Feza's shirt pocket. 'It was not used in evidence,' Marais had told me in explanation of his willingness to hand over the intriguing tape.

At the beginning of the recording is a phone conversation between Feza and Sabrina in which she implores him not to call her at her brother's house. It is the night following Beverley's funeral. Tatum is asleep beside Sabrina. Allister is talking to his wife in another room. The house is very quiet. 'They're looking for you,' hisses Sabrina, terrified that her brother will hear the conversation. 'There are cops all over the place. They phoned last night to say they had caught you,' she tells Feza, who quickly ends the call.

The tape goes dead, turning round and round until a phone starts to ring. In the emptiness of my living room comes Sabrina's confident pre-murder, pre-recorded message, the mundane sound of her life as it used to be and will never be again. 'Hi. This is Sabrina. I'm not available at the moment. Please leave your name and number.'

The recorder, which is being controlled by a specialist police undercover unit, is then switched off. When it resumes, again with a ringing mobile, Feza speaks after Sabrina answers in a sleepy tone. 'Sabrina, I need cash,' he whispers. 'There are police all over. I need R1 000 to go away.'

Sabrina's voice is full of fear. 'Don't call me here,' she says faintly. 'I'll see you tomorrow and give you R3 000. Nine o'clock.' The line goes dead.

It is creepy listening at home alone for conspiratorial voices on the tape, which is winding ominously onward. Suddenly, another ringing phone pierces the night. 'Hello.' Sabrina's voice sounds wary.

'Sabrina, nè? I want to meet you,' says Feza.

'Where are you?'

'I'm here in town, in Westbourne. Do you know where's Westbourne?'

She sounds both scared and irritated. 'No, I don't want you to meet me at all. Hold on. Gino's going to come to me and I'm going to give him the money for you.'

Feza answers firmly: 'No, I don't want to come to Gino. I just want to meet you somewhere. We can go to the Caltex garage.'

Sabrina agrees. 'Okay. At nine.' There is a pause before she adds urgently: 'At the back (of the garage)'.

'Okay, at the back.'

The tape winds soundlessly forward until Feza breaks the silence. 'Sabrina,' he says tentatively. His voice is now echoing in one of two adjoining cells at Queenstown Police Station, where Inspector Rheeders has locked them up together after Sabrina's arrest in the hope that they will discuss the murder and that she will incriminate herself.

'Please come here,' Feza says.

'Why?' she asks. Her voice is weary, resigned.

'I just want to ask you …'

'What?' She is sharp with him, suddenly annoyed.

'Do you know what you did?' Feza asks.

'What?'

'You gave the cops the right description (of me).'

'Me?'

'That's why the cops caught me.'

'Do you know how bad I feel, Feza?' she admonishes him. 'I killed my mother.'

'What about me?'

'I'm going to jail, Feza.'

'You? Why?'

'Yes, because you told Stephen (Rheeders) it was me who told you to do it.' She yells the investigating officer's name, a sudden angry sound that makes me jump, 'Stephen!'

'It was not me,' he insists. 'It's me going to jail.'

'You told them what I did.'

'And then?'

'And then! I'm going to jail because I did something wrong.' She shouts again for Rheeders.

'I'm in trouble,' Feza insists petulantly. 'I've lost my girl-friend – everything. I'm going to jail now.'

She replies more calmly, slowly, as if gradually coming to terms with her fate. 'I know that but it's my fault.' Then her mood veers and her voice is screaming out again, 'Stephen'. There is no response. The tape rolls on mutely until she confides: 'I need to go to the toilet.'

'It's just here … the toilet,' he says.

'Ja, I know.' Their practical discussion sounds pitiful amid the tension. There is a pause and she asks, 'Are you locked in? Did they lock you in?'

'Yes.'

'I'm going to jail,' she announces, testing the idea on herself rather than on him. 'Do you know that?'

An indistinct discussion follows, punctuated by another scream: 'Stephen!' Then Sabrina asks Feza, who apparently has a better view out of his cell into the police station beyond, if anyone is approaching down the passage. He gives her an indistinct commentary on what he can see. In an attempt to attract attention, he whistles deafeningly just when I have my ear very close to the muffled tape. The two of them wait in

208

silence. Nobody comes. Sabrina yells again for Rheeders.

She asks Feza: 'If you didn't want to lose your girlfriend, then why did you go and phone me this morning from the police (station)?'

He answers: 'The police caught me yesterday. The time I was phoning you, I was here. They know everything.'

'How did they know?' she asks in a theatrically suspicious tone.

'I don't know.'

'Gino!' she exclaims. 'Gino told them!'

'I don't know,' says Feza neutrally.

Their conversation continues indistinctly for some time. It is hardly an entrapment of 007 precision despite an entire technical team having had to come to Queenstown from East London to set it up. Sabrina screams repeatedly for Rheeders, at one point rattling the gate of her cell noisily.

'Who's coming?' she demands.

'No one is coming,' says Feza, sounding tired.

'Feza, (remember) when Gino came to me and he pushed me and he said if I don't do it then I'm going to get hurt?' Sabrina seems inspired now.

He responds with another question. 'You remember that day, that morning, when I said we must just leave everything?'

'What day?' she asks boredly. Hearing footsteps, which sound briefly on the tape, she shrieks: 'Are they coming?'

'No.'

She screams again for Rheeders, then asks, 'Feza, who told you to kill my mother?'

'Gino.'

'Gino?' She considers his answer and goes on excitedly: 'I told Gino I don't want to do it. Then he came to me and he said you told him that if I don't do it he's going to hurt me or my child.' An indecipherable exchange follows before she adds

209

in a shrill, authoritative voice: 'That's why I did it, because I didn't want my child to be killed. I love my child. Gino forced me. Gino kept on coming to me, every day; phoning me every night. I told him to leave it.'

Sabrina has become tearful during the tirade against Gino. She yells again for Rheeders. 'I didn't want to kill my mother,' she sobs. 'I told Gino; I told him to scare her. I just wanted to scare my mother. I didn't want to kill her. That's why you were just supposed to break in. I didn't want you to kill her. I loved my mother. But Gino kept on and kept on ... Gino was the one who decided, not me. Gino asked me how he could get into the house, remember?'

'Ja.'

'Gino decided it, not me,' she insists again.

*

It was Sabrina's failure to accept responsibility for her mother's murder that Professor Mark Welman cited as the most compelling proof of her psychopathy. Although I am quite willing to believe that she suffers from this most devilish of conditions, she does not seem to me to have exhibited its symptoms unequivocally or for long enough to warrant Mark Welman's certainty. According to the *Diagnostic and Statistical Manual of Mental Disorders*, the symptoms of psychopathy include stealing, lying, substance abuse, financial irresponsibility, an inability to deal with boredom, cruelty, running away from home, promiscuity, fighting, lack of remorse. The most profound characteristic of all psychopaths is that they have no concept of guilt. Devoid of a conscience, they cannot feel remorse.

In Sabrina's case, there does seem to have been remorse. She has expressed it verbally to me many times and I have regularly seen her eyes well up with tears when she talks about her mother and the murder. Her half-brother Allister, while implacably hostile towards Sabrina, refuted without hesitation my suggestion to him that Sabrina was a psychopath. He couldn't explain why he rejected the idea, however.

Malherbe Marais, on the other hand, is convinced that Sabrina is a psychopath – and he is competent to judge the syndrome. Stressing in our interview that attention-seeking is a dominant symptom of psychopathy and that the packed courtrooms in State vs Van Schoor were a stage from which Sabrina could tell her story, Advocate Marais nevertheless sighed deeply when I asked him if Sabrina had looked as if she was enjoying the limelight. 'When she spoke about her mother, she was in tears all the time. I won't say she was enjoying it – that would be wrong of me. I think she went through a hard time.'

International prison statistics indicate that one in four convicted criminals is psychopathic, a condition once known as moral insanity. Characterised by the lack of a conscience, it enables those afflicted by it to act entirely in their own interests. Psychopathy is classified as a disease by the World Health Organisation and is more dominant in males than females, as well as being five times more likely to occur in a male offspring of a father suffering from the disorder. Since Louis van Schoor has often and with good cause been labelled a psychopath, it is possible that Sabrina might have been predisposed to the condition.

Most psychopaths are incapable of love, according to psychiatric textbooks. When displaying regret or sorrow, these expressions originate from selfish needs rather than consideration for others. Because they are often highly intelligent and understand the emotional needs of regular people, psychopaths are master manipulators. Even highly trained psychiatrists report sometimes falling prey to the charms of their psychopathic patients. They are uniquely different from each other: one psychopath might be promiscuous and lie but be financially responsible while another tortures animals though touches neither drink nor drugs.

In Sabrina's case, there is no evidence of cruelty prior to Beverley's murder: she appears to have been unfailingly kind to her pet cat and dogs. There is evidence that she was a liar, though. Her friends Cherie van Heerden and Navin Neermul say she could not always be believed, although her lies were usually in pursuit of self-aggrandisement, they believe. There is evidence that Sabrina stole, too. Her aunt, Beverley's sister Jenny, described to me in an interview in East London how she was able to prove that Sabrina had stolen money from the takings at her mother's coffee shop in Queenstown's Pick 'n Pay Mall.

However, Beverley appears to have been both a liar and a petty thief herself. The family's questionable ethics seem to have accommodated selective lying and stealing. While working for Beverley at the coffee shop, Cherie van Heerden observed her employer's dishonesty on a number of occasions. Having reported valuable jewellery stolen and claimed the insurance payout, says Cherie, Beverley started wearing the missing jewels again a few years later. Cherie also told me that Beverley, who used to pay her staff's wages weekly, once insisted against all evidence that she had given her employees their pay packets – a blatant lie, according to Cherie, who was forced to forgo her wages.

There is much evidence of Sabrina's abuse of alcohol as well as the promiscuity that often characterises psychopaths. However, as social worker Mike Earl-Taylor admits, alcoholism is rife among South Africans who live in a culture of despair. He concedes, too, that Sabrina's promiscuity did not necessarily point to psychopathy. 'Sabrina mistook sex for love and became promiscuous: that is the way she hoped to get the affection she'd never had before.'

Although I have no doubt that Sabrina deserves to be in prison and that her 25-year sentence is, if anything, quite lenient for premeditated matricide, I do not believe that she is a psychopath. Someone else who, like me, has examined all the evidence with no axe to grind is the documentary film-maker from Cape Town. When I call her to discuss whether or not Sabrina is a psychopath, she says she is in a quandary on the issue. She seems to be leaning more towards Professor Welman's view than I am, though.

We talk for an hour on the phone, bouncing the symptoms of psychopathy back and forth. The thrust of the film-maker's belief in the opinions of the state's three wise men – Rheeders, Marais and Welman – seems to be the pragmatic argument that the defence's main witnesses – family friend Maggie Riggien, prison evangelist John Stoltz and Sabrina's former lover Navin Neermul – are implausible show-offs whose opinions will not convince television viewers of her documentary, *Sabrina*.

We discuss how difficult it is to weigh different interpretations of events from different sources. I admit that I am also struggling with the small-town vulgarities of some of my Queenstonian interviewees, whose evasions and embellishments might be tantamount to dishonesty. I sometimes find it as hard as she does not to despise them, I tell her.

Despite being only one generation away from European working class or poor Afrikaner agrarian roots, the whites among them are nevertheless affluent and pretentious. This is not only because apartheid afforded whites the opportunity to enrich and elevate themselves but also because coloureds and Asians are historically the second-class citizens of South Africa. Blacks have always trailed way behind in third position in the skewed social hierarchy that persists throughout the country.

Among our most important informants in the investigation of Beverley van Schoor's murder are the same hapless coloured Queenstonians who have confounded us by failing to meet commitments, by contradicting themselves endlessly, and by making claims they cannot prove. They are not the most reliable of witnesses. While the film-maker and I discuss how tempting it is to view those who do not share one's own value system as 'the other', whether on racial or class lines, we agree that we are both acutely keen to ensure that our own prejudice neither discounts the ragtag Queenstonians' interpretations nor makes the views of the cool-headed professionals automatically right.

We agree that it is probably as difficult for lawyer Marais, policeman Rheeders, and psychologist Welman as it is for us – a film-maker and a writer – to make sense of another's personality. No one can ultimately prove or disprove that Sabrina van Schoor or any other criminal is either a psychopath or a normal person goaded beyond endurance. Nor can anyone say for certain that the state's three wise men – who collectively labelled Sabrina a psychopath outside the courtroom if not in so many words at the trial itself – did not judge her from the hidden depths of their own prejudice.

The overwhelming impression I get reading the court transcript and talking to Marais, Rheeders and Welman is that they despise Sabrina. In my view, it is at least possible that the three conservative white men responsible for bringing Sabrina to justice were influenced by their repugnance not only of the horror of matricide but also of the uncodified South African crime of mixed-race sex. My impression of all three of them is that, where loyalty to a long-held belief is involved, pity ceases to function. Of all the fears to which conservative white men raised to believe in segregation would be prey, the deepest is intimate contact between the races. Apartheid's sexual control, embedded in the Immorality

Act, was, after all, at the core of racial control. Implicit in the implementation of the law was the idea that white men could have intimate contact with blacks on their own terms but not vice versa. Whites in both apartheid South Africa and the southern states of America 50 years ago feared that once black men were their sexual equals – once blacks had white female sexual partners – their whole social structure would collapse.

Proving that Sabrina felt remorse for her mother's murder seems impossible. There are no criteria left to explore in this regard, only opinions. Left with an overriding sense of the inevitability of evil in the wake of apartheid, I realise that it might be necessary to obscure the moral contrast between victim and murderer by finding fault on both sides. I wonder if, in attempting to understand a crime like Sabrina's, we risk explaining away the behaviour of murderers. By locating its causes in society, are we not implicitly making violence more acceptable? While our explanations invoke sympathy for the murderer partly because we all know that someone like Sabrina is a human being like us, recent efforts to understand Hitler, for example, have been described by philosopher Claude Lanzmann as 'the obscenity of understanding'. Can we counter his argument by asking how we will ever learn from history if attempts to understand monstrous murders are not allowed?

With a feeling of simultaneous distance from and identification with the killer, I believe Sabrina is genuinely sorry for what she did. I believe she has experienced a painful awakening to the wrongfulness of the murder she committed: remorse, a psychological phenomenon that, like forgiveness, remains understudied throughout the world. I also believe that the white community of Queenstown ought to share the remorse for Beverley's murder. It was, after all, her own community's disdain that made unloved, oversized

Sabrina an outcast after she defied apartheid's sexual taboo. It was white Queenstonians who gave Sabrina the reckless I-couldn't-take-it-any-more sense that she had little left to lose.

In his essay, *Decline of the English Murder*, George Orwell discusses murderers whose stories are known in their general outline to almost everyone and which have been made into novels and rehashed over and over again by Sunday papers. The ideal murder should 'excite pity for both victim and murderer', he wrote. One of the criteria for memorable murders is that the killer should only come to the point of murder after 'long and terrible wrestles' with her conscience.

Most readers of Beverley van Schoor's murder will probably sympathise with the sad daughter as well as with the dead mother. How long the murderer wrestled with her conscience is known only to Sabrina. In trying to decide if she is truly sorry for what she did, I am hoping that my penultimate interview is the one that finally seals her moral fate.

Chapter Eight

On the morning of my meeting with Beverley's killer, Feza Mdutshane, I keep remembering the investigating officer speculating that Feza used excessive violence because he hated white people. The prospect of talking to such a man face to face is not only unappealing but frightening. Considering that he had never even seen Beverley before he murdered her and that he barely knew Sabrina, Feza's crime reflects the chillingly violent nature of South African society. On the other hand, if financial gain was his sole motive, as he claimed in his testimony, Feza's failure to secure any advance payment from Sabrina for the murder of her mother suggests his desperate circumstances, his gullibility, or both.

I had hoped to avoid meeting Feza altogether until I read the former barber of Queenstown's claim in court that Sabrina, with her baby on her hip, had been 'peeping' around the half-open door of Beverley's bedroom while he was killing her mother. On the face of it, Feza is the person who can shed light on Sabrina's state of mind at the time of the murder. It is he who can perhaps tell me if, by her actions, Sabrina is a psychopath, a monster, an irredeemably wicked person, as the prosecutor and the psychologist believe, or not. Such a cold-blooded act by a daughter as voluntarily watching while her mother, in the judge's words, 'was slaughtered like an animal' would, if true, warrant the psychopath label indisputably and make any further speculation about Sabrina's motive redundant.

Sabrina denied Feza's 'peeping' charge from the moment she heard it, according to her lawyer. She also insisted during my first meeting with her at Fort Glamorgan that Feza had lied, making the allegation in the hope of convincing the judge – who had commented on the excessively brutal nature of the killing – that his cruel culpability was equally hers. According to the investigating officer, Sabrina had always maintained that she did not see Feza take the knife from the kitchen dresser and that she did not, therefore, know how he planned to murder her mother. In her testimony and in successive interviews, Sabrina said it wasn't until she wondered in a panic if Beverley was still alive that she went into her mother's room after Feza had left and saw how brutally he had ended Beverley's life.

Middledrift Prison, where Feza is serving his 25-year sentence, is a grim place. A two-hour drive from East London, it is just outside a small town called Alice, site of the University of Fort Hare, where many of the country's leaders, including Nelson Mandela, were educated. It makes Fort Glamorgan, where Louis and Sabrina are incarcerated, look like a holiday camp. The 'maximum security' compound comprises a cluster of grey buildings inside several perimeters of steel, spiked fencing and razor wire. It is surrounded by bare fields in which a fleeing, orange-clad prisoner would be spotted easily. The guards have bulky handguns strapped to their waists. The visitors lined up to see inmates are silently bowed, tired perhaps from walking long distances or weak with hunger. The place reeks of poverty and despair. Even on a spring day in September 2004, the icy draught blowing through the entrance permeates the visitors' room and presumably the cells beyond. It must be hard to get to sleep here on bitter winter nights.

I go through the security checks into the visiting section and follow a warder to the cubicle allotted to Feza. He is a good-looking young man, with large, clear eyes framed by thick lashes; a smaller man than I expect a violent killer to be. None of the microphones fitted into the barred glass in the visitors' booths is working. I can barely hear Feza's voice, or he mine. I lean ever closer to him in order to listen through five small holes situated alongside the useless speaker. After a while, we are cheek to cheek and I can hear him faintly. Fortunately, he speaks English quite well.

Having considered simply asking Feza to confirm that Sabrina was 'peeping' around the door when he attacked her mother, or alternatively asking him bluntly if his testimony to that effect was a lie, I decide instead to invite him to talk me through the events leading up to the killing. That way, he will not feel challenged or unduly defensive and I will have the opportunity to compare Sabrina's version of the countdown to murder with his and confirm whether or not she has been truthful in her discussions with me.

As soon as I start to question Feza, pen in hand, a scowling warder tells me to put away my notebook. At first, it is hard to concentrate on what Feza is saying because other prisoners, all of them young, keep coming up behind him and grinning or waving at me. I am probably the first white woman they have seen in a while, perhaps in years. Or they may be enjoying the strange sight of my face pressed against Feza's in a parody of intimacy. The warder who searched me at the entrance to the prison told me that many of these men are rapists or murderers and I am initially reluctant to greet them. But they are so persistent and clearly so pleased to see me that

I begin to feel churlish maintaining a vinegary expression. So I wave back and then smile, at which point Feza becomes irritated by the distraction. He calls a guard somewhere behind him, who pushes the prisoners back, literally, and slams the gate at the entrance to the cells. For a while, they crowd up against the bars, still waving, one of them blowing kisses. I stop responding and they wander away.

I have been told that most of these prisoners were convicted of armed robbery. Virtually all come from deprived communities and belong to gangs that hold a subcultural mirror and two fingers up to the society from which they have been marginalised all their lives. In referring during a recent survey to guns as the tools of their trade and to their criminal activities as 'going on duty' or 'doing business', they mock the world of employment from which they are excluded. Describing their acquisitive criminal activities as the desire to have the latest in fashion clothing and cars, they talk of 'keeping up with the syllabus' and ridicule the world of education to which they once forlornly aspired.

Prisons all over the world impose punishment and revenge on the social victims who become trapped in a cycle of deprivation and violence. As *TIME* magazine once noted: 'Each year jails take large numbers of hopeless people and turn them into bitter hopeless people.' A recent report on prison conditions in South Africa found that young offenders in jail 'have a 99.9% chance of being raped'. Many inmates refer to jail as 'the university of crime', just as political prisoners used to call Robben Island 'the university of liberation'. Incarceration works only if going to jail brings stigma and shame to the offender. You have to wonder if some form of restorative justice with indigenous roots might not produce better results.

Somehow, against all odds, the solution to youth criminality must be found in contemporary youth identity and culture. It needs to create a sense of belonging to counter the impact of marginalisation. This – for Sabrina as surely as the predominantly young black offenders at Middledrift – is a process of human development; of recreating the social fabric that has been destroyed. It involves rebuilding family relationships and redressing the legacy of race-based inequity. A tall order indeed.

Feza talks for 45 minutes in a low voice, glancing constantly behind him to make sure the other prisoners are not listening. I strain to hear him, my face pressed against the glass, watching his mouth in an attempt at partial lip-reading. Sometimes I interrupt for clarification. Everything he says is exactly as I have heard it in detail, often more than once, from Sabrina.

We get to the moment when he is about to kill Beverley. He walks into her room, sees her on the bed and jumps on top of her, clasping both hands around her throat. She struggles and they fall onto the carpet, he sitting on top of her, legs astride her bulky body. He tries to strangle her; she fights for her life. He cannot keep his grip around her neck. He demonstrates how he tries to press his thumbs against her windpipe. She struggles free again and again. Finally, he whips the knife from his tracksuit pants and slits her throat. The murder takes him ten minutes, he estimates.

So, according to his own account, Feza slit Beverley's throat because he had failed to hold her down long enough to strangle her, not because – as the investigating officer believed – he hated whites. More relevant is the fact that there is no mention in his account of Sabrina watching him murder her mother.

Feza is still talking. He walks down the passage and stops outside Sabrina's room. She hears him and opens her bedroom door. 'Is she dead?' she asks. He assures her that he has killed Beverley. 'Are you sure?' Sabrina repeats. He turns to go back to Beverley's room to check her pulse.

At this point, Feza's story differs for the first time from Sabrina's. He says she comes out of her own bedroom and follows him into her mother's room. He feels for a pulse and shakes his head. According to Feza, Sabrina then takes her mother's hand and monitors the lifeless wrist. 'She was crying,' he adds.

During their planning of the murder with Gino, it had been agreed that Feza would take Beverley's cellphone as well as Sabrina's car in order for the murder to seem part of a robbery rather than an assassination. Feza now tells me that Sabrina was standing in Beverley's room when he informed her that he had not found the phone. He claims she took her own mobile from her pocket to dial Beverley's number. It rang under the bed, close to Beverley's body. Sabrina reached across her mother's corpse for it, according to Feza, and handed it to him.

According to Sabrina, however, she remained either inside or later in the doorway of her own bedroom throughout the time the murder was being committed and in its immediate aftermath. She says she dialled Beverley's number from her own room so that Feza could locate the phone after he told her from the passage that he had not found it. Sabrina insists that she did not enter the room where her mother's bloodied body lay until later, after she had heard Feza driving away in her car. She backs her version with the claim that she waited inside her own room, ready to slam the door shut and lock it, because she was scared of Feza and what he might do to her and Tatum, especially after his suggestion that he tie her up in order to make the scene resemble robbery rather than pre-planned murder.

I ask Feza if he is absolutely sure that his memory is clear on this point: Sabrina came from her own bedroom into Beverley's room after the murder? He nods firmly. She had been inside her bedroom up to the time she entered her mother's room? He nods again. So Sabrina was not peeping around the door watching him commit the murder, as he claimed in court?

'No,' he admits.

Since Feza did not mention during his testimony that he had seen Sabrina feeling her dead mother's wrist for a pulse, this is probably untrue. It was, in fact, Sabrina's version of events that Feza confirmed when he told the judge: 'She said I must go and check her pulse to certify that she is really dead. I went and checked her. She said where is the cellphone. I said I do not know ... She phoned for her mother's cellphone and it alerted and I took it (from) under the bed – I heard it under the bed and I took it.'

My hour with Feza has almost expired. As I stand up to leave, he yells out: 'Wait, wait!' He is waving his hands frantically as if flagging down a passing car. I stare at him in surprise. 'You must help me,' he demands. When I arch my brows, he issues a torrent of swear words and his eyes fill with tears. He is speaking quickly and very loudly, imploring me to find out why Gino, who planned Beverley's murder and 'forced' him to kill the victim, has not been punished. 'If he is free, I must be free also,' he insists. I try to explain that the police cut a deal with Gino and Kello. It seems unfair, I agree, but it happens routinely because public prosecutors would otherwise lack the evidence to convict at least some dangerous criminals.

'Me? Dangerous?' he asks incredulously. 'I am not dangerous.' A watery smile spreads across his face and he flutters his eyelids. 'I agreed to do this thing for the money. I support my younger sister and my mother; now I am here I cannot work and they have nothing. The one who must be in prison is Gino, not me. Or me and Gino but not only me. I am not the one who (made the) plan to kill this lady.'

The guard standing nearby is glaring at me and tapping his watch. I pull my handbag onto my shoulder resolutely and turn to go, waving goodbye to Feza. He opens his mouth and bellows into the holes in the window: 'You do not want to help me because I am black.'

I sit in the car for a while trying to calm down after Feza's outburst and begin the return journey. His accusation of racism implies the worthlessness that he, like millions of his countrymen, feel throughout their lives. I regret not having brought him either the supply of toiletries and magazines I regularly take to Sabrina or something else to indicate some sort of regard. He murdered Beverley in cold blood partly because those whose own lives are poorly valued will themselves devalue life. Not even Sabrina – who indirectly ruined Feza's life just as surely as Beverley ruined hers – feels sorry for him. I recall once mentioning Feza to her and asking if she felt guilty about him. She looked indignant and mumbled something about having offered him a large sum of money to do a job, which he accepted. Tough luck, she implied in the shrug of her shoulders. Feza feels utterly betrayed, according to a warder I talk to on the way out of Middledrift. He believes that, if only he had the wherewithal to engage a good lawyer, he could try to launch an appeal against the justice system for using him to trap Sabrina without giving him a sentence reduction in return.

An hour later, driving past a silvery glimpse of the Buffalo River winding its way to East London, I am greeted by a massive sign, *Jesus Loves You*, on the outskirts of King William's Town. The high street is a collection of tall, once elegant houses alongside an oversupply of nineteenth-century churches. The town's early history is of military conflict between British forces and Xhosa warriors.

Deciding to visit the grave of martyred Steve Biko, I stop in nearby Ginsberg, the township where he was born. His tragic death on 12 September 1977 at the age of 30 has just been commemorated all over the country, particularly in the Eastern Cape. Biko's achievement was extraordinary despite his short life. He spread the powerful idea that no one can make you feel inferior without your consent. Like Nelson Mandela, he was consistently free of hatred, bitterness and resentment, often saying with a laugh that these feelings took up too much time and energy. He believed, like Mandela and Martin Luther King, in the liberation of the oppressor as well as the oppressed.

Fresh wreaths cover Biko's grave. He is remembered as an outstandingly courageous man, who never missed an opportunity to confront apartheid head-on. He wrote about the many encounters – often violent – he had with policemen and prison guards, in which he tried unfailingly to engage them as human beings. In the end, he fought bravely for his life against men whose dehumanised condition made them more dangerous and unpredictable than wild animals. Even the medical doctors who should have treated him for wounds inflicted in a terrible beating by police chose instead to collude with the state to cover up the cause of his death, which was brain damage. I've often wondered about the source of courage: are we born with it as surely as we inherit our brown eyes? Or do we acquire it a bit at a time, day by day, by confronting our fears? If Sabrina had conquered her fear of lifelong domination by Beverley and found the courage to call her mother's bluff, she might have found a way to negotiate Beverley's twisted love without resorting to violence.

The road winds through land scarred by erosion and stripped by drought of everything except thorn scrub. Here and there are hardy goats searching for stems and aloes flowering unexpectedly in the baked red earth. Mountains rise high and then melt into hazy horizons as the sky becomes overcast. White-faced huts cling to the slopes. Occasionally, there are cheerful people in dusty clothing waving from the roadside.

On the journey back to East London, I assess the interview with Feza. It seems that he lied to the court when he said Sabrina had watched him murder her mother. It seems, too, that Sabrina has been substantially if not wholly truthful in her account to me of the murder itself. My meeting with Feza has in no way strengthened the charge of psychopathy made against Sabrina by the state prosecutor and the psychologist.

Even if it is true that she felt for her mother's pulse, crying, and that she located Beverley's phone in the manner described by Feza, it would prove that she wanted her mother dead, not that she was a psychopath. According to Sabrina's version as related to the judge and subsequently to me, she saw her mother's body only after Feza had gone, when the full horror of what she had done began to sink in. Sabrina claims that she immediately telephoned the emergency services – despite having promised Feza that she would wait ten minutes to give him time to escape before she called for help – in the desperate hope that Beverley might be resuscitated.

In East London, driving along Settlers Way onto the bridge over the Buffalo River which was renamed by Nelson Mandela in honour of Biko in 1997, I decide to go shopping for more toiletries for Sabrina. The supplies I have brought from Johannesburg seem mean now that I have heard in a phone call from the Cape film-maker that Sabrina has no visitors apart from the two of us. Hesitating in front of a shelf full of hair dyes, which she has asked me to bring her in various letters, I consider the frivolity and conclude that it is important to preserve my professional distance by taking her only essential items and reading matter. An hour later, though, I feel mean again at having rejected her request for hair dyes when she has so few pleasures.

When I enter the visitors' room to see her, Sabrina is already standing in one of the booths waiting for me. The trolley bearing items for purchase by visitors is parked immediately behind her. Both she and the shopkeeper are looking tense. Sabrina barely greets me before asking me to buy stuff for her from the trolley. The other woman keeps glancing at her watch and I assume – since it is nearly 2.00, the visiting deadline – that the shopkeeper is agitating to close up. 'Can I have smokes?' Sabrina asks tersely. Sure, I say. 'A carton?' I nod. The two women exchange glances and the shopkeeper says, 'There are only three cartons left: can she have them all?' I shrug: why not? The list grows. Coffee, tea, sugar, biscuits. I give R400 to a warder who is now standing beside me, her hand held out to receive the cash in this vulgar transfer of resources. I don't mind paying, however. I don't blame Sabrina for trying by all possible means to make her stay in prison more bearable.

We talk about her life in prison. 'The hardest thing is not having my daughter with me,' she says. 'I will never get used to that. But you get used to everything else. There are 24 girls in my cell. I am the only white, there are five coloureds and the rest are blacks. Some speak English, some Afrikaans and we all speak Xhosa. I have had a lesbian relationship, although I am back to preferring men now, and six others in my cell are involved sexually with each other.'

She explains that their first chore every morning is to polish the cement floor of the cell. 'If it doesn't shine, our TV is taken away. That is the highlight of our lives, television, which we have only for a week every three weeks. There are two toilets and one shower. I miss having a bath. We have flasks to keep coffee or tea hot in the cell – if we're punished, the flasks are taken away.

'We have breakfast at 7.00, lunch at 11.00 and supper at 2.00 in the afternoon. Then we are locked up at 3.00. In the last few weeks, we have eaten supper and lunch together at 12.00 because there is a staff shortage or they are having meetings. We go into the dining room and put our food into a plastic dish. Then we eat it with a plastic spoon, which we must supply ourselves. We're often searched for kitchen spoons, which disappear all the time. We are issued with toilet paper, soap, a face cloth, toothbrush and toothpaste, sanitary pads, prison clothes and bedding. That's all. Anything else must come from outside or be bought for you with your own money.

'The girls in my cell don't have money. They might get a bit when someone visits them but that doesn't happen much. They are all poor. I get hardly any visitors. I see my dad once in the second week of every month. I used to see him every fortnight but now he's doing other stuff to do with his parole so he can't see me more at the moment. I see my daughter maybe once every six months.'

Sabrina says that when she first came to Fort Glamorgan she was studying a course called Life Orientation, which she did not find stimulating. When she left school, she recalls, she had wanted to become an accountant. 'I got accepted at the University of the Free State but my mom and my brothers decided it was too far from home for me to go. They said they could not keep an eye on me there so I couldn't go.' Sabrina reminds me of a conversation she and I had soon after I met her, in which we discussed her need for more psychotherapy than was available through prison channels. It occurred to me at the time that studying psychology might be the next best thing to prolonged psychoanalysis, perhaps giving her a second chance to grow up. 'After you suggested I do psychology,' she continues, 'I applied for it and I've just started the course. It's very interesting, so thanks for that.'

She says she is excited at the prospect of Louis leaving Fort Glamorgan, not least because she is hoping that he will adopt Tatum. When I tell her I doubt that the state will give him custody of the child, she looks upset but agrees. 'I don't think so either. He's been punished and I have forgiven him because I love him so much but I don't think society has forgiven him. The way I see it, he was just doing his job. It was all in the line of duty. He was doing what he thought he was meant to do. The people in East London – whites – all used to say he was the best cop. But seeing my daughter is not white, and my dad shot all those blacks, well ...' She shrugs, looking helpless.

'My brothers were so angry with me not only for killing my mother but for saying in court that my family was racist. I think they reacted that way because they don't know what it means to be racist; they don't realise it applies to them because they don't see anything wrong in the way they treat blacks. All their friends are the same; all the whites in South Africa are the same way so they think it's okay.'

Sabrina cites the fact that her brothers approved of the murders her father committed as proof of their racism. 'They were all in favour of him killing blacks, same as most whites in East London were. Now, if they talk to journalists, they might say, no, they disapproved of Louis but that wasn't true at the time.

'You'd think my mother knew she was being racist when she paid Shanine much less to do a computer job than she would have given a white person for the same work. But when I asked her about this because Shanine was my friend she said, no, it wasn't racist – she was giving a coloured an opportunity. If she had to pay her the same salary, she would definitely employ a white instead, so what did Shanine want?

'Shanine became my sister, my best, best friend but Mom didn't approve at all. We worked in the same office but we weren't allowed to sit together. We had to stay at our own desks. So we used to talk for hours on our office computers. Whenever I could, I used to sneak out and visit Shanine. Her mom and dad treated me like one of their own children. I loved them all so much. I will always be a part of that family – if they will still have me.

'But it wasn't all about racism in Mom's case. Even when I was a little girl at junior school I was allowed friends to visit me but I wasn't allowed to visit or sleep out, even though they were all white kids. I think my mother felt threatened and I guess it was a problem she had thinking she was going to lose me. I don't know why but that is how she was.

'The coloureds accepted me for me, not for what I had or what my surname was. Van Schoor may have been a great surname because it came from someone the whole of East London's and Queenstown's whites admired – my father, Louis – although Mom thought people looked up to the name because of her. There are certain standards you had to have for the white people in Queenstown to approve of you: if you were thin, if you were beautiful or if you had money. And you had to hate blacks and coloureds. That is where I drew the line. Gladys was mine and I wouldn't hate her. I was taken in by blacks and coloureds and loved by them, more than by my family. I wouldn't change it even if I could because you saw the precious baby they gave me. Even though my whole family has abandoned me, I cannot say I did wrong to mix with blacks and coloureds.'

*

One member of the maternal family who has not turned her back on Sabrina is Beverley's sister Jenny. I find her in a remote suburb of East London called Sunrise-on-Sea. Arranging to visit her involves taking a lot of directions the evening before from her husband, who sounds suspicious and resentful of the interview to which she has agreed.

Jenny is a meek woman. She wears old clothes: a shapeless green pullover, baggy pants and scuffed sandals. Her long, dark hair, streaked with grey, hangs limply around her tired face. Her skin is weather-worn, her hands cracked from physical work. She tells me she loves to knit, earning a little income from making baby and doll's clothes for sale to neighbours.

We talk in my car on a Sunday morning because her husband is showering in their tiny bed-sit. They live in a corner of Jenny's half-brother's house, which is still under construction after ten years or more, according to a neighbour. Jenny is a year younger than Beverley, whom she describes as 'a super person on the surface'. Having lived and worked with Beverley and Sabrina for eight months in 2000, she says she was often upset at the way Beverley treated her daughter. 'She never spoke to her sons the way she talked to Sabrina, so harshly and crudely. She would just turn around and slap Sabrina across the face. Once, Sabrina came running to me and said, "I wish she was dead." I hugged her and told her, "No, you don't mean that."

'Bev hated Sabrina's coloured friends. As far as I was concerned, Sabrina was at a multiracial school so what did her mother expect? I think if Bev hadn't pushed so hard over the friends, all this might never have happened. Sabrina had to be chaperoned everywhere, often by me. Her mother would hardly even allow her to go shopping by herself.

'Bev pushed hard about everything, though. When you worked for her, as I did, she didn't have the decency to take you aside and tick you off on your own. When Bev was going on a diet, we all had to go on a diet. I remember her looking at me in a funny way when my skirt was two sizes too big because I was the only one who had lost weight. She didn't like that. It was hard to please her.

'When I first moved into Bev's home in Queenstown to help her in her businesses and try to make some money because we were having a hard time in East London, she promised me a salary of R4 000. But once she had deducted board and lodging – which had never been mentioned – I only had R1 000 left. She told me that Sabrina didn't get a salary because she was given everything she needed. The car Sabrina drove was not actually hers: it belonged to her mother. So although Sabrina was always saying she wanted to leave home, Bev wouldn't let her go. She kept her there under her control by making sure Sabrina had no independence. I don't think Sabrina hated her mother. I think she had to get away from her and she didn't know how to do it without a job or a car or anything to her name.'

Jenny heard about her sister's murder from one of her neighbours twelve hours after it had happened. She also learnt of Sabrina's arrest on the grapevine. 'Nobody in the family bothered to tell me. Bev and the boys considered themselves a rank higher than us. If you didn't have everything they had, the jewellery and the money, they looked down on you. Not Sabrina; she always tried to stay in touch. Lester, Allister and Shane used to come to East London regularly and stop for ice creams at a shop a few hundred metres from where I lived but they never ever called in to see me.

'After I went to work for Bev but found I couldn't stand the bickering, fighting and Bev's nagging any more and left Queenstown, I told Sabrina that if she ever needed a friend, someone to talk to, she could always come to me. After the murder, I said to my husband, "Why don't we adopt her, seeing we have no children?" But he is still very upset about it all; that a daughter could kill her own mother.'

Throughout our meeting, Jenny keeps wiping her eyes. Blaming her mascara for the tears, she goes into the house to fetch tissues. When the fresh supply runs out, she opens the car door to go inside for more. I follow in order to see photographs of Sabrina as a child. As we walk up the front steps, she tells me: 'Sabrina called me from prison the other day. She told me she was very sorry for what she had done and asked me to visit her. I'd like to but I don't have any transport to get there.'

Jenny seems nervous in the room she shares with her husband, glancing around for him and muttering that he seems to have disappeared. A puppy sprawled on the bed senses her anxiety and starts to whine. Squeezing around a double bed and a couple of dressers, one with a two-plate cooker on top, I sit on a collapsed armchair to look at the photo albums. Jenny points to a picture of Beverley in uniform, newly qualified as a nurse, looking proud, stout and severe; not the sort of person you would want to find at your hospital bedside.

I stare at Beverley's steely expression for so long that Jenny comments, 'She looks like a Nazi, doesn't she?' There is certainly something very hard in Beverley's eyes; a look of unfathomable anger or disappointment. Perhaps it is the long shadow cast by ancestors who, arriving traumatised, guilty or inadequate from beleaguered circumstances in Europe, battled to hack new meaning out of their frontier farms or gold-rush aspirations while learning to disregard the suffering of others.

One photograph stays in my mind; of Sabrina aged about seven, wearing a pretty white dress with puffed sleeves. She is standing on top of some steps, the sun on her golden hair, looking tentative, as if not quite sure what to make of the camera. A serious child? 'She was quite serious but sweet-natured,' says Jenny. 'I never saw anything wrong with her although she used to talk a lot, such a lot, as if nobody ever listened to her.'

On the way back to my car, I ask Jenny about her childhood.

It was difficult, she says hesitantly. Her mother was 'terribly hurt' by life in general and her husband in particular, who lived with his girlfriend and wife simultaneously for a number of years. 'It always annoys me that Bev used to say my mom had a drinking problem,' she adds with sudden vehemence. 'She drank, yes, but she always got up in the morning and did what she had to do. And she looked after Sabrina very well.'

Driving away, I stop to ask one of Jenny's neighbours for directions to the airport. We chat briefly, long enough for her to confirm that I have 'come about the murder' – even though it is well over two years since Beverley's death.

The neighbour seems to know that Beverley lived in fear of Louis' fists, to the point of hospitalisation on more than one occasion. Later, it was Danie Nel, the senior police officer Beverley dated in Queenstown, who terrorised her. Domestic violence is rife in South Africa, where a woman is killed by her intimate partner every six hours, according to a recent survey. It is just one form of brutality among many, including rape on an unprecedented scale, armed robberies and car hijackings, that regularly claim lives. Drunk driving, an act of violence in itself, is commonplace.

The way in which violence and lawlessness were systematically used for political gain by both sides in the struggle has made antisocial and brutal responses the norm in South African society. Like the motives of the IRA in Northern Ireland, it is sometimes hard to separate the politicisation of crime from the criminalisation of politics.

Crime has always tormented South Africans, however. Says author-journalist Jonny Steinberg, currently researching the subject at the Centre for the Study of Violence and Reconciliation in Johannesburg: 'Crime, and the fear of crime, is as old as South Africa itself ... our preoccupation with crime is testimony to how this country was stitched together with violence, to how we worry that malevolence is our most abiding pedigree. Fear in this country is saturated with politics; it is the product of generations of estrangement between races, classes and individuals. We are preoccupied with revenge; we worry that it will burst its walls.'

Given how many South Africans greeted democracy homeless, hungry and jobless, says Steinberg, it is extraordinary that the country's formal institutions are stable and its polity reasonably settled. 'Could it be, though, that the rage so many expected found expression after all, not in the formal arenas of politics but in the underworld of crime?' he asks.

*

Fort Glamorgan is close to the airport and I have a little time to spare so I drive into the prison and board the bus that is about to depart for the inner gates. I walk across to the men's section, where the warders are sucking green lollipops, to talk to Louis. Again, he refuses to discuss his life and crimes. He does not want to talk about his intentions regarding Tatum or where he will live once freed. He says he has 'frozen all discussion' about his family until he is out of prison. 'I can't make any decisions in here,' he says irritably. He is willing to tell me how frustrated he has become with Sabrina, though. 'I have tried to teach her by sharing my experiences of prison life but she is very stubborn and seems determined to make her own mistakes,' he grumbles.

Maybe this is because she was never allowed to grow up?

'Ja, maybe.'

Beverley buried herself in her work and her pursuit of material things in order to earn the respect of outsiders while neglecting the needs of her own child. Sabrina became a desperately insecure attention-seeker. Her main source of comfort, Gladys, was treated with a mixture of indifference and disdain by Beverley. Sabrina could not have failed to notice that her white mother did not really like her black mother. Her anger with Beverley grew and grew.

However, according to several people who knew her well, Beverley was herself insecure, badly needing to be needed. According to an independent psychologist with whom I discussed the mother-daughter relationship, Beverley may have systematically alienated her daughter because she suffered from a common inferiority principle which makes the parent believe that, once the child no longer needs her, she will be redundant. To protect her ego from acknowledging this basic fear of redundancy, Beverley may have tried everything in her power to control and keep Sabrina dependent. Sabrina, in her natural maturation process, rebelled against Beverley's domination, partly by befriending mixed-race and black people in defiance of Beverley's racist taboos and partly by adopting a lifestyle that was unacceptable to the parent who was trying to impose competing social values.

International case studies show that the most common single trigger for matricide among children is the parent objecting to the child's romantic liaisons. Add to this the bleak history and still bleaker prognosis of Sabrina's family relationships and a crisis was undoubtedly looming years before Beverley's murder.

While a child does not necessarily need two good parents in order to develop into a healthy adult, it does need one. Sabrina was cursed with not one but two inadequate adults to set her standards and boundaries. It is hard to imagine a worse role model than Louis. Beverley's intolerance of Sabrina's preference for disreputable bars where she drank far too much and slept with coloureds fuelled the mutual anger of mother and daughter against a backdrop of lifelong estrangement.

Having looked at Beverley's murder from every possible angle, I am convinced that Sabrina's motive for matricide was the fear of losing Tatum. The more threatened Beverley felt by Sabrina's rebellion and the more embarrassing Sabrina's conduct became to her mother in bigoted Queenstown, the more Beverley resorted to psychological blackmail in order to manipulate her daughter. Once her tactics included the threat to deprive Sabrina of baby Tatum, their relationship could only end in disaster.

Louis shrugs as I outline this scenario. 'Bev was a bitch,' he states flatly. He is not a good listener and has other thoughts on his mind. He thinks Sabrina must forget about the past and focus on her future, as he has done. In particular, she must stay out of trouble in prison. He says he believes the warders resent the fact that Sabrina mixes so easily across the racial divide, she having asked to share a cell with coloureds and blacks. 'They are happier when the lines are drawn,' he claims. 'Then they can play one off against the other. I will never understand them. They've always got an ulterior motive.'

'They' and 'them' refer to black people; 'the other' as far as white South Africans are concerned. Is Louis saying that Sabrina is an outcast even in prison, ironically on the basis of race despite being virtually colour-blind herself? 'She might not see it like that but that's what I hear when she describes all the fights she gets into, not only with warders but also with the prisoners in her cell,' replies Louis. 'There is almost always a racial issue involved.'

Here is further confirmation of the tragic extent of Sabrina's alienation, assuming Louis is to be believed (which, on the subject of his daughter, he probably is). A few months away from her 25th birthday, Sabrina has grown up without the most basic of human rights: her mother's love and approval. She has lived in the horrible shadow of an infamous father whose racist attacks and murders may have provided the bleak inspiration for her attempt by all possible means, including acute promiscuity, to atone for his sins, in the process of which she turned Beverley's half of her family, including her three brothers, against her. She has consigned herself to prison for the remainder of her youth by committing matricide, the motive for which she does not fully understand. Largely as a result of the love she received from her black surrogate mother, she has broken with the tradition of racism in her family, only to be denied acceptance by black and coloured people once she lives among them in prison. And, worst of all, she has virtually lost the daughter she adores.

A few weeks after I saw Louis van Schoor in prison for the last time, he was released on parole from Fort Glamorgan. A small contingent of media, mainly Eastern Cape journalists, were waiting to meet him at 9.00am on October 29, 2004, in the visitors' reception area at the perimeter gates. A prison van drew up and offloaded a folded trestle table. A warder pulled a crumpled white linen cloth from under his arm and threw it over the table. Shortly afterwards, Louis, aged 53, looking robust and tanned from working in the prison's vegetable patch, stepped out of an unmarked car and strode into the building.

'How are you feeling, Louis?'

'Butterflies,' he replies.

Wearing new blue jeans and a bright red shirt, he looks supremely confident. There to welcome him with a lingering kiss, her arms wrapped around his neck, is his tall blonde fiancée, 38-year-old Eunice de Kock, a lawyer who giggles like a nervous teenager. She is dolled up for the occasion in a charcoal pinstriped suit, sheer black stockings with perfectly straight seams, blue toenails and stiletto sandals.

The head of the prison and the media liaison representative

for Correctional Services, both black women, sit on either side of Louis at the table set up for the occasion. His former jailers tell reporters that he is 'a natural leader' who became a born-again Christian in prison. No one among the watching warders can remember anything like the press conference taking place in Louis' honour: most departing prisoners are intent on anonymity, says one. The local journalists, all white, greet Van Schoor like the apartheid hero he became as the country's most prolific mass killer of black people. 'When are you getting married, Louis?' they shout. 'What would you like to eat for your first meal as a free man?'

Louis reads out his press statement. 'I am happy that the time has come to join society again,' he says. Speaking in a deep, clear voice, he hopes the public will forget about his past and 'not judge me on it but judge me on my future'. He says he will not go back to work in the security field because he wants to farm. Eunice has earlier told the reporters that her family has a farm near Clanwilliam in Namaqualand, where she hopes to settle with her new husband.

Survivors of his three-year shooting spree and relatives of his victims, who were mostly poor and uneducated, are not there to protest at Louis van Schoor's freedom, possibly because they are unaware of the news. There is nothing in the *Daily Dispatch* that morning about the release of East London's most infamous prisoner after serving only 12 of his 20-year sentence thanks to a sentence reduction issued to all convicts by Nelson Mandela when he was president. Only when prompted does Van Schoor express sorrow to the relatives of his victims. He says he tried to contact them four years earlier through a radio programme during which he apologised 'for any of my actions which caused them inconvenience or hurt'.

Saying he will miss Sabrina once out of jail, Louis promises to look after her little daughter Tatum. 'I saw Sabrina on Wednesday. She's very excited for me but just because I am gone the bond between us won't be broken. We're still a family. We'll still keep in touch.' He will not confirm that he intends to adopt his granddaughter.

After 'addressing the media', as he puts it, Louis goes to court to sign agreement to his parole conditions, which confine him to the magisterial district of East London for the time being, as well as preventing him from discussing either his trial or his experiences at Fort Glamorgan. Then he suggests a meeting to discuss his future at – of all places – the Wimpy Bar on East London's Esplanade. Incredibly, he chooses the very restaurant where in June 1988 he shot dead teenager Liefie Peters and wounded his friend, John Swartbooi.

White East Londoners eating at the Wimpy either stare or smile at Louis. Describing his plans to write a book about his life to 'set the record straight', Van Schoor says he is neither a mass murderer nor a serial killer but a 'crime fighter'. He supports this claim by explaining defiantly: 'I called the police after each encounter.' Despite claiming that his prison experiences have convinced him of the irrelevance of racial difference, that 'people are people', nothing seems to have changed in Louis van Schoor's coldly calculating view of his criminal record.

Denying that his killings were motivated by bloodlust or racism, he insists he was just doing his job as he thought right at the time. 'It was nothing to do with race. I was purely protecting people's property,' he says. Louis refers to his multiple murders as 'incidents', saying he was the product of his society, his police training and his paramilitary experiences in South Africa's border wars during the 1970s.

So how many people did he shoot?

'I don't remember. I don't really know.'

How does one shoot a single person, never mind scores?

'I can't say it is easy, but I suppose the time I spent in the police made me used to shooting and killing,' is his reply. In fact, Louis spent his police years as a dog handler with scant scope for shooting and killing. Although he claims to have been conscripted into military duty on the borders of Namibia and Angola, his second wife Beverley told friends at the time that he had volunteered for service. During the investigation conducted by *Daily Dispatch* journalist Patrick Goodenough into Van Schoor's murders, the reporter learned that Louis had tried unsuccessfully to rejoin the police force after leaving his job in the dog unit and failing to make a go of civilian life. Why he was unacceptable even among the ranks of the brutalised apartheid police has never been revealed.

Does he recall the faces of any of his victims?

'None. I don't remember faces. I remember some events, sequences of things.'

Is he sorry?

'In 2000 because of the rehabilitation and progress I felt on my side, and in the light of so much bad publicity and so on, I made an effort to contact the victims, their families. We couldn't do it. I then went to the media and made a public apology, rightly or wrongly. I apologised for the pain, suffering my actions caused them. I meant this sincerely. There was a huge public response (from whites) but to this day I've had no contact with them (victims' families and survivors).'

It was as a result of this broadcast that Louis' fiancée Eunice first wrote to him. Letters became phone calls and then a visit on his birthday turned the friendship into love, followed by a marriage proposal. They were allowed contact visits in prison, he says.

Having fudged the question of whether he intends to adopt his granddaughter Tatum during his prison press conference a few hours earlier, Louis finally decides to deal with it. He says he hopes to get to know the child but will not try to take her away from her foster home. 'Let her stay where she is happy and secure,' he announces magnanimously.

Louis says he is pleased not to have had any contact since his arrest with Patrick Goodenough, the young *Daily Dispatch* reporter whose tenacity, despite the obstruction of his editors, eventually forced the apartheid state to charge Van Schoor with multiple murder. Having tried unsuccessfully over the months to locate Goodenough myself, I am pleased to get an unexpected message from him in the United States, where he now lives. The email, dated a few days after Louis' release, refers to an article I had written in *The Guardian* of London and offers to contribute his version of the events that led to Louis' trial and imprisonment.

I write back, telling him I have almost finished my book and adding: 'I couldn't believe how feeble the *Daily Dispatch* was in covering Louis' release last weekend – not even an editorial! He came out a folk hero ...'

Goodenough replies: 'Actually, I'm not surprised at all. My years at the *Dispatch* ... were marked by frequent battles with editors to get contentious stories published, and the Louis story was only the first (hit squads, homeland coup plots, racist murders, seriously corrupt crooks with friends at the highest levels of government ...)'

Noting that '... it doesn't sound as though VS has done too much soul-searching in prison ...', Patrick Goodenough guesses that it was Louis who chose the Esplanade Wimpy as the venue for his first interview after his release. 'He'd very likely have found it amusing to talk to a reporter about, oh, three feet away from where he shot to death Liefie Peters,' he wrote.

What is equally clear, I told him in response, is that many of the whites of East London continue to see no reason to distance themselves from Louis van Schoor, a blatant symbol of apartheid. Only one of the ten I spoke to on the day of his release condemned his actions and parole. Perhaps they are still unable to understand that he was their creation; that he was pandering to their wishes when he shot so many people in the name of crime prevention. Those who encouraged Louis van Schoor to kill would doubtless agree that a crime as serious as murder – never mind 39 such crimes – should have strong emotions behind it. How, then, do they feel indifferent to what Louis did and not even notice their own culpability in his actions? And how do they justify the virtually equal sentences given to Louis and Sabrina: 39 blacks v one mother. Are we to assume that whites' lives are more valuable, or that Sabrina's crime was *so* heinous?

Chapter Nine

The youngest Van Schoor faces the same challenge as her country: how to overcome a terrible history. Her grandfather is a mass murderer; her mother killed Tatum's grandmother. The community which shaped her family still has a long way to go in overcoming the racist attitudes that gave rise not only to Louis' multiple murders but to the death of Beverley as well. While Tatum is not white and not responsible for the sins of her elders, she is a child of South Africa and will have to construct her future from the devastation of the past.

I am once again in East London, this time to visit Tatum as well as Sabrina. Waking before dawn, I push back the curtains of the vast window of my room at Dolphin View Lodge and watch the sun rise beneath thick clouds over a restless sea. After a while, the clouds drift apart and the morning light is briefly blinding on the horizon. A glossy starling tiptoes along the window ledge; a ship is steaming across the blue.

Tatum lives with her foster mother Lynne Hall in Molteno, a small mountain hamlet in a region known as the Stormberg. It is a three-and-a-half-hour drive from East London via Queenstown, where I have arranged to meet Lynne and follow her home. The road is empty on a Saturday morning. Arriving in Queenstown with time to spare, I visit Justina to say hello and goodbye on my last research trip.

She tells me her hospitality business is doing so well that she plans to expand Longview Lodge. She worries that the neighbour living opposite, a white woman who has to date literally turned her back whenever Justina has tried to approach her, might withhold the permission that is required for building approval. 'She is my only hostile neighbour now,' explains Justina. 'When I first moved in with my family, she put up a garden screen to block her view of my house and mine of hers. The staff working for her told me that's why she put up the barrier – because we were blacks. The white policeman living next door to me eventually made friends after I invited him in to watch rugby on my TV once when his wasn't working. And the woman on the other side, also white, has a B&B and is in the same business as me so we have always cooperated with each other.'

We talk for a while about prejudice and intolerance. There are not many ideas more damaging than the belief by individuals or groups that they alone know how to live, what to do or who to be. It is an idea that abounds among white South Africans even ten years after they relinquished political power. The same illusion in the form of intolerance, especially of criticism, is becoming more and more evident among the country's new black elite, says Justina, even though they know only too well from their own lives under apartheid how ruinously arrogant it is to believe that since you alone are right, others cannot be right if they disagree. 'The black elite are becoming just like the whites; superior and indifferent to the problems of others less fortunate than them. It's unbelievable,' says Justina. 'I pray they won't forget that a rich person is only a poor person with money or that a white person is only a black with a different skin colour.'

Lynne Hall arrives at the appointed time at Whistle Stop, a diner attached to a service station on Cathcart Road. Trailing slowly behind her foster mother is Tatum, her enormous brown eyes exploring my face. She is a pretty child in a yellow dress with a mop of soft black curls and very long legs. We get back into our cars and drive through the spectacular scenery of the Penhoek Pass into a region renowned for sheep farming. It is an area, as the name Stormberg implies, that is known for extreme weather but also for the profusion of yellow flowers that suddenly spring up at the end of winter, filling the valleys with wild beauty and the hillsides with fragrance on days when the wind is warm.

As we approach Molteno, clouds of white butterflies float over the road not far from the site of an epic clash between the British and the Boers. It is not the first time I have travelled through this lonely landscape to Lynne Hall's home. I came uninvited several months earlier with Cherie van Heerden, Sabrina's schoolfriend and Tatum's godmother. After hearing from the Cape film-maker that Lynne was implacably opposed to talking to journalists or allowing them to see Tatum, I had decided that I must meet the child in her new surroundings, if only for a brief encounter.

It was unthinkable to write a book about the Van Schoor family without seeing Tatum, whose future, in view of her past, remained tantalisingly uncertain. Not wishing to contact Lynne and be told directly that I was not welcome, I suggested to Cherie by phone from Johannesburg that we drive together to Molteno. I knew she felt guilty about not seeing her godchild and calculated that she would be tempted to visit Tatum with me. I told her the truth about my dilemma and motive from the outset, promising to reveal my deception at the earliest opportunity once we were in Lynne's family's midst. Cherie was initially dubious, understandably, and I suggested she think it over.

She agreed quite readily, though, explaining how both her boyfriend and her father had urged her 'not to get involved', whereas her mother understood the attachment she felt to Sabrina's child, whose birth she had attended. It was Cherie who had told me, months earlier, how sad she had felt when Tatum was born. Beverley was crying bitterly once she realised that the baby was dark-skinned, having inherited the father's colouring rather than Sabrina's, Cherie recalled. 'Tatum came out blue-black and wriggling weirdly,' she said. 'I remember the doctor going up to Bev to comfort her. He told her the baby would get lighter after a while.'

That the attending doctor, Fanwell Chimsoro – a Ghanaian-born gynaecologist who is blacker than the darkest South African – felt pity for Beverley in these crushing circumstances is an extraordinary testament to his magnanimity and compassion. That he had become over the years the physician of choice of so many of the white women of Queenstown in the most intimate aspect of their health care is one of the bizarre contradictions of life in South Africa. For many years the only professional black person in Queenstown, Dr Chimsoro's acceptance among diehards proves at least that class criteria can on occasion triumph over race even in the least hospitable circumstances.

Molteno has a few wide, dusty streets, police and railway stations, a hotel, several shops, a takeaway food outlet and two enormous churches – one of them Dutch Reformed and the other Wesleyan Methodist – as well as a smaller Anglican chapel. Chickens peck nervously along the pavements of the main street. The town has no notable sons that anyone can think of but its most famous stepson, according to some residents, is William Plomer, a British writer who spent his formative years there. He wrote of Molteno: 'Everybody knew everybody else's business, and small scandals took on colossal proportions; Europe seemed a conception as remote and unreal as heaven or hell; and the cats, asleep on the windowsills or hearth-rugs, looked as tranquil and detached as so many images of Buddha.'

The faded bungalow where Lynne Hall lives, with its long shady veranda and peeling tin roof, is not only in urgent need of a coat of paint but is, on closer inspection, falling to bits. The front door wobbles on loose hinges as Tatum rushes out of the house and onto the grass in front of our parked car. I am hoping to remain incognito as long as possible on that occasion, hovering at the wheel while Cherie steps out into the sunshine to greet her little goddaughter. Lynne is behind the child with her two adult daughters alongside, all grinning broadly as Tatum dances around Cherie. When she refers to her godmother as her stepmother by mistake, we all laugh. Tatum twirls around shyly, her thumb in her mouth, head cocked to one side beguilingly; a charming child dressed entirely in pink.

It is a Saturday and Lynne is busy preparing Sunday lunch. 'We go to church so early that I have to cook today for tomorrow,' she explains. We traipse into the kitchen, Cherie and I sitting on the floor with Tatum as she begins to unpack a large bag of presents brought by Cherie. Once over the initial caution she felt about connecting with her coloured godchild, Cherie has flung herself joyously into her new role as aunty to this most controversial of Queenstown's children. She strokes Tatum's hair, admires her new shoes, helps her draw pictures for me to take to 'Beena', as Tatum calls her birth mother. I watch, waiting for the opportunity to reveal my identity and thinking that, of all the characters I have interviewed, Cherie is the only one who seems metaphorically to have grown during the two years I have known her, presumably as a result of her private exploration of the moral dilemmas surrounding Beverley's murder. Not that Cherie isn't bigoted: her description of Tatum's birth included her dismay on noticing that the newborn had a 'flattie', an insulting reference to the shape of the baby's nose.

Lynne is delighted at Cherie's visit and says so repeatedly. Her daughters, 24-year-old Kelly and 21-year-old Christine, gush over Tatum's gifts and tell Cherie endearing stories about their new sister. Tatum smiles self-consciously at Cherie whenever her name is mentioned and folds the wrapping paper carefully after opening each of her presents.

A tidy little girl?

'Oh, no,' says Lynne. 'She's just showing off, aren't you, Tatum?'

Lynne's eyes are squarely on me now. The child has run to her mother's side to show Lynne a new book as she stirs tomorrow's stroganoff. She glances down, cooing perfunctorily, and then stares straight back at me. 'And where do you fit in?' she asks finally.

Cherie freezes. I can see her blushing in my peripheral vision as I answer.

'So you tricked your way in,' says Lynne.

I am half off the floor by now, feeling sure she is about to ask me to leave and explaining hurriedly that it was entirely my idea to come uninvited; nothing to do with Cherie. Lynne continues to stare at me as I stand up but then a sudden smile spreads across her face. 'Actually, your timing is very good,' she says. 'If you had pitched up a few months ago I'd have been very annoyed. But lately I've been thinking that it's maybe time that I got to know everything about this Van Schoor family.'

I tell her jokingly that she is looking at the world expert on the Van Schoors. The tension vanishes. Tatum has left the room and Lynne starts to question me closely. I tell her the truth as I see it. No, Beverley was not the genteel woman her public image suggested. No, Beverley was not wealthy: Sabrina's brothers took over the main business she started and then cut her out of the profit chain. No, Sabrina cannot identify Tatum's father with any accuracy.

We talk and talk. Lynne describes the arrival of 18-month-old Tatum in Molteno. It was Chantelle, Sabrina's sister-in-law, who brought the child from Queenstown a fortnight after Sabrina's arrest. The large vehicle she was driving was piled high with Tatum's belongings stuffed into seven packing crates. 'There was nothing that tiny girl lacked,' recalls Lynne. 'Chantelle gave me so many instructions about what Tatum ate, the brand of yoghurt and so forth, and how to look after her. She said Beverley was always very particular about Tatum's routine. Poor Chantelle was in such a panic trying to remember to tell me everything. Kelly, Chrissie and I were here together to welcome Tatum into our family and, when Chantelle left, we went a bit silly, playing with all the toys, throwing her things around like children ourselves. We were so overwhelmed at the amount of stuff that had been bought for one baby.'

Lynne says: 'Tatum was very ill with pneumonia when Chantelle dropped her off. She was so sick. The doctor told me he had the impression that she had lost the will to live, as small as she was; she was that traumatised. She had been with her uncle Lester and his wife since Sabrina's arrest but they had no children of their own then and they couldn't cope.

'The social worker in Queenstown warned me that the baby was very ill. She said that one of the reasons she chose a foster home in Molteno was because we have a very good doctor and hospital here. I took Tatum straight to the doctor and he watched her closely for the first few days. We hardly left her side. Then she started to get stronger and take an interest in us.

'I just took one look at her when she was first put in my arms and decided to make her my own. I don't think much about her history and all that stuff. I think of her in exactly the same way as I did Kelly and Chrissie. If I treat her like my own, she will respond like my own. It was supposed to be a temporary (social welfare) placement and we didn't know how long she would be staying but we all loved her from the word go. And, basically, she's never looked back. A psychologist told me that the development of a child's personality depends more on its experiences than on genetics. This child's experiences from 18 months onward are all going to be good, that I can assure you.'

Although she struggles financially and gets the most modest of cheques from the welfare authorities each month, Lynne says she does not use the maintenance money for the intended purpose but banks the payments in Tatum's name whenever they arrive. 'She was born into wealthier circumstances than I can provide,' she explains, 'and I feel she should inherit some money of her own some day. This isn't going to be much but it will accumulate. I can manage very well without it.' One of her daughters asks coyly what she and her sister will inherit. Lynne smiles and puts her arm around the pretty young woman's shoulders. 'You have inherited both a mother and a father who adore you,' she replies gently.

Twice divorced from the same man – who left her for another woman the first time and went insolvent before the second infidelity, leaving her destitute – Lynne nevertheless speaks well of her former husband. Both her daughters live with their remarried father in a nearby town while Lynne claws her way back to liquidity. 'Mine are not the ideal financial circumstances for foster care and I am not the ideal foster mother for a small child,' she admits. 'I'm divorced with grown-up children and really too old to be Tatum's mother ...' She confesses to having had an earlier unsuccessful foster care experience. 'He was a troubled boy several years older than my own girls. Unfortunately, it didn't work out because he interfered with Kelly and Chrissie and we had no choice but to send him back. It was the same social worker who sent us Tatum so she knew the history. She knew how hard we tried to make it work with that boy but it wasn't to be.'

At 47, Lynne is energetic and likeable. She says her parents were 'as racist as everybody else at the time' so she grew up feeling superior to black people. 'But my church has taught me to think differently. I know now that we are all just people.' She says she longs for the day when South Africans accept, as Britons, Dutch and Scandinavians reputedly do, that there are many ways of living, believing and behaving. Lynne being a teacher, we talk about the value of education; the knowledge available in history, literature, anthropology and law which shows that the similarities between cultures are just as deep as the differences. People benefit from variety; it enriches their minds, making them wiser and happier. Equally, as Lynne points out, lack of knowledge makes people prejudiced, fearful of difference, resistant to change.

Tatum is bonding with her godmother, popping in and out of the kitchen busily, her tiny hand held tightly in Cherie's. She is neither black nor white. Or both black and white. A beautiful child. The real beauties in the world are of mixed race. Evolution has only happened because of the vigour of hybrids. Extremes don't work; their limitations eventually destroy them. For that matter, there is no such thing as racial purity. Human pigmentation is neither black nor white but brown. We may have more of it or less of it but we are all just various shades of brown.

Tatum knows Sabrina well and talks a lot about her, says Lynne. 'The first time I took her to see Sabrina I was struck by how close the two of them were. They belong naturally together and you can see it.' Far from feeling threatened by their biological and spiritual connection, Lynne wants to foster it. 'If Tatum feels okay about the Van Schoors as well as about us, she will be whole. You can't change her past or what happened to Sabrina or Beverley or Louis. You can't wish it away or run from it. Much better to give Tatum the knowledge to understand what happened.'

On my second visit to Molteno some months later, Lynne described her most recent visit to Fort Glamorgan with Tatum. 'She was chattering away about Sabrina in the car beforehand. I told her that Sabrina was in jail and she asked: "What is jail?" I told her and when she demanded to know why Sabrina was in jail, I said she should ask Sabrina. Sure enough, it was the first thing she said: "Why are you in jail?" Sabrina replied that she had done something very bad but it was a mistake. Afterwards, Tatum told Kelly and Chrissie and everybody else that Sabrina had done something very bad but it was a mistake. Perhaps next time she sees Sabrina she'll ask about the bad thing she did, and Sabrina will have to tell her. In that way, some of Tatum's knowledge about the Van Schoors will come from me but some will come directly from Sabrina. Gradually, she'll get the whole picture.'

Lynne took Tatum to meet her grandfather Louis in prison, too. 'I only did it once. I didn't like him. My ex-husband knew him in East London and said he was okay but I didn't take to him at all.' The only other person Lynne dislikes in Tatum's biological family is Shaun Ortell, one among several of Sabrina's lovers who, according to Sabrina, could have fathered her child. Shaun has verbally accepted paternity but, since he has been unemployed virtually all his life, he has made no effort to take responsibility for Tatum. 'When he was visited by a TV crew recently, he went on camera saying he loved Tatum so much and was longing to raise her. I don't believe him because he has made absolutely no effort to contact her so far and she is nearly four years old. I hope he doesn't show up, frankly. I don't think I would allow him to tell Tatum he is her dad until he has got to know her and shown that he intends to take fatherhood seriously. She is longing to have a dad. When she particularly likes a man, any man, she'll sometimes ask him, "Will you be my dad?" I don't want her to meet someone she thinks is her real father and then never hear from him again.'

I have been invited to spend the night in Lynne Hall's home. Before supper, she takes me on a tour of Molteno. We drive in her battered Opel through the black township, Nomonde, where several people greet her and Tatum. Lynne, who has lived in Molteno for 12 years and says there are few residents, even on the farms, she does not know by name, responds in foghorn Afrikaans or Xhosa. Tatum is tired, her thumb in her mouth, a doll hugged tightly in the other arm. We drive on to the home of family friends: he is a sheep farmer, totally deaf, while his wife is loud and jolly. Their youngest daughter, Lindy-Lou, is Tatum's best friend, explains Lynne as Tatum tumbles out of the car and a tiny, round blonde child her own age trips towards her. They hug each other, whispering and giggling.

As the evening progresses, the little girls' voices rise steadily above ours. Like her new mother, Tatum's is particularly raucous, one among many ways in which the child is beginning to resemble her foster family rather than her biological one. We watch them playing. They argue a lot. 'All the time,' says Lindy-Lou's mother, who is related to the Van Schoors by marriage. 'They are opposites in every way: ebony and ivory.'

It was because of Lindy-Lou's parents' connection to the Van Schoors that Lynne Hall first heard about Tatum's need for a foster family. Her immediate thought was to offer a home to the baby with the terrible history. 'I have a personal fascination with children,' she says. 'Every child is entitled to love and everything it needs in life. It hurt me to hear of a baby with nothing.'

Lynne recalls one of her friends not only looking aghast at the thought of her raising Tatum but warning: 'She will end up killing you.' Kelly and Chrissie thought it a great idea to give Tatum a fresh start. The two young women nod enthusiastically when Lynne keeps telling me how smart Tatum is. 'Once she asked me if she grew under my belly button. I told her no, she grew under Sabrina's belly button. The next day she came and said: "So you're not my mother." I told her, "Of course I am. Who looks after you all the time and loves you but me? You're just lucky to have two mothers." She is so clever and responsible for such a little thing,' says Lynne, 'more so than Sabrina ever was, as young as she is.'

Once back at Lynne's house, I can't help noticing how untidy it is. Every surface is piled high with stuff, even though it is a large house for just the two of them and there seem to be plenty of cupboards and drawers. On my previous visit, when Tatum had wanted to show me her bedroom, Lynne had objected mildly and with a laugh, saying it was too messy. Now, while Lynne cooks in the kitchen, I wander around with Tatum. The toilet doesn't flush; there is a large sticky stain of something spilt a while ago on the passage floor. The beds are unmade. Cobwebs dangle everywhere. I am not particularly fastidious but this place is a shambles.

Lynne brings our food through to the dining room, pushes all the junk on the table to one side and plonks plates in front of us. 'There is nothing ceremonious about our meals,' she jokes. 'I'm not much of a housekeeper, am I?' When we have finished eating, Tatum starts getting cranky. 'She is used to having my undivided attention,' explains Lynne, suggesting that I accompany the two of them to Tatum's room while she reads a story. It is long past the bedtime of most three-year-olds, though Lynne says she does not worry about other people's norms. 'Tatum goes to bed late and sleeps late in the morning. If she goes to school in her pyjamas, well, what does it matter. I am raising her intuitively, just trusting my intuition.'

When Tatum is tucked up, we return to the dining room and I ask Lynne for the third time if there is a black role model in Tatum's life. The reason I am persisting with this line of questioning is that a mixed-race friend in Johannesburg, whose opinions I respect, has told me that it is particularly important for a coloured child raised in a white family to be able to relate to a significant black parental figure of the appropriate social class, which makes sense to me. Lynne replies again, rather irritably this time, that Tatum attends preschool every day with black kids, knows their parents and sometimes plays at their homes. 'The colour of a person's skin is so not an issue,' she grumbles.

Lynne's irritability grows when we talk about Tatum's three uncles – Sabrina's half-brothers, Lester, Allister and Shane. Although only Allister has ever agreed to talk to me, my overall impression of the brothers is unflattering. They rejected Tatum at a time when the baby was dangerously ill and distressed, after all. Lynne counters that the three had initially intended to adopt their niece collectively. It was only once newspaper reports began quoting Sabrina's murder defence of racism that they turned against the idea of raising Tatum, she claims, giving as the source of this knowledge little Lindy-Lou's parents, who maintain close contact with the Van Schoors.

Why is the accusation of racism against the Van Schoors an acceptable reason for them to reject Tatum?

'Because it is unfair. Everybody in their community was and is equally racist,' says Lynne forcibly. 'I grew up a racist but my church taught me it was wrong. Sabrina's brothers didn't want any more to do with the case after her lawyer made all those accusations of racism against them and against Beverley, as if they were somehow to blame for what happened. They just wanted Tatum out of their lives. Who is to say that you are obliged to love the child of the person who murdered your mother? I don't blame them. They told the social worker that they wanted Tatum to be free of the Van Schoor name, to be adopted, but Sabrina wouldn't agree to that. So they gave me money to help raise her. I took it but told them I didn't want any more. I may ask them later to help with her education. That is her right and I am sure they will support her if she wants to go to university.'

But they don't want anything to do with Tatum at a personal level?

'No, that's true. That's their choice. I keep the door open. Shane's wife Chantelle is the only one who seems a bit interested so I take Tatum to visit her whenever possible. I think it's important for Tatum. She needs the Van Schoors. She needs to know them or she won't feel complete; she won't know who she is later in life.'

These are good reasons for Lynne to stay on cordial terms with Tatum's uncles. I tell her I will gladly note her goodwill towards Lester, Allister and Shane although I do not agree with her assessment of them. She then tries to convince me, by quoting Jesus and various scriptures, that I have misjudged the Van Schoors. I should find it in my heart to understand them, she claims. I reply that it is my function to make assessments from the head not the heart. Part of my job as a writer is to examine people's motives.

At this point, she starts to rail at me. 'I hope you aren't examining my motives,' she protests. 'I don't want someone coming into my home and judging me. Whose right is it to judge? Only the Lord can judge. Why can't you have some heart for the Van Schoors? What happened to them should be private, not recorded in a book. Sabrina's brothers were doing their best. Beverley was just doing her best, too.'

On the contrary, I insist: even if Beverley was doing her

best, she was woefully misguided in a number of respects. At the very least, she was a pretentious hypocrite, so intent on portraying herself as superior that she boasted constantly about her wealth, especially her collection of diamond rings. Beverley taunted Sabrina with these jewels and the power they represented, promising them to her daughter one minute and withdrawing them the next. When she told people in Queenstown that she had purchased her tenth diamond, they used to joke that she didn't need any more because she had only ten fingers. After Beverley's death, when her sons took the rings to be valued, however, they discovered that all ten were made of glass, according to a local jeweller.

Such a person, who so obviously prized outward shows more than intrinsic worth, was ill-equipped to tolerate her daughter's provocative choice of black and coloured friends over whites in a racist community. My arguments do not impress Lynne and, after a time, she pushes back her chair abruptly, virtually telling me to mind my own business. We agree to differ. The atmosphere between us has cooled markedly, Tatum is yelling for her mother and I retire to my room, reminding Lynne that I will be leaving early the next morning as planned.

I grope my way down the dark passage, trying to switch on several lights which are not working. Feeling in the darkness along the wall of the room next to mine in the hope of illuminating the bathroom at the end of the passage, I suddenly find myself in Lynne's lit-up schoolroom. There are 20 miniature chairs and desks, painted in bright colours, bold curtains at the windows, nursery characters hanging from the ceiling. Taped to the walls are dozens of kids' crayon pictures with the names of Lynne's pupils pencilled on top: Sange, Landile, Chwayita, Pamela, Mehle, Uzu, Tatum, Thando, Kazi – most of them Xhosa names. I realise that Tatum's home is full of middle-class black people most of the time, which explains Lynne's impatience with my dogged questioning about a black role model for Tatum. I had assumed that Lynne's preschool catered mainly for white children. My intuitive certainty, aka prejudice, has meant that I have only now by chance stumbled on the knowledge that Lynne is the teacher of the town's elite black kids. However unusual it is to find a white woman in a conservative rural area with a predominantly black, middle-class preschool inside her home, here she is.

I go to bed thinking about stereotyping, the source of so much conflict in the world. Since time began, we humans have turned against neighbouring groups who threaten us in some way. Rationalising our fears, we label each other inferior, evil or ridiculous, emphasising the difference between 'them' and 'us'. A profoundly damaging tendency, it continues to occur in twenty-first-century USA in the wake of 9/11 as well as in newly democratised South Africa. The sole antidote is understanding how other societies do things and accepting that it is possible to lead very different lives yet remain equally human and deserving of respect. Stereotyping is conquered most effectively via free speech, which is why totalitarians who manipulate people through fear immediately silence independent thinkers.

Stereotypes can change quite quickly in the right circumstances. Achieving compromise with those whose manners one doesn't fully understand or with whose causes one does not entirely sympathise is a vital characteristic of successful, open societies. The British, for example, are remarkably free of racial fanaticism when you consider that they were cruel imperialists arrogantly oppressing Africa's 'nig-nogs' during the nineteenth century.

In the morning, Lynne taps on my door, proffering a tea tray and her apologies. 'You were right to stick to your guns over Sabrina's family,' she says. 'We don't all have to think alike.' She sits on the bed opposite mine, spots the book I have been reading, *Beyond Belief: The Moors Murderers* by Emlyn Williams, and shrugs. 'What a job you have,' she exclaims. 'I don't know why you want to think about murderers all the time, but still ...'

I open Emlyn Williams' famous book and read to her from the author's foreword: 'For me, just as no physical aberration can ever be too extraordinary to interest the medical scientist, so no psychological phenomena can be forbidden to the serious and dispassionate writer, however "unsavoury" the details. Who expects savour from a story of noisome evil? When a shocking scandal blows up, with all the attendant sensationalism, there is in some people a tendency to avert the head and shovel the whole thing under the carpet, "I don't want to know." But some of us *do* want to know, and it is salutary to enquire: the proper study of mankind is Man. And Man cannot be ignored because he has become vile. Woman neither.'

Although I am intending to leave Molteno early on Sunday morning, Lynne wants to show me her church. I am keen to patch up the previous night's altercation. Though wary of a repeat of her sermon after supper on the way the Lord would regard the Van Schoors, I decide to go with her.

The service starts at ten but people are already arriving, some to prepare flowers and food for the all-day event; others to be sure of a good seat. A trio of young black women dressed in lace and chiffon ask me timidly where they should sit. Lynne steps forward to direct them. There are several middle-aged white women officiating in one or other capacity. They go out of their way to welcome a group of township dwellers disembarking uncertainly from a banged-up car. Another group of black congregants arrives, this time jaunty women with casual waves. 'You can see that all races and classes are welcome here,' says Lynne. 'All denominations, too. We share one culture, our Christian culture. Church is church and God is God. It's wonderful: it works for everyone. People really help each other. We collect clothing for the poor and stock it in our church boutique, where people can go and choose what they like, not just be given handouts. Respect is important, so important. I really think we're onto something here.'

The band is warming up. Allen Wilson, the born-again banker-turned-priest who started this movement called Churchnet and is accused by some in Molteno of setting himself up as a cult figure, is standing in front of the musicians. A regular looking guy, a little stern, perhaps. A pretty vocalist begins to sing: 'The holy spirit told me that things are gonna be all right ...' Lynne points to a notice board heralding upcoming events, all concerned with charity. 'He who has pity on the poor lends to the Lord,' says a quote from Proverbs in bold lettering.

I have been vaguely aware all morning of insect bites incurred during the night. Realising now that my torso has been attacked not by mosquitoes, as I assumed at first, but by bedbugs, I feel secretly amused. Here is the foster mother of one of the most publicised children in South Africa, as unsuitable a parent on the surface as you could find if you undertook a search for the mother from hell. Her home is grubby and chaotic; her life fractured; her personality eccentric in the local context. She has not enough money in the bank and too much faith in esoteric phenomena. However, despite all these drawbacks, Lynne Hall's values are impeccable. She adores Tatum. She is spiritually generous enough to nurture Sabrina's biological bond with the child and to maintain links with the wider Van Schoor clan because she believes this to be in Tatum's interests. And, despite the teachings of her tribe, she is not a racist.

'Tatum is very interested in family relationships because we talk about it all the time,' says Lynne. 'We saw Allister and Lester in Queenstown by chance recently and Tatum remembered them: she ran up to them with her arms held high and they both hugged her. They looked surprised but I think they were quite pleased. It is surprising how much she seems to remember from her previous life. She often talks about Beverley. What happened before is tragic but it is part of her history and I am trying to make it as normal a part of her life as possible. We don't know for sure how she will turn out. In 15 years' time, we'll see who Tatum is.'

Is it likely that this child will triumph over her terrible history? Living with Lynne, who would probably be classified 'the good enough mother' by psychologists, Tatum has the best possible chance of conquering the ghosts of her grandfather's mass murders and her biological mother's matricide. She will have a good education and be loved unconditionally by her foster family. 'You can see already how clever and beautiful she is,' says Lynne. 'I have no doubt she will be a wonderful adult.'

You have to hand it to this fearless woman. Not for her the superficial spoils of success such as Beverley van Schoor's spotless home, maintained not by one domestic worker but two, or the fake jewels that set Beverley apart in her relentless search for significance. Lynne has set herself the goal of making the difference in one little girl's life. She wears the same tired trousers two days in a row, eats pap and beans like her township neighbours when the pantry is bare. I see her hand a beggar a fistful of notes she can ill-afford when she doesn't realise I am watching. I hear her explaining patiently to a ragged man who has wandered through her front door claiming to be looking for a drink of water that he should ring the bell rather than walk straight in. Tatum is at her side all the time absorbing manners that are radically different from the alternately rude and cruel or bogusly polite behaviour observed by Sabrina throughout her childhood.

Driving back towards Queenstown, I spot a road sign showing the way to Tarkastad, where Gladys Nontombi, Sabrina's black mother, was born. It reminds me of the multiple phone calls I have had over the months from Gladys, always asking for 'assistance'. Having tried unsuccessfully to call her on the incoming journey to Molteno, thinking then that she might like to accompany me to Lynne's house and spend time with Tatum overnight, I dial the number she has given me again. This time it is answered and I hear a stranger's voice initially, then some shouting and, after a long pause, Gladys on the line. Meet me at Whistle Stop in an hour, I suggest, and she agrees to get a taxi to Cathcart Road. As I draw up at a petrol pump outside the diner, I spot her through the window, sitting primly at a table, hands folded in front of her, staring straight ahead.

We have breakfast together. Gladys needs money, inevitably. She is also very concerned about the maid's job Sabrina undertook to arrange for her with Louis. Taken aback at her eagerness to work for a mass murderer, I explain that Louis has not been long out of prison and might take time to set himself up in a home in East London. Does she know about Louis' crimes, I wonder. She listens intently as I tell her that Louis might be moving to the Cape before long. She does not mind moving there, she assures me.

Having thought of respecting the fact that Louis has served his time, I decide to ask if she knows why Sabrina's father was sent to prison. Gladys shakes her head. When I explain that Louis killed a lot of people, black people, she receives the news calmly. 'Sabrina showed me her father in the newspaper. I know him. I want the job,' she says as if I have warned her about Louis' propensity for untidiness.

The lengths to which poor people will go to earn money is sad and alarming, I reflect. Feza was prepared to slaughter Beverley for a large sum; Gladys does not mind living alongside a mass murderer for a paltry amount. Her attitude is another example of a nation with its values in turmoil. I watch her get into a taxi that will take her back to her township shack and wave, though she is not looking my way but staring resolutely ahead.

It strikes me again on the drive back to East London how closely little Tatum van Schoor's story reflects the uncertain future of the wider society in which she lives. How likely is it that South Africa will overcome its devastating history any time soon? Like Tatum in the custody of Lynne Hall, the country was offered its best chance of a new beginning in the care of its revered first president, Nelson Mandela. More recent events may herald challenging times ahead, however.

'The past is not dead. In fact, it's not even past,' wrote American novelist William Faulkner. A decade into South Africa's first democracy has seen the statute books stripped of apartheid laws as well as the dramatic growth of a well-heeled black middle class, thanks to the economy's buoyancy. But much remains the same. The new constitution – repository of the nation's values – has been lauded by human rights lawyers everywhere yet is still far ahead of the country's mood. South Africa remains the most racist society on earth. State-sponsored brutality has ceased but violence among the citizenry has increased. Unemployment, which rose to an alarming 40 per cent in 2004, means unacceptably high levels of inequality exacerbated by HIV/Aids. Black economic empowerment policies, while certainly necessary in the short term, have the unfortunate effect of re-racialising a society that urgently needs to focus on unity. Ongoing shortcomings in state schools leave the ill-educated majority both frustrated and unequal to modern tasks, as reflected in the fact that one in four officers in the country's feeble police force is functionally illiterate.

In the second decade of its hard-won democracy, South Africa must conquer not only the continuing legacy of apartheid and endemic poverty but also the unexpected intolerance that has become apparent among its new rulers. Whether the country tiptoes towards authoritarianism and squanders the Mandela legacy or opts decisively for democracy over the next few years will depend largely on whether South Africans resist the state's growing insistence on patriotic loyalty.

In an unseemly clash between President Thabo Mbeki and Archbishop Desmond Tutu at the end of 2004, the nation's leader publicly insulted a universally respected churchman for reasonable criticism on vital issues. The Archbishop had incurred Mbeki's wrath by expressing anxiety over the government's failure to deal effectively with the HIV/Aids pandemic and its failure to condemn human rights abuses in neighbouring Zimbabwe. Tutu's remarks were a challenge, from one of the world's moral guardians, for South Africans to avoid becoming a nation of yes-men and women. His comments, including concern that the poor are getting poorer, were echoed by the head of the country's trade union movement who, despite being the popular leader of the ANC's largest single constituency, came in for similar abuse from the president's office.

Disdain for the opinions and dignity of others gives impetus to rampant nationalism. If two world wars and apartheid have not proved that, what on earth will? By far the most dangerous influence in many countries – including the United States today – nationalism tends to be built on a wound inflicted by one tribe on the national psyche of another: the incalculable trauma white racism unleashed on black South Africa is one example; the appalling atrocities inflicted by Muslim terrorists on America in September 2001 and on London in July 2005 are others. Fundamentalism is often a form of nationalism in religious disguise.

As I write these final paragraphs, I am mindful that little Tatum van Schoor will someday read about her family's history. I hope she understands that, as surely as Sabrina's tragedy reflects all that was wrong and damaging in apartheid society, so her own story might become a metaphor for what is right and good and growing stronger with each passing year. Archbishop Tutu has said over and over again that there is no future without forgiveness, an idea that South Africans have debated more than any other nation and which many have embraced as the core of a new belief system. Tatum may well find that to forgive her original family is not only to be altruistic. 'It is the best form of self-interest,' according to Tutu. It is also possible that Sabrina's brothers might benefit from forgiveness.

During what I intended to be my last visit to Sabrina in prison in February 2005, she was in a jaunty mood as we exchanged pleasantries. All of a sudden, deliberately catching her off guard, I asked if she regretted killing her mother. Her eyes clouded with tears and her shoulders slumped as she nodded. 'It's nearly three years ago now but I still wake up most days wishing that I could turn the clock back. But I can't and that's that. I used to think that if people could only realise how mean my mother was to me they would understand. I actually thought that most people would have done what I did if they had had the same experiences. But now I just wish I hadn't hurt my brothers and Mom's sisters so much. I'm glad my gran wasn't alive to see the terrible way Mom died. I think Tatum will understand when she is older and realises that Mom threatened to take her away from me, and I just couldn't bear that.

'I think a lot about forgiving myself,' she says. 'Although I am locked up and reminded every minute of every day what I'm here for, I feel freer than I ever did at home with Mom. I think that's because I feel that my past is behind me now. I don't have to prove anything to Mom or try to make people love me. I am close to my father and I can just be myself. I have asked my family over and over again to forgive me and maybe they will some day.'

Listening to Sabrina in this heartfelt mode with tears in her eyes, I believe it is entirely possible that the paradoxical freedom she feels in prison is the result of her remorse having made her feel part of the human universe once more.

Those who deliberately inflict pain are not easy to forgive, especially if they do not accept full responsibility. Very few perpetrators who came before the Truth and Reconciliation Commission showed remorse for their crimes. South African leaders like Thabo Mbeki accuse white South Africans of putting the issue of racism out of sight and out of mind: the warm welcome accorded Louis van Schoor on his release from prison by many of East London's white community amply proves the charge. Surely whites would be wise to hear Mbeki and confront the remnants of the ideology that enabled them to claim the right to rule so cruelly for so long?

One of the ways to assess a society's weaknesses is through its misfits. Sabrina's major failing, according to Queenstown's white community, was the very colour-blindness that makes her a tragic figure to the rest of the world. She tells me at the end of my visit: 'I wish I had been born in another country; one without racism. If those who dish it out knew what it is like to have people looking right through you as if you don't even exist, or talking down to you as if you're a dog, maybe they would think about their racism. I despise our family's friends in Queenstown who used to phone my mom every time they saw me talking to a black, just to cause trouble. Or some would whisper, loud enough for me to hear, "There goes the little hotnot bastard's mother." You might not believe me but I have had more kindness and consideration in prison from hardened criminals than I ever got from the whites of Queenstown.

'What I feel all the time is regret for that Queenstown stuff and other things. I wish more than anything else that I had not killed my mother. I can't tell you how much I miss my mother. Every day, I realise how much I needed her. And my daughter ... And my brothers ... The head of the prison phoned my oldest brother recently to ask if they would come and see me so that I could say sorry properly but Lester said they never want to see me again. I thought if so many people could go to the Truth and Reconciliation Commission and forgive what happened to them under apartheid, maybe my brothers could forgive me, but they say no. I will carry on begging and pleading with them whenever I can because I just can't accept that I've lost my entire family. I think if Mandela could forgive us for keeping him in prison for nearly thirty years and for murdering so many people who opposed apartheid, my brothers will forgive me some day.'

While it will take much more than conciliatory words from Nelson Mandela and Desmond Tutu to break the cycle of hatred in South Africa, the dialogue initiated by the Truth and Reconciliation Commission will continue to seek a spirit of compromise and tolerance. 'Listening to one another and acknowledging the experience of loss on both sides would be a start,' says former TRC commissioner, author and psychology professor, Pumla Gobodo-Madikizela of the University of Cape Town. 'The task of picking up the pieces of a society shattered by violence is not easy. It needs patience ... Perhaps the most enduring effects of totalitarian rule and systematic oppression under apartheid cannot be measured in terms of numbers of the dead, but in immeasurable losses of the human spirit,' says Gobodo-Madikizela. 'That is what has to be restored.'

How does a society restore its humanity in the aftermath

of such a terrible past? Perhaps, as a start, by understanding why some whites feel a sense of loss in the new South Africa and by understanding why the liberation movement, despite having committed some human rights abuses, was necessary in an unjust society. By discussing why so many white people supported apartheid long after the international community had condemned it, according to Pumla Gobodo-Madikizela. And by understanding that, while systematic injustices have to be remedied through positive discrimination, there should be continual questioning about the memory of that suffering in the present: about its uses as well as its abuses.

Given the finest of lines between remembering and forgetting the past, perhaps South Africa can only repair its broken heart by examining how white supporters of apartheid reflect on their history. Are they sorry? If they acknowledge their part in an evil system, how should black South Africans respond? asks Pumla Gobodo-Mazikizela. Should they spurn the apology and carry on punishing whites with their hatred, knowing that neither side will benefit from revenge? Or can they find in the abundant compassion demonstrated by Nelson Mandela an idiom of humanity common to all South Africans who, regretting their past, sincerely wish to mend it.

Although I had not intended to do so, I suddenly decided to visit Sabrina again in April 2005 because there was a question I had forgotten to ask her. She appeared in one of the visitors' booths looking pale and a lot thinner than I had ever seen her. Her hair was its natural, light brown colour and cut like a child's, tidy but blunt and unflattering. Her nails and lips were unpainted. She looked tired and troubled. When I smiled, her eyes filled with tears.

She told me she had been ill with an undiagnosed malady for some time. When I pressed her, she said she thought it dated back to October the previous year – the month Louis was released. No, she admitted reluctantly, her father had not come to see her as often as she had hoped. In fact, he had been only twice in six months. 'He would come more often if he could,' she insisted. The prison doctor could find no physical explanation for her weight loss, she told me. She was having nightmares that left her sobbing in her sleep, waking the other girls in the cell night after night, so she was shortly to be transferred to a prison in Port Elizabeth for a period of intensive psychotherapy.

My final question to Sabrina drew an immediate response. Three years after she murdered her mother, was there anything left to frighten her? 'I'm scared of myself,' she replied. 'I'm afraid of how I'll react once I'm in the outside world if, say, some of the things that happened to me happen to Tatum. I can hear my mother's voice sometimes when I'm alone. She is still asking me why all the time and I still don't really know why. That's scary. I have tried to explain what it felt like to be me in my life with only my baby to live for and even Tatum belonging more to my mother than to me, if Mom had her way. I'm scared sometimes that people will take revenge against my father. And I worry that my brothers might seek revenge against me when I am released. I still write to them on their birthdays and at Christmas. They told me never to write again but I will never stop. I am scared they will never forgive me so I have to keep trying.'